FARM BUSINESS TENANC

AGRICULTURAL TENANCIES ACT 1995

FARM BUSINESS TENANCIES

AGRICULTURAL TENANCIES ACT 1995

Angela Sydenham MA, LLB, SOLICITOR
Chief Legal Adviser
Country Landowners Association
London

and

Neil Mainwaring BA, FRICS, PARTNER
Chartered Surveyor
Smiths Gore
London

JORDANS
1995

Published by
Jordan Publishing Limited
21 St Thomas Street
Bristol BS1 6JS

British Library Cataloguing-in-Publication Data
A catalogue record for this book is available from the British Library.

ISBN 0 85308 313 4

Typeset by Create Publishing Services Limited, Bath
Printed in Great Britain by Bookcraft (Bath) Ltd, Midsomer Norton

FOREWORD

Following detailed consultations with the agricultural industry organisations, the Government has carried out a radical reform of the legal framework within which the agricultural tenanted sector is to operate. The new legislation will have far-reaching effects on the way in which agricultural land is let in England and Wales. I was greatly privileged to be the Government Minister responsible for introducing the Agricultural Tenancies Bill in the House of Lords in November 1994.

As well as accepting the overwhelming case for reform in the light of a serious long-term decline in the tenanted sector, almost all of the main farming organisations were also able to agree on the provisions contained in the Bill itself. Clearly, most people in the industry no longer see the agricultural let sector simply in terms of landlords on one side and tenants on the other. They recognise that both must share a common sense of purpose if their respective businesses are to flourish. That will in turn revitalise the wider rural economy.

The Agricultural Tenancies Act 1995 gives more freedom for the parties to a tenancy agreement to agree provisions which suit their particular circumstances. But with freedom comes responsibility; and so it is vital that landowners and prospective tenants alike understand the full implications of the new legal framework. In this book, Angela Sydenham and Neil Mainwaring have provided a detailed, readable and astonishingly speedy explanation of the new legislation and how it will operate in practice. I am sure it will prove to be an invaluable guide to the Act which will benefit anyone who is likely to enter into or advise upon a farm business tenancy.

THE EARL HOWE
Parliamentary Secretary (Lords)
Ministry of Agriculture, Fisheries and Food
(1992–1995)

PREFACE

The aim of this book is to set out as clearly as possible the new law on farm business tenancies. It is directed primarily at professional advisers, solicitors, surveyors and others who are qualified to draw up and prepare farm business tenancy agreements under section 35 of the Agricultural Tenancies Act 1995. In addition, we hope that the book will be useful for students studying agricultural law and for landowners and prospective tenants contemplating entering into farm business tenancies.

The emphasis of the book is on the practical application of the law. Where appropriate, reference is made to the political and legal background to the legislation.

The law relating to agricultural tenancies has remained largely unchanged since 1948. During that near half century, farming and the use of rural property have evolved at a remarkable rate. In 1948, the horse was still an important source of motive power; now, there is no arable operation which is not mechanised. On livestock farms perhaps there is still some way to go, although machines have removed much of the drudgery.

In 1948, there was no negotiating balance between the landlord and tenant. The tenant might have known much about the practical ways of farming, often simply learned from an earlier generation, but rarely would he have had technical and financial training. His grasp of what science could provide in the way of crop and livestock yield improvement would have been superficial. The landlord, by contrast, in most cases would have had ready access to professional skills and would have been altogether better versed in the application of new ideas.

All that has changed. Today, whilst the landlord continues to have access to advice, so does the tenant. Farmers have shown a remarkable facility for adopting all manner of technical change. Their crops grow better as a result of the activities of plant breeders and agronomists; their machines are sophisticated, reflecting the achievements of mechanical and electronic engineers; their livestock are bred and reared with the aid of a highly developed veterinary service. In addition, as financial acumen seems to be ingrained, so farmers readily embrace the new financial management techniques proffered by bankers and other lenders. Few farms would have boasted an office in 1948; it would be difficult to find one that did not have a computerised accounting facility today.

The nature of the farm business has changed too. In the 1950s, a great many farms were run with a mixture of enterprises which were not carefully analysed. The notion was that, with seasonal variations, some ventures would fail but others might prosper and given favourable weather conditions perhaps the total would be profitable. Now, there is a much greater degree of specialisation and after a few decades of enterprise costing, not much is left to chance. There is further specialisation in the provision of certain services by contract. With modern farm buildings and powerful machinery, dependence on favourable weather conditions is much reduced. Even where land has been neglected, it is possible to bring about restoration quite swiftly.

Against this background, it is no longer necessary to have a legal system which defends one party in a leasing negotiation at the possible expense of the other. The game is evenly matched in the sense that both sides are aware of the need for technical or professional advice; both have access to similar sources of finance; both hear or read what the media have to say about current issues national or international and can react accordingly.

In these circumstances, it seems sensible to remove the inhibitions of post-war years and to leave the parties to a letting negotiation free to work out what best suits their circumstances and requirements.

The landlord must decide in the first instance what terms would be attractive causing him to let the property as opposed to retaining it for his own use or selling it so as to reinvest the proceeds. After that elementary point has been passed then it becomes equally important for the prospective tenant to decide how he is to use the property so as to generate a profit. This will dictate the length of term which he requires and the amount of rent which he is willing to offer. It will determine a whole host of other conditions relating to the manner in which the land is cultivated, what buildings are to be erected and how these are to be kept in repair. Open negotiation will determine what is permitted and what is prohibited in the use of the property. It will produce agreement between the parties on when, if at all, and how the rent is to be reviewable. The tenant is likely to contemplate farming or trading so as to improve the property and that will appeal to the landlord but the tenant will need to know that he will be rewarded adequately for such improvement.

It might be argued that none of these things requires intervention by the legislator but the industry has become accustomed to a large degree of regulation and perhaps approaches change with a little caution. For that reason the new Act creates a broad framework within which the parties can operate quite freely. There is virtually no restriction on the way in which property letting arrangements need be organised to comply with statute. The parties will be entirely free to determine all the main features of a tenancy and that is how it should be. We shall see later that there are certain specific areas where, if the parties do not make contractual arrangements, then there is what has become known as a 'fallback procedure' but those instances are few. Certain things remain mandatory even after this welcome reform, but they are fewer still. Consequently, the new tenancies will to a large extent be subject to the general law of landlord and tenant. We have taken a deliberate decision therefore to set out, where relevant, the underlying legal principles which will affect farm business tenancies.

Many firms of solicitors and surveyors will be drafting leases under the new Act. It is important that the opportunity is taken to rethink the standard terms which were incorporated in the leases under the Agricultural Holdings Act 1986. Some of these terms will no longer be appropriate. Others may suit the individual agreements which have been reached by the parties. There should be many options, not one form of standard agreement. The Royal Institution of Chartered Surveyors has been in-structed by Parliament to prepare Guidance Notes and some precedent agreements. Care should be taken not to follow these precedents blindly without adapting them to the particular needs of the clients.

We have been fortunate to be involved from the very beginning in the process of reforming the law, which has resulted in the Agricultural Tenancies Act 1995. In this context, we record our thanks to those with whom we have worked. First, to the team from the Ministry of Agriculture Fisheries and Food (MAFF) and, in particular, John Osmond, Helen Baker, Cliff Netten, Mark Edwards, Christine Cogger. In writing the book, much use was made of the notes to clauses produced by the MAFF. Secondly, to the members of the Tenancy Reform Industry Group who monitored the legislation as it went through Parliament and added to our understanding of the new law. The Group included Tim Key, Paul Joseland, Jane Adderley, Barney Holbeche, Jeremy Moody, Julian Sayers and Nick Way. Within the Country Landowners Association, we are indebted to three Presidents, Rodney Swarbrick, John De Ramsey and Hugh Duberly.

We acknowledge also the seminal work of William de Salis who produced the *Landlord/Tenant Survey* for the Country Landowners Association in 1989 which showed the urgent need for reform if the tenanted sector in agriculture were to survive.

We are grateful for the helpful comments from Professor C P Rodgers on the Housing chapter and Professor J E Adams on the Dispute Resolution chapter. Any errors, however, are those of the authors.

Special thanks are due to Patricia Goodwin, Senior Secretary in the Legal Department of the Country Landowners Association, who gave up her weekends to typing and retyping the manuscript. Thanks too are due to our publisher, Martin West, and to our editor, Mollie Dickenson of Jordans, for their support and enthusiasm.

Finally, we are grateful to family and friends who put up with our obsessional interest in the new legislation, boring them with our interminable conversations on the subject.

The law is stated as at 24 June 1995.

O fortunatos nimium, sua si bona norint agricolas (happy beyond measure are farmers did they but know their good fortune) Virgil Georgics II 458.

ANGELA SYDENHAM
NEIL MAINWARING
Midsummer 1995

CONTENTS

TABLE OF CASES

TABLE OF STATUTES

References are to paragraph numbers except where they are in *italics* which are references to page numbers

TABLE OF STATUTORY INSTRUMENTS

GLOSSARY

This glossary covers the terms used in the narrative of this book. The statute may define the terms differently.

Administrators	Persons authorised to administer the estate of an intestate.
Assignment	A disposition or transfer of lease or reversion.
Assignee	The person to whom an assignment is made.
Assignor	The person who makes the assignment.
Covenant	An obligation contained in a deed.
Deed	A document which shows that it is intended to be a deed and which has been signed and delivered.
Demise	A grant of a lease.
Determine	Terminate, come to an end.
Distrain, distress	The lawful seizure of goods, to enforce a right, eg payment of rent.
Emblements	Growing crops which an outgoing tenant may take away in certain circumstances.
Equity	Body of law which developed to mitigate the common law rules.
Executors	Persons appointed by testator to administer his estate.
Incumbrance	A liability burdening property.
Intestacy	Failure to dispose of property by will.
Landlord	Person who grants lease or holds reversion.
Lease	(1) Document creating a leasehold interest.
	(2) The leasehold interest.
Lessee	Person to whom lease is granted, same meaning as tenant although lessee is usually used for the original grantee of the lease rather than an assignee of the lease.
Lessor	Person who grants lease. Same meaning as landlord although lessor is usually used for the original grantor of the lease rather than the assignee of the reversion.
Licence	Permission to occupy which does not create a tenancy or interest in land.
Mesne	Intermediate.
Personal Representatives	Administrators or executors.
Privity of Contract	The relationship between parties to a contract. Used especially between original lessor and lessee.
Privity of Estate	The relationship between the landlord for the time being and the tenant for the time being.
Restrictive Covenant	A covenant restricting the use of the land.
Reversion	The interest remaining in the lessor after granting a leasehold interest.

Sub-lease **Sub-tenancy**	A leasehold interest carved out of a superior leasehold interest.
Tenancy	The leasehold interest.
Tenancy Agreement	Document creating tenancy or lease.
Tenant	Lessee, person to whom lease or tenancy is granted.
Waste	Acts which alter the nature of land.
Ameliorating Waste	Alterations which improve the land, eg converting redundant buildings into dwellings; a farm into a market garden.
Permissive Waste	Failure to do that which ought to be done, eg non-repair of buildings or failure to clean out ditches.
Voluntary Waste	Positive acts of destruction.
Equitable Waste	Acts of wanton destruction.

Chapter 1
NEED FOR LEGISLATION

1.1 HISTORICAL BACKGROUND

Since 1908, there has been a continuing decline in the amount of tenanted agricultural land in the UK. There are many reasons for this, social, economic and fiscal. However, the major reason in the post-war period has been legislation giving security of tenure to tenants.

The history of statutory intervention began in 1875. The Agricultural Holdings (England) Act 1875 introduced statutory compensation for improvements and gave the tenant the right to remove fixtures erected at his own expense. Until the coming into force of the Agricultural Holdings (England) Act 1883, it was possible to contract out of the compensation provisions. This later Act also amended the common law rule that six-months' notice was needed to terminate an annual tenancy, by providing that for agricultural tenancies at least 12-months' notice was necessary, unless there was an agreement to the contrary.

The Agricultural Holdings Act 1900 provided for an arbitration procedure to settle disputes where the parties had not agreed otherwise. (The 1875 Act had provided for the settlement of disputes by referees and umpires with an appeal to the county court.) This Act was amended and supplemented by the Agricultural Holdings Act 1906. It extended the list of improvements for which compensation could be claimed and introduced compensation for disturbance and game damage.

These Acts were followed by consolidating and amending Acts in 1908 and 1923. A major departure was made in 1947 when the Agriculture Act of that year gave the tenant security of tenure. This Act also established Agricultural Land Tribunals. It was replaced, almost entirely, the following year by the Agricultural Holdings Act 1948.

Again, there was much amending legislation. By far the most significant amendment was by the Agriculture (Miscellaneous Provisions) Act 1976 which applied to existing as well as future tenancies. This Act enables certain close relatives of a deceased tenant to apply for a succession tenancy provided they can prove that they are eligible and suitable. It also extends the succession right to a further generation of eligible and suitable close relatives.

The result of the 1976 legislation was that very few landowners were prepared to let land. If they did so, they would be putting the land out of the family control for up to three generations. The Agricultural Holdings Act 1984 was passed to deal with the problem. It gave effect to some of the recommendations of the Northfield Report[1] and was based on agreement between the Country Landowners Association and the National Farmers' Union. Succession rights were abolished for all tenancies granted after 12 July 1984. In return, a new rent formula was introduced. The 1986 Act made minor amendments and consolidated 10 statutes.

---

[1] Report to the Committee of Inquiry into the Acquisition and Occupancy of Agricultural Land (1979) Cmnd 7599.

In the event, as many people had anticipated, the 1984 legislation did not go far enough to encourage landowners to let land. In particular, the artificial rent definition proved to be a singular disincentive. A survey carried out by the Country Landowners Association in 1989 showed that 1.6m acres would be let if there were legislation based on freedom of contract. Discussions took place between the Ministry of Agriculture Fisheries and Food and the organisations representing landlords and tenants. In December 1993, a Joint Statement was issued by the Country Landowners Association, National Farmers' Union, the Tenant Farmers' Association and the National Federation of Young Farmers' Clubs. It is set out in Appendix II. On the basis of this industry agreement, the proposed legislation was announced in the Queen's Speech on 14 November 1994.

The Government, committed to deregulation, wanted simple legislation limited to essential safeguards. It recognised the importance of legislation based on freedom of contract, a principle supported by the main agricultural organisations representing both landlords and tenants, not least the young farmers who foresaw opportunities to enter the industry.

Lord Howe, Parliamentary Secretary for Agriculture, Fisheries and Food, on the second reading of the Bill in the House of Lords quoted the Master of the Rolls in a case before the Court of Appeal in 1875 who had said:

> 'If there is one thing which more than any other public policy requires, it is that men of full age and competent understanding shall have the utmost liberty of contracting and that their contracts when entered into freely and voluntarily shall be held sacred and shall be enforced by the courts of justice.'

He went on to quote from the Northfield Report on the importance of preserving the landlord and tenant system:

> 'Many people believe that agriculture, like any other industry, needs a continuous infusion of "new blood" from outside the industry to provide a fresh and innovative outlook, energy and drive.'

> 'Letting represents a relatively low-cost route into the industry and one which prevents agriculture being a closed shop. A healthy let sector allows good young farmers to extend and develop their potential, with benefits for the industry as a whole.'[2]

The Act has effect from 1 September 1995. It has 41 sections and one Schedule, in contrast to the Agricultural Holdings Act 1986 which has 102 sections and 15 Schedules.

Landowners contemplating the grant of farm business tenancies will be reassured by the undertaking given in the House of Commons for the Opposition by Dr Gavin Strang MP. He made it clear that any Labour Government would not interfere retrospectively with the terms of a letting under the Act, nor cause the period of such letting to be extended. Later, these assurances were repeated in the House of Lords by Lord Carter.

---

[2] HL Deb, 2nd reading, cols 485, 487, 28 November 1994.

'Dr. Strang: I am happy that the right hon. Gentleman has clarified his position.

I am coming to what I regard as the crunch point. We want to give the legislation an opportunity to work. That means in essence that people who let land after 1 September 1995 must have the prospect of their contract remaining. Despite the fact that I have not used the word "retrospective" in the context of the Bill, I accept the right hon. Gentleman's use of the word on this issue.

In that sense, I am happy to give an undertaking that a Labour Government will not legislate retrospectively, and any new tenancy created after 1 September 1995 will be honoured. If we can treat the tenancies as contracts, a contract for five years will last for five years if the legislation provides that it can continue by mutual agreement. The same will apply should the contract be for 10 years, 50 years or whatever. No Labour Government will legislate to break that contract or tenancy. I cannot be clearer than that.

We are saying to the industry—including the Country Landowners Association, the National Farmers Union, the Tenant Farmers Association and the young farmers organisations in Wales and England which supported the agreement that provided the basis for the legislation—that we will honour the position that they have adopted and that the Government have put into the legislation, and we will give it an opportunity to work.'[2a]

'Lord Carter: Perhaps I may repeat the undertaken given in another place by my honourable friend Dr. Gavin Strang. We know that the Labour Party has been pressed hard to state its actions regarding the Bill. We explained that when the Bill completed its course through both Houses we would make our position clear. We have stated that the next Labour Government will not seek to overturn any of the contracts entered into under the Bill after 1st September 1995 and before we change the legislation, if we do so. There will be no attempt to amend retrospectively any of the agreements reached.'[2b]

1.2 REASONS FOR FARM BUSINESS TENANCY

Farm business tenancy legislation was needed for four main reasons:

(i) to encourage landowners to let land;

(ii) to allow tenants to diversify into other businesses whilst still remaining agricultural tenants;

(iii) to enable the effective enforcement of environmental and conservation covenants;

(iv) to abolish the recourse to unsatisfactory short-term arrangements which were being used to avoid the security provisions of the Agricultural Holdings Act 1986.

1.2.1 Lack of let land

Changes in social conditions
The security provisions were first introduced shortly after the 1939–45 war. At that time, there was a need to encourage farmers to farm efficiently and to produce more

---

[2a] Hansard vol 258 no 88 col 526.
[2b] Hansard vol 563 no 80 col 1359.

food. Tenants therefore needed every incentive to make a personal and financial commitment to the land. Today, shortages have given way to surpluses, although at some cost to the taxpayer. The farming industry does not need protection but rather deregulation and competition.

Statistics

Security provisions designed to protect tenants have operated to the disadvantage of prospective new tenants. This is because landlords are not prepared to let land to tenants who will receive lifetime security.

The decline in let land from about 90% at the turn of the century to less than 35% of the total by 1993 is well documented. See for instance the Northfield Report; the annual CAAV statistics; and the 1994 RICS Survey of Farm Business Tenancies: New Farms and Land 1995–97 which charts the decline in let land since 1908. In the summary, it states:

> 'The number of rented agricultural holdings in Great Britain continues to decline from 31% in 1984 to 26% in 1992 and from 40% of the agricultural area by 1984 to 37% in 1992 (Figures 1 & 2). In England and Wales they amounted to 24% of holdings and 35% by area in 1992.'[3]

Projected lettings

The survey of RICS members managing more than 3.26m acres revealed that 155,955 acres (603 units) would be let for five years or more within two years of the new legislation becoming law. Extrapolating these figures, the RICS estimates that this will mean that a further 1m acres will be available for letting. Although much of this land may be let to existing tenants, it is anticipated that some of the land will be let to new entrants.

Tax

Under Chapter II, Part V of the Inheritance Tax Act 1984, owners who have occupied agricultural property for the purposes of agriculture for two years or more qualify for 100% relief from inheritance tax. Where the land is let, however, the landlord is eligible after seven years of ownership for only 50% relief unless, exceptionally, he is able to obtain vacant possession within 12 months.[4] However, for new farm business tenancies and succession tenancies beginning on or after 1 September 1995 there will be 100% relief for let land provided that the landlord has owned the property for seven years immediately before death (or any lifetime transfer).[5]

---

[3] It is generally considered that of the 35%, many are family arrangements or short-term lettings.
[4] By extra-statutory concession issued 13 February 1995, this period is extended to 24 months.
[5] Finance Act 1995, s 116(2)(C), Inheritance Tax Act 1984.
    When the relief was first introduced in 1981, the Government at that time recognised the need for the net-of-relief taxable value for let and in hand land to be roughly equivalent. Sir Geoffrey Howe said in his 1981 Budget speech 'it is important to maintain a proper balance between owner-occupier and let land, allowing for their different value... The difference in the rate of relief recognises the lower value that let land commands...' The introduction of 100% relief in the Finance (No 2) Act 1991 disturbed that balance.

1.2.2 Diversified farm businesses

Degree of farming activity

With European Union restrictions on production in some sectors of the industry and competitive pressures elsewhere, it has become necessary for many farmers to diversify into businesses other than farming. It is a question of degree whether these non-farming activities take the tenancy outside the traditional agricultural tenancy. Where the original letting was agricultural then the presumption is that it will continue to be so. In *Short v Greaves*,[6] 60% of the turnover was non-agricultural but on the facts this was held not to be sufficient to deprive the holding of its agricultural status.

New definition of farming business

A tenant contemplating diversification needs to know with certainty whether he will continue to be an agricultural tenant. It is unsatisfactory if his position can be determined only by the courts. The wider definition of farm business will enable him to develop his farm enterprises without the possibility of finding himself converted into a business tenant under the Landlord and Tenant Act 1954, Part II, or being in breach of any obligation he may have to farm the property in accordance with the rules of good husbandry. The conventional form of agricultural tenancy is unsuited to businesses other than farming.

1.2.3 Environmental and conservation covenants

The problem

The agricultural holdings legislation has always been directed towards the efficient production of food. Much of it pre-dates current concerns for the environment and conservation. The rules of good husbandry often are in conflict with the aims of environmental land management.

The Agriculture Act 1947

Section 11 of the Agriculture Act 1947 lays down statutory standards of good husbandry:

'(1) For the purposes of this Act, the occupier of an agricultural unit shall be deemed to fulfil his responsibilities to farm it in accordance with the rules of good husbandry in so far as the extent to which and the manner in which the unit is being farmed (as respects both the kind of operations carried out and the way in which they are carried out) is such that, having regard to the character and situation of the unit, the standard of management thereof by the owner and other relevant circumstances, the occupier is maintaining a reasonable standard of efficient production, as respects both the kind of produce and the quality and quantity thereof, while keeping the unit in a condition to enable such a standard to be maintained in the future.

(2) In determining whether the manner in which a unit is being farmed is such as aforesaid, regard shall be had, but without prejudice to the generality of the provisions of the last foregoing subsection, to the extent to which—

    (a) permanent pasture is being properly mown or grazed and maintained in a good state of cultivation and fertility and in good condition;

---

[6] [1988] 1 EGLR 1, [1988] 08 EG 109, CA.

(b) the manner in which arable land is being cropped is such as to maintain that land clean and in a good state of cultivation and fertility and in good condition;

(c) the unit is properly stocked where the system of farming practised requires the keeping of livestock, and an efficient standard of management of livestock is maintained where livestock are kept and of breeding where the breeding of livestock is carried out;

(d) the necessary steps are being taken to secure and maintain crops and livestock free from disease and from infestation by insects and other pests;

(e) the necessary steps are being taken for the protection and preservation of crops harvested or lifted, or in course of being harvested or lifted;

(f) the necessary work of maintenance and repair is being carried out.'

Agricultural Holdings Act 1986

Although the sanctions for non-compliance with the good husbandry rules have been removed from the Agriculture Act 1947, the rules are still relevant to the agricultural holdings legislation. A landlord can apply to the Agricultural Land Tribunal for a certificate of Bad Husbandry. Within six months of obtaining a certificate, the landlord can serve a Case C incontestable notice to quit.[7] If the tenancy agreement incorporates the good husbandry rules then a Case D notice may be served.[8] A tenant may be in breach of the rules if, in order to comply with a management agreement (ie an agreement made by the occupier with Government or statutory body under legislation providing for the designation and protection of special areas), he reduces stocking levels, or does not make full use of his arable land. It has been suggested that an Environmentally Sensitive Area designation order which requires a farmer to refrain from ploughing, reseeding and applying herbicides or pesticides might also result in the tenant not complying with the rules of good husbandry.[9]

The good husbandry rules are also relevant to the statutory rights which a landlord has to claim compensation at the end of a tenancy for dilapidation or deterioration of, or damage to, the holding. Compensation is payable if the deterioration or damage is due to the failure of the tenant to comply with the rules of good husbandry.[10] If a tenant has diversified into non-agricultural activities, he may be in breach of these rules.

Contractual provisions

At common law, there is an implied condition that a farm tenant will cultivate the land in a husband-like manner according to the custom of the country.[11] It is possible for the parties to have express provisions to override the implied conditions. Where there is an express conservation covenant, or a separate agreement with the landlord, then the Agricultural Land Tribunal when deciding whether to issue a certificate of bad husbandry must disregard any practice adopted by the tenant in pursuance of such a term.[12] The covenant must have the object of furthering the conservation of flora and fauna, the protection of buildings or other objects of architectural, archaeological or

---

[7] Agricultural Holdings Act 1986, s 26, Sch 3, Pt I Case C, Pt II, para 9.

[8] Ibid, s 26, Sch 3, Pt I Case D.

[9] Rodgers *Agricultural Conservation and Land Use* (University of Wales Press, 1992) p 156.

[10] Agricultural Holdings 1986, s 71.

[11] *Powley v Walker* (1793) 5 Term Rep 373 *Onslow v* — (1809) 16 Ves 173, *Horsefall v Mather* (1815) Holt NP7.

[12] Agricultural Holdings Act 1986, Sch 3, Pt II, para 9.

historic interest, or the conservation and enhancement of the natural beauty of the countryside or the promotion of its enjoyment by the public. For the purpose of possession proceedings for remediable, Case D, or irremediable, Case E, breach of covenant, the Act provides that any conservation covenants:

> 'shall (if it would not otherwise be so regarded) be regarded as a term or condition of the contract which is not inconsistent with the tenant's responsibility to farm in accordance with the rules of good husbandry.'[13]

However, it is not possible for a landlord to enforce a conservation covenant if it overrides the statutory right to freedom of cropping of arable land.[14]

1.2.4 The disadvantages of short-term tenancies

Statute and case-law enabled landowners, who did not wish to give tenants lifetime security, to enter into short-term tenancies. Frequently, these arrangements were not consistent with the long-term sound management of the land, or necessarily what the parties wanted. There are many cases where the landlord failed to comply strictly with the rules for short-term tenancies and was held by the court to have conferred full statutory protection on the tenant.

Section 2 Ministry consent tenancies

Where the Minister of Agriculture, Fisheries and Food, or, in Wales, the Secretary of State approved an agreement for the letting of land for a period of less than one year then such an agreement was not converted into a full Agricultural Tenancy under s 2 of the Agricultural Holdings Act 1986. It was important that the approval was obtained before the agreement was entered into.[15] It was also important that the approval was for a tenancy rather than a licence. As a matter of law, where an occupier is given exclusive possession of the land, he will have a tenancy not a licence.[16] Although s 2 envisaged that Ministry consent could be given for a licence of any length, this was effective only where the occupier did not in practice have exclusive possession of the land. In *Ashdale Land & Property Co v Manners*[17] the Minister gave consent to a licence for approximately three years. The court held that the agreement had all the characteristics of an agricultural tenancy. Therefore, it was outside the Minister's approval and so the tenant was entitled to security of tenure.

Section 5 Ministry consent tenancies

Section 5 of the Agricultural Holdings Act 1986 provided that the Minister or Secretary of State could give consent for a tenancy of not less than two years and not more than five years. Again, it was essential that the consent was obtained before the tenancy was granted. The contract of tenancy subsequently entered into had to have a statement endorsed upon it that s 3 of the Act (the section which provided that a fixed-term tenancy of more than two years was to continue from year to year) did not apply to the tenancy.

---

[13] Ibid, paras 10 and 11.
[14] Ibid, s 15.
[15] *Bedfordshire County Council v Clarke* (1974) 230 EG 1587.
[16] *Street v Mountford* [1985] AC 809, [1985] 2 All ER 289, [1985] 2 WLR 877.
[17] [1992] 34 EG 76.

In August 1989, a joint announcement by the Agricultural Departments, the Ministry of Agriculture, Fisheries and Food (MAFF) and the Secretary of State for Wales set out a policy for applying the discretion on whether or not to grant consent. Broadly, approval was to be given where development was pending or where temporary arrangements were necessary before a reorganisation of the holding. Ministry consent was also likely to be granted where land was required for specialist cropping. In many cases, the Minister was reluctant to grant consent to more than one such letting and certainly not more than two.

New legislation
There will be no Ministry consent tenancies under the new legislation.

Grazing and mowing tenancy
Grazing and mowing tenancies of less than one year were excluded from protection by s 2 of the Agricultural Holdings Act 1986. The limitations on these agreements were twofold. First, the letting had to be for grazing and/or mowing. Although ancillary activities were permitted, this did not include ploughing or reseeding or the use of buildings other than as shelter for animals. Secondly, the tenancy had to be for a specified period of the year. It was essential therefore that the letting did not continue and that the grazier removed his animals at the end of the period.

The new legislation
Under the new legislation, parties may enter into grazing or mowing agreements. There will, however, be no statutory restrictions as to length or activity.

Gladstone v Bower tenancies
One of the most widely used short-term devices was a *Gladstone v Bower*[18] tenancy. This was an agreement for a fixed term of more than one year but less than two years. Again, care had to be taken that these arrangements were not allowed to run on at the end of the fixed term or that the landlord did not agree to grant further tenancies in the future. In both of these situations, it would be possible for the tenant to claim a full agricultural tenancy. Another trap, which the landlord had to avoid, was signing the agreement after the tenant was in possession. A grant of a tenancy cannot operate retrospectively so as to confer an interest on the tenant before the agreement is made. In one case, by the time the agreement was entered into the tenancy had only a few days left to run. Since it was a tenancy for less than one year, it was automatically converted into a tenancy from year to year under s 2 of the Agricultural Holdings Act 1986.[19]

At one stage, it was considered that a *Gladstone v Bower* tenancy might not be within the definition of an agricultural holding at all but a business tenancy under the Landlord and Tenant Act 1954, Pt II. However, a unanimous Court of Appeal decision in *EWP v Moore*[20] held that a *Gladstone v Bower* tenancy was an agricultural holding, albeit one without security of tenure.

---

[18] [1960] 1 QB 170, [1959] 3 All ER 475, [1959] 2 WLR 815.
[19] *Keen v Holland* [1984] 1 All ER 75, [1984] 1 WLR 251.
[20] [1992] QB 460, [1992] 2 WLR 184, [1992] 1 All ER 880.

Although it may be that the *Gladstone v Bower* tenancy escaped the security provisions because of defective drafting in the agricultural holdings legislation, it provided a means of letting land and buildings which would otherwise not have been let. Whilst some eleven measures have been passed since the decision in *Gladstone v Bower*, when the law could have been amended, it was not. This appears to indicate that there is a need for short-term lettings without security.

New legislation

Under the new legislation, it will be possible to enter into fixed-term tenancies of any duration without giving the tenant security of tenure. Thus, these special forms of tenancy have become otiose.

1.2.5 The disadvantages of other short-term arrangements

Quite apart from short-term tenancy agreements, landowners have also attempted to avoid the security of tenure provisions of the legislation by what might be called joint ventures. These have included partnerships, contract farming agreements and share farming. They have also purported to grant licences rather than tenancies.

Partnerships

Section 1(1) of the Partnership Act 1890 defines a partnership in these terms:

> 'Partnership is the relation which subsists between persons carrying on a business in common with a view of profit.'

The consequence of a partnership is that each partner is jointly and individually responsible for all the debts and obligations of the firm and for any wrong-doings. This means, for example, that any one partner can be sued by a creditor for the whole of the debt incurred by the partnership, even if that partner had nothing to do with the transaction personally. The same applies in respect of any contract or civil wrong (tort) made or done in the partnership business.

A partnership will be appropriate where the landowner wants to run a business jointly with someone else. This is likely to be a particularly suitable arrangement where a family business is concerned. Frequently, however, partnerships were entered into with the sole purpose of avoiding the security provisions of the Agricultural Holdings Act 1986 and preceding Acts. This was so even where the parties were not related and where one party certainly did not want to guarantee the business debts of the other.

Contract farming

Farming by contract can take many forms. A common arrangement is one where an established farmer provides services and machinery for a landowner in return for a fixed remuneration. A specified slice of the profits, after the payment of that remuneration, is paid to the landowner and then the remaining profit is divided between the landowner and farmer in agreed proportions. There is always a danger, with contract farming agreements which are not carefully drawn up, that the contractor will be able to claim a tenancy.

Share farming

The essence of a share-farming agreement is that a landowner and farmer run their own separate businesses on the same area of land.[21] The landowner provides the land and the fixed equipment, and he pays for a share of certain input costs. The share farmer provides the working machinery and the labour, and he pays for a share of the input costs. Because there is not a business in common and the gross produce rather than net profits are shared, a partnership is not created. Nor is there a tenancy. The operator is not given exclusive possession of the land, an essential pre-requisite of a tenancy. The landowner retains possession through the crops which remain vested in him until severance and by his percentage ownership in each individual livestock animal. Although it is perfectly possible to draw up an agreement which avoids both a partnership and tenancy, a share-farming agreement is very difficult to operate correctly in practice.

New legislation

In future, it will not be necessary to resort to partnerships, contract farming and share-farming agreements, or other less defined arrangements, for the purpose of avoiding the security of tenure provisions of the Agricultural Holdings Act 1986. Farm business tenancies will run for the period which has been agreed between the parties; no more and no less.

Contractual agreements are a legitimate means of organising farming and other businesses; doubtless they will continue to be used in appropriate circumstances.

Licences

In order to avoid giving a tenant security of tenure under the Agricultural Holdings Act 1986, many landowners purported to grant non-exclusive licences. A myth surrounds so-called specialist cropping licences. In practice, where crops are grown, the occupier will have exclusive possession. Where there is exclusive possession, there is a tenancy.[22] The genuine non-exclusive licence arises where the landowner shares occupation or where several unconnected people have the right to use land. Under the new legislation, the true nature of the relationship will depend, as before, on whether or not exclusive possession is granted. There will be no point in purporting to grant licences which are, in reality, tenancies simply to avoid security. However, there may be occasions when a landowner will wish to grant a licence for tax reasons.

---

[21] See Stratton, Sydenham and Baird *Share Farming* (CLA publication, 1992).
[22] *Street v Mountford* supra; AHA 1986, s 2, exclusive licence confers security.

Chapter 2

APPLICATION AND OUTLINE OF THE AGRICULTURAL TENANCIES ACT 1995

2.1 APPLICATION

The Agricultural Tenancies Act 1995 applies to farm business tenancies, both written and oral, beginning on or after 1 September 1995.[1] Excluded from the Act are:

(a) existing tenancies protected under the Agricultural Holdings Act 1986;[2]

(b) succession tenancies to the above where two successions have not already taken place;[3]

(c) variations of tenancies in (a) between the same landlord and the same tenant where the law implies a surrender of the old tenancy and a regrant of a new tenancy;[4]

(d) tenancies beginning on or after 1 September 1995 pursuant to a written contract of tenancy before that date indicating that the 1986 Act is to apply to that tenancy;[5]

(e) tenancies granted to tenants under the Evesham custom.[6]

2.2 OUTLINE

2.2.1 Meaning of 'farm business tenancy'

The Act defines the term 'farm business tenancy'. In order to be a farm business tenancy, the tenancy must comply with the business conditions and either the agriculture or notice conditions. The business conditions require that at least part of the land must be farmed for the purposes of a trade or business and has been so farmed since the beginning of the tenancy.[7] The agriculture condition requires that the tenancy must be primarily or wholly agricultural.[8] Alternatively, the landlord and tenant must have exchanged notices before the parties enter into the tenancy agreement or, if earlier, the beginning of the tenancy identifying the land to be comprised in the proposed tenancy and confirming their intention that the tenancy is to be and will remain a farm business tenancy.[9] So long as the use was primarily or wholly agricultural at the start, it does not matter that there is a subsequent shift to non-agricultural use provided the business conditions continue to be fulfilled. Excluded from the definition are those tenancies set out at para 2.1 above.[10]

---

[1] Agricultural Tenancies Act 1995, ss 2, 4, 41. 'Beginning' is defined by s 38(4).
[2] Ibid, s 2.
[3] Ibid, s 4(1)(b), (c), (d).
[4] Ibid, s 4(1)(f).
[5] Ibid, s 4(1)(a).
[6] Ibid, s 4(1)(e). See para **3.3.5**.
[7] Ibid, s 1(2). A farm business tenancy is specifically excluded from the Landlord and Tenant Act 1954; see s 43(1) as amended by the Agricultural Tenancies Act 1995, Sch, para 10.
[8] Ibid, s 1(3).
[9] Ibid, s 1(4).
[10] Ibid, s 4.

2.2.2 Termination of tenancies

Fixed-term tenancies of two years or under expire automatically on the term date. A notice of at least 12 but less than 24 months is required to terminate a tenancy of over two years. Failure to serve a notice means that the tenancy will continue as a yearly tenancy.[11] A yearly tenancy, whether granted initially or arising after a fixed-term tenancy, can be terminated only by a notice of between one and two years.[12] A break clause in a fixed-term tenancy of over two years will operate only if notice of at least 12 but less than 24 months has first been served.[13]

2.2.3 Fixtures

Fixtures and buildings may be removed by the tenant during the tenancy or at any time when he remains in occupation as tenant.[14] The tenant is not entitled to remove fixtures or buildings which were affixed under an obligation, or replaced existing fixtures. Nor may he remove fixtures or buildings for which he has received compensation or where the landlord has consented to the fixture or building on condition that it will not be removed.[15]

2.2.4 Rent review

The parties can as a matter of contract decide that the rent will remain fixed throughout the term, or be increased to specified amounts at specified times or varied in accordance with objective criteria such as the Retail Prices Index.[16] The parties can also agree contractual terms on the frequency and dates of rent review.[17] There are fall back provisions providing for the rent to be reviewed at not more than three-yearly intervals on the anniversary of the beginning of the tenancy.[18] However, any agreement on a formula for assessing the rent can be overturned by an arbitrator. If either the landlord or tenant refers to an arbitrator the rent payable from the review date, the arbitrator must ascertain the rent on the basis of the open market value. That is the rent which might reasonably be expected if the holding were let on the open market by a willing landlord to a willing tenant disregarding the tenant's improvements, dilapidations caused by the tenant and the fact of the tenant's occupation.[19]

2.2.5 Compensation

The tenant is entitled to compensation for improvements which add to the letting value of the holding at the termination of the tenancy.[20] Improvements are defined to include physical improvements and intangible advantages such as planning permission.[21] No compensation will be payable unless the landlord, or, for improvements

---

[11] Ibid, s 5(1).
[12] Ibid, s 6(1).
[13] Ibid, s 7(1).
[14] Ibid, s 8(1).
[15] Ibid, s 8(2).
[16] Ibid, s 9.
[17] Ibid, s 10(4), (5).
[18] Ibid, s 10(6).
[19] Ibid, s 13.
[20] Ibid, ss 16, 20, 21.
[21] Ibid, s 15.

other than planning permission, the landlord or arbitrator, has given consent to the improvement.[22] There are special provisions dealing with compensation where there are successive tenancies[23] and where the landlord has resumed possession of part[24] or there has been a severance of the reversion.[25] The Act provides that disputes on compensation shall be referred to an arbitrator agreed on by the parties or appointed by the President of the Royal Institution of Chartered Surveyors.[26]

2.2.6 Resolution of disputes

In three situations, arbitration under the Arbitration Acts 1950–1979 is compulsory. These are for the determination of rent following a statutory review notice,[27] (if the parties after the service of the notice have not agreed that the rent shall be determined by a person acting not as an arbitrator); applications for consent to improvements where the landlord refuses or fails to give his consent or imposes unacceptable conditions;[28] and disputes concerning compensation for tenant's improvements.[29] The landlord and tenant can agree in the written tenancy agreement that an independent third party can resolve disputes relating to other matters. Once the dispute has arisen, there must be a joint reference to the third party. If one party only makes a reference, he must serve a notice informing the other party that a reference has been made. The recipient of the notice, if he does not want the third party to have jurisdiction, can within four weeks apply for the appointment of an arbitrator or go to court.[30]

The arbitrator for the purposes of the Act is a sole arbitrator appointed by agreement of the parties or in default of agreement by the President of the Royal Institution of Chartered Surveyors.[31]

2.2.7 Mortgages of agricultural land

Section 99 of the Law of Property Act 1925 is amended to enable a mortgagee to exclude the mortgagor's power of leasing in mortgages of agricultural land granted on or after 1 September 1995. However, the power to grant a lease of an agricultural holding which is governed by the Agricultural Holdings Act 1986 by virtue of s 4 of the Agricultural Tenancies Act 1995[32] cannot be excluded.

2.2.8 Limited owners

There are special provisions for landlords who are trustees under Trusts For Sale or tenants for life under Strict Settlements. They are able to give consents and enter into

---

[22] Ibid, s 17.
[23] Ibid, s 23.
[24] Ibid, s 24.
[25] Ibid, s 25.
[26] Ibid, s 22.
[27] Ibid, ss 10, 28.
[28] Ibid, ss 19, 28.
[29] Ibid, ss 22, 28.
[30] Ibid, s 29.
[31] Ibid, s 30.
[32] Ibid, s 31.

agreements under the Act as if they were absolute owners.[33] Capital money can be invested and raised by mortgage for improvements executed by such landlords and also for compensation paid to tenants for improvements carried out by tenants.[34] Where there are statutory provisions in other legislation requiring a landlord to obtain the best rent, tenants' improvements can be disregarded.[35]

2.2.9 Preparation of documents by surveyors

Section 22 of the Solicitors Act 1974 is amended to allow full members of the Central Association of Agricultural Valuers, Associates or Fellows of the Incorporated Society of Valuers and Auctioneers and Associates or Fellows of the Royal Institution of Chartered Surveyors,[36] to draw up farm business tenancies even where they exceed three years.

2.2.10 Notices

A notice is duly given if it is delivered to a person, left at his proper address or given to him in a manner authorised in a written agreement between the parties. A notice or document to a company is duly given if it is given to its secretary or clerk. A notice given to an agent or servant responsible for the control or management of the landlord's holding is deemed to have been given to the landlord. Likewise, a notice given to an agent or servant of a tenant responsible for the carrying on of a business on the holding is deemed to have been given to the tenant. Where there has been a change of landlord, notices given to the original landlord are deemed to have been duly given to the original landlord unless notice of the change with the name and address of the new landlord has been given to the tenant.[37]

2.2.11 Crown land

Crown land is covered by the Act. There are special provisions dealing with the Duchy of Lancaster and the Duchy of Cornwall.[38]

2.2.12 Definitions

Most of the definitions use the word 'include' and so are not exhaustive.[39] Unusually, there is also an index of expressions defined in the various sections of the Act.[40]

2.2.13 Consequential amendments

There are consequential amendments to 21 other Acts; mostly they are adding farm business tenancies to the special provisions in other legislation dealing with agricultural tenancies under the Agricultural Holdings Act 1986.[41]

---

[33] Ibid, s 32.
[34] Ibid, s 33.
[35] Ibid, s 34.
[36] Ibid, s 35.
[37] Ibid, s 36.
[38] Ibid, s 37.
[39] Ibid, s 38.
[40] Ibid, s 39.
[41] Ibid, s 40, Sch.

2.2.14 Commencement and extent

The Agricultural Tenancies Act 1995 has effect from 1 September 1995. It extends to England and Wales.[42]

---

[42] Ibid, s 41.

Chapter 3

MEANING OF FARM BUSINESS TENANCY

3.1 NEED FOR DEFINITION

One of the main aims of the legislation is to allow tenants to diversify without their tenancies being converted by operation of law into business tenancies which are protected under the Landlord and Tenant Act 1954, Pt II.[1] The simple solution would have been to allow the parties to state that the tenancy was a farm business tenancy. This, however, would undermine the Landlord and Tenant Act 1954, Pt II. It would allow the landlord to let, say, an industrial plant whilst invoking the provisions of the Agricultural Tenancies Act 1995. The drafting difficulty was to produce a definition which was wider than that of an agricultural tenancy under the Agricultural Holdings Act 1986 and yet was distinct from a business tenancy under the 1954 Act.

The term 'farm business' was used in the Farm Business Specification Order 1987, SI 1987/1948 made under the Agriculture Act 1970, and the Farm Business Non-Capital Grant Scheme 1988, SI 1988/1125 made under the Farm Land and Rural Development Act 1988. For the purpose of those orders, a list is given of farm businesses. This was not considered to be a sufficiently flexible approach for the purposes of the Agricultural Tenancies Act 1995. Indeed, it proved impossible to devise a list of businesses which was wide enough to cover all that the landlord and tenant might want the agreement to cover. On the other hand, the definition in s 1 of the Farm Land and Rural Development Act 1988 was not considered sufficiently precise. That definition is as follows:

> '"farm business" means any business consisting in, or such part of any business as consists in, a business which—
>
> (a) is carried on by a person who also carries on an agricultural business at the same time and on the same or adjacent land; and
>
> (b) is not itself an agricultural business.'

The device adopted by the 1995 Act avoids both these defects. There is no list of businesses but the definition, which stipulates that there must be some farming activity, albeit minimal, on the holding throughout the term, precludes confusion with other business tenancies.

3.2 THE DEFINITION

In order to come within the Act, written and oral tenancies, beginning on or after 1 September 1995, must satisfy the business conditions and either the agriculture or notice condition.[2] 'Beginning' is defined as the day on which, under the terms of the

---

[1] HL Deb, 2nd reading, cols 488, 1092, 28 November 1994.
[2] Agricultural Tenancies Act 1995, ss 1, 2, 4(1), 41. Farm business tenancies are specifically excluded from the Landlord and Tenant Act 1954, Pt II. See s 43(1) and the Agricultural Tenancies Act 1995, Sch, para 10.

tenancy, the tenant is entitled to possession under that tenancy.[3] Excluded from the Act are the tenancies set out in para 3.3 below.

Where planning permission for opencast mining has been granted, subject to a restoration condition and immediately before the permission was granted any of the land was comprised in a farm business tenancy, then while it is occupied or used for the permitted activities it is deemed to be used for the purposes for which it was used immediately before such use or occupation.[4] In other words, provided the business and either the agriculture or notice conditions were fulfilled when the opencast mining activities started it will continue to be a farm business tenancy.

3.2.1 Business conditions

There are two business conditions. Since the beginning of the tenancy, all or part of the land must have been farmed for the purpose of a trade or business. 'Farmed' is defined in s 38(2) to include references to the carrying on in relation to land of any agricultural activity. The definition of agricultural is similar to that in the Agricultural Holdings Act 1986. Both definitions use the word 'include' and are not therefore exhaustive. It is considered that the expression 'farming of land', because it includes agricultural activity, may be wider than 'agriculture'. The other condition is that, at the time when the status of the tenancy is challenged, all or part of the land comprised in the tenancy must be so farmed.[5] Provided this second condition is fulfilled at the time of challenge then it is presumed that the first condition has been fulfilled unless the contrary is proved.[6] This presumption may be of assistance where proceedings have arisen in respect of another issue but while that issue is being determined one of the parties questions whether the business condition has been fulfilled at all times since the tenancy was granted. This could be difficult to prove and therefore without the presumption would impose an unreasonable burden on the party challenged.

It is not necessary for the same part of a holding always to have been farmed for the purpose of a trade or business. The business conditions will be satisfied if farming for a trade or business has been carried out on different areas of the holding during the tenancy, provided that at all times there has been some part of the holding in use for commercial farming. The business condition does not require the farming activity to be predominant. Any farming activity will suffice provided it is not de minimis.

If all agricultural activity ceased then the tenancy would no longer be a farm business tenancy under the Agricultural Tenancies Act 1995. It would become a business tenancy under the Landlord and Tenant Act 1954, Pt II. There would be no opportunity for the parties to make a joint application to the county court to contract out of the security provisions of the 1954 Act. This is because such an application has to be made before the tenancy is granted.[7] A tenancy which ceased to be a farm business tenancy automatically would become a business tenancy without a further grant.

---

[3] Agricultural Tenancies Act 1995, s 38(4).
[4] Opencast Coal Act 1958, s 14B; Agricultural Tenancies Act 1995, Sch, para 14.
[5] Agricultural Tenancies Act 1995, s 1(2).
[6] Ibid, s 1(7).
[7] Landlord and Tenant Act 1954, Pt II, s 38(4)(a).

The Landlord and Tenant Act 1954, Pt II:

> 'applies to any tenancy where the property comprised in the tenancy is or includes premises which are occupied by the tenant and are so occupied for the purposes of a business carried on by him or for those and other purposes.'[8]

Business is widely defined. It:

> 'includes a trade, profession or employment and includes any activity carried on by a body of persons, whether corporate or incorporate.'[9]

Therefore, although land let for non-commercial farming will not be a farm business tenancy, it could be a business tenancy. Premises for the purposes of the 1954 Act include bare land.[10] Expressly excluded from the Landlord and Tenant Act 1954 are agricultural tenancies and farm business tenancies.

Where the tenancy becomes a business tenancy under the 1954 Act either because it fails to comply with the business conditions or the agriculture condition (discussed below) then the tenant has a right to apply to the court for a new tenancy at the end of his lease.[11] However, a landlord can oppose the grant of a new tenancy on the ground that he intends to occupy the premises for the purpose of a business carried on by himself[12] (or by a company which he controls) or as his residence.

If the farming activity does not amount to a business then the tenancy will simply be a common-law tenancy without any statutory protection. It will not be governed by the Agricultural Tenancies Act 1995 nor by the Landlord and Tenant Act 1954.

3.2.2 Agriculture condition

The agriculture condition, unlike the business condition, does not need to have been satisfied at all times since the tenancy was granted. It must be satisfied only at the date of challenge. The agriculture condition is that, having regard to:

(a) the terms of the tenancy;

(b) the use of the land comprised in the tenancy;

(c) the nature of any commercial activities carried on on that land; and

(d) any other relevant circumstances,

the character of the tenancy is wholly or primarily agricultural.[13]

There is no single test or any weighting given to the elements which make up the condition. One criterion, taken alone, could give a misleading answer as to the overall character of the holding.

---

8 Ibid, s 23.
9 Ibid, s 23(2).
10 *Bracey v Read* [1963] Ch 88 [1962] 3 WLR 1194.
11 Landlord and Tenant Act 1954, Pt II, s 24.
12 Ibid, ss 29, 30.
13 Agricultural Tenancies Act 1995, s 1(3).

The drafting of the condition enables the court to use reasonable discretion in judging the character of the tenancy, by having regard to the range of factors specified. The terms of the tenancy will not necessarily be in writing and there may be a dispute over what oral terms and conditions were negotiated by the parties. The terms of the tenancy would then be a matter for the court to determine on the evidence. Where there is a written agreement, the terms of the agreement will be relevant in deciding what is the character of the tenancy.

If the status of a tenancy is challenged early in the tenancy, discretion may need to be exercised to determine what use is being made of the holding. For example, non-agricultural crops may have been sown on certain areas within a holding or non-agricultural use may take place for part of a year. It may be that at the time of the challenge there is no financial evidence available (or the evidence may not cover a reasonably representative period of time) to enable the respective contributions to the business of the agricultural and commercial activities to be assessed. For instance, in a given year, income from agriculture might be virtually non-existent and thus out-weighed by only modest non-agricultural revenue.

The judge or arbitrator will have to consider all these matters and any additional relevant circumstances, including allowance for exceptional circumstances, in determining whether or not the agricultural condition is fulfilled at the date of the challenge.

3.2.3 Notice conditions

The purpose of these conditions is to ensure that the parties, especially the tenant, are aware of the nature of the tenancy before they become contractually bound. However, failure to give notice will not prevent the tenancy being a farm business tenancy provided the tenancy complies with the business and agriculture conditions. The notice is not therefore so crucial as the notice which has to be given before the grant of an assured shorthold tenancy of a dwelling.

Nevertheless, it will be more satisfactory if the parties do in fact comply with the notice conditions. This will ensure that the tenancy will remain a farm business tenancy and therefore within the legislation as intended and contemplated by the parties. If the notice conditions are not fulfilled then there is a danger that on the development of a non-agricultural business by the tenant, the tenancy will cease to be a farm business tenancy and become a business tenancy governed by the Landlord and Tenant Act 1954. Well-advised landlords and tenants will ensure therefore that there is compliance with the notice conditions, to avoid uncertainty. In practice, it is likely that where there are written tenancies the notice conditions will be fulfilled but where there are more informal arrangements, resulting in oral tenancies, they will not. Also, where there are fixed-term tenancies of two years or less with a covenant restricting the use to agriculture, the parties may decide to dispense with notices.

There are two conditions which must be fulfilled. On or before the day upon which the parties enter into any instrument creating the tenancy, other than an agreement to enter into a tenancy on a future date, or before the beginning of the tenancy, if this is earlier, the parties must give each other a written notice which:

(i) identifies the land to be comprised in the tenancy whether by name or in some other way (such as Ordnance Survey parcel reference numbers, or by means of an attached plan); and

(ii) contains a statement to the effect that the person giving the notice intends that the tenancy is to be and remain a farm business tenancy throughout the term.[14]

The notice does not have to be in a prescribed form and there is no need for it to be signed. The intention of the legislation is that the notice procedure should be kept as simple as possible. However, the notice cannot be included in the tenancy agreement itself.

The second condition is that at the beginning of the tenancy the character of the tenancy is primarily or wholly agricultural. In deciding this question, regard has to be paid to the terms of the tenancy and any relevant circumstances. There is no obligation to have regard to the use of the land comprised in the tenancy or the nature of any commercial activities on the holding, being the other two factors which have to be taken into account when assessing whether the agriculture condition has been fulfilled. This is because the notice condition applies at the beginning of the farm business tenancy and there may be no valid evidence at that time regarding those matters which could be applied to an incoming tenant. However, where the tenancy is a new tenancy, but granted to the same tenant on the same terms and conditions as the tenancy which immediately preceded it, there may be evidence about the use of the land or any non-agricultural activities carried on by the tenant. These could be relevant circumstances which have to be taken into account in deciding whether the use was primarily or wholly agricultural at the start of the tenancy.

Provided that the notice condition has been fulfilled then it does not matter that there is a subsequent shift in emphasis of activity away from agriculture. In the words of Lord Howe '... provided that at least some of the land is farmed in the conventional sense, for a trade or business throughout the term of the tenancy, no matter what the balance of farming and non-farming activity is on the holding as time goes on, the tenancy will remain a farm business tenancy in law.'[15] This would be so even if the parties were to keep only a small area of land for farming, for the sole purpose of maintaining the status of the letting as a farm business tenancy.

It should be stressed, though, that the use must be primarily or wholly agricultural at the beginning. So a tenancy granted for a riding school, even if it included grazing land would not qualify as a farm business tenancy but would be a business tenancy governed by the Landlord and Tenant Act 1954.

The Act sets out circumstances in which the notice conditions will be deemed to have been complied with, where a new tenancy follows immediately upon a previous tenancy which met the notice conditions. The effect is that where there is a surrender and regrant of a farm business tenancy in respect of which notices were exchanged before that tenancy was granted, the parties do not have to exchange further notices in respect of the new tenancy.[16]

---

[14] Ibid, s 1(4).
[15] HL Committee, col 1990, 12 December 1994.
[16] Agricultural Tenancies Act 1995, s 3.

The deeming provision applies to both express and implied surrenders and regrants. An implied surrender and regrant is most likely to occur where there is a minor change in area of a holding which is otherwise occupied under identical terms to those contained in the original tenancy. The parties do not always appreciate that in such circumstances a new tenancy has been created and might not think of serving new notices.

The rule that no new notice need be served applies only where the following conditions are met:

(1) notices must have been exchanged by the landlord and tenant in respect of the original tenancy;

(2) the new tenancy must be between the same landlord and the same tenant;

(3) the terms of the new tenancy must be substantially the same as the old except

    (a) for changes in area which are small in relation to the size of the holding and do not affect the character of the holding; or

    (b) the only difference is that the new tenancy is for a fixed term which expires earlier than the fixed term under the old tenancy.

Consequential changes or change in area, or reduction in term, agreed by the parties are permitted. An example might be a small increase in rent to cover a small increase in the area of the holding.

If, on the other hand, there is a substantial alteration in the terms, or the new tenancy is for a longer fixed term than the original tenancy, new notices must be exchanged. New notices will also be necessary where there are a series of short-term tenancies which expire by effluxion of time.

3.2.4 Effect of breach of covenant

A tenant who is in breach of any of the terms of his tenancy as to the use of the land, the commercial activities or cessation of commercial activities on the holding, cannot challenge either the business conditions or the agriculture condition by relying on his own breach.[17] For example, a tenancy agreement might prohibit the tenant from carrying on any commercial activities on the holding. If the tenant began such activities and sought to challenge the agriculture condition on the basis that the holding was no longer primarily or wholly agricultural in character, the court would disregard the effect of the breach when applying the agriculture condition. There might also be a requirement in a tenancy agreement that part of the land would at all times be farmed for the purposes of a trade or business. A breach of this requirement would be disregarded when applying the business conditions. However, the position would be different where the landlord, or a previous landlord, had consented to or ac-

---

[17] Ibid, s 1(8).

quiesced in the breach. In those circumstances, the breach would not be disregarded in applying the business conditions or the agriculture condition.

3.3 EXCLUDED TENANCIES

3.3.1 Tenancies beginning before 1 September 1995

The Agricultural Tenancies Act 1995 is not retrospective.

Specifically excluded from the Act are tenancies beginning before 1 September 1995.[18] They will continue to be governed by the Agricultural Holdings Act 1986 if they come within the definition of agricultural tenancies under that Act. Otherwise, if they are tenancies of land which is not substantially agricultural, then probably they are business tenancies covered by the Landlord and Tenant Act 1954, Pt II. Where there is no business element, then they will not be governed by the Agricultural Holdings Act 1986 nor by the 1954 Act.

3.3.2 Succession tenancies

The 1995 Act preserves the succession rights of tenants which have themselves been preserved under the Agricultural Holdings Act 1986. Without such specific provision the statutory rights and legitimate expectations of a tenant with those rights would have been lost and the result would have been to introduce legislation with retro-spective effect.

The Act deals with three situations where a succession tenancy might be granted. First, where it is obtained by a direction from the Agricultural Land Tribunal;[19] secondly, where it is granted directly by the landlord following a direction;[20] and thirdly, where the parties agree, without obtaining a direction from the Agricultural Land Tribunal, that there shall be a succession tenancy.[21]

Section 36 of the Agricultural Holdings Act 1986 enables an eligible person (ie a close relative of the deceased, being spouse, brother or sister, child or child of the family, who has derived his livelihood from agricultural work on the holding for at least five of the last seven years ending with the date of death and who does not already occupy a commercial unit of agricultural land) to apply to the Agricultural Land Tribunal for a direction entitling him to a tenancy.

Section 50 of the Agricultural Holdings Act 1986 enables a nominated successor of a tenant to apply to the Tribunal for a direction to succeed to the tenancy on the retirement of the tenant. The nominated successor must be an eligible person on similar criteria to applications for succession on death.

---

18 Ibid, s 2.
19 Ibid, s 4(1)(b).
20 Ibid, s 4(1)(c).
21 Ibid, s 4(1)(d).

Succession rights apply as a matter of law to tenancies granted before 12 July 1984 (ie the date when the Agricultural Holdings Act 1984 came into force, this being the Act which abolished succession rights for future tenancies). However, the 1984 Act and the Agricultural Holdings Act 1986 enable the parties to contract into the succession provisions where the tenancy was granted after the 1984 Act.[22]

In order to maintain the principle of no retrospective interference with established rights, the draftsman had to preserve existing rights by agreement as well as the statutory rights. The drafting which was required to do this was extremely complex as it had to cover new tenancies which were granted pursuant to original or succession tenancies granted before the 1995 Act. There was therefore a need to incorporate many of the definitions under the Agricultural Holdings Act 1986.

3.3.3 Implied surrender and regrant

Where because of the operation of the doctrine of implied surrender and regrant on a purported variation an existing tenancy to which the 1986 Act applied has been replaced by a new tenancy without the parties deliberately deciding to enter into a new tenancy, then that new tenancy will continue to be governed by the 1986 Act.[23] However, this provision will apply only where the new tenancy is granted to the same person who was tenant of the holding immediately before the grant, and the holding must be substantially the same in respect of both tenancies. The regrant must arise by operation of law, for example where a small increase in the area of the holding has given rise to an implied surrender of the old tenancy and a regrant of a new one. Where there is an express agreement to surrender the old tenancy and grant a new one, the new tenancy will be a farm business tenancy under the Agricultural Tenancies Act 1995.

3.3.4 Tenancies granted pursuant to written contracts before 1 September 1995

The Agricultural Holdings Act 1986 will apply to a tenancy granted pursuant to a written contract of tenancy entered into after 9 May 1995 (when the Agricultural Tenancies Act received Royal Assent) but before 1 September 1995 and which indicates (in whatever terms) that the 1986 Act is to apply in relation to that tenancy.[24] Apart from this limited exception, it is not possible to contract into the Agricultural Holdings Act 1986. The aim of the legislation is to simplify and not to continue indefinitely two forms of agricultural tenancy law.

3.3.5 Evesham custom

The 1986 Act will apply where a tenancy is created by the acceptance of a tenant in accordance with the Evesham custom on the terms and conditions of the previous tenancy.[25]

---

[22] Agricultural Holdings Act 1986, s 34(1)(b)(iii).
[23] Agricultural Tenancies Act 1995, s 4(1)(f).
[24] Ibid, s 4(a).
[25] Ibid, s 4(e).

Mr Michael Jack, Minister of State at the Ministry of Agriculture, Fisheries and Food, explained the Evesham custom as follows:

'That is a rather esoteric subject, and a few words of explanation may be helpful for Hon. Members. The custom grew up last century in the Evesham area, where there were a considerable number of very small market garden holdings and the larger landowners did not find it cost-effective to be closely involved in their management. Where the custom applies and the tenant wants to quit the holding, he or she can, in effect, sell a new tenancy to a substantial and otherwise suitable person, if the landlord is willing to accept that person as a tenant. The payment made by the new tenant covers all compensation for past improvements that is due to the outgoing tenant and also generally includes a premium in return for receiving a tenancy, conferring lifetime security. As my Hon. Friend explained, the premium may, at present, be as much as £300 an acre, which is a substantial sum. An existing tenant has the expectation of recouping that when he, in turn, sells out to another tenant. In the meantime, the expectation of recouping the premium can be used as an asset if, for example, a loan from the bank is needed.

The problem that my Hon. Friend highlighted stems from the fact that, if the Bill were enacted in its present form, any new tenancy would be a farm business tenancy and would not really be on the same terms and conditions as the previous tenancy, which is what the Evesham custom requires. Even if the landlord were prepared to offer excellent terms, there could be no guarantee that such terms would be repeated ad infinitum for each successive tenant. Therefore, it is likely that an incomer would not be willing to pay a substantial premium. As a result, the existing tenant would suffer financially if he wanted to quit the holding under the custom. Moreover, tenants to whom the Evesham custom applies could suffer an immediate loss as their holding would become much less valuable as an asset if, for example, they needed a loan.

Having considered all the implications, we concluded that, if we did not make some provision for the Evesham custom, the 1986 Act tenants would be prejudiced by the introduction of the Bill, even though they remained on their existing holdings under their current tenancy agreements. The amendment that I have tabled addresses that problem. Where the custom applies and is used to create a new tenancy, that new tenancy will remain subject to the 1986 Act. The custom will be able to continue from tenancy to tenancy, until there is a break in the sequence. That could happen if, for example, a tenant dies, or the tenancy is terminated by a notice to quit served by the landlord. Any further tenancy after that would then be a farm business tenancy. The Tenancy Reform Industry Group agrees with that approach, and I hope that it will resolve the problems in relation to that small group of market garden tenants whom we would not want to suffer financial loss by reason of an unintended effect of the Bill.'[26]

The point to emphasise is that the custom applies only where the tenant terminates the tenancy. The custom was developed to protect the landlord from paying the extra compensation to which a tenant of a market garden would be entitled under the Agricultural Holdings Act 1986, in circumstances where the tenancy is brought to an end by the act or financial default of the tenant.

---

[26] HL Committee Stage, col 38, 21 February 1995.

3.3.6 Tenancy at will

Tenancy is defined in the 1995 Act to include a sub-tenancy, and an agreement for a tenancy or sub-tenancy but excludes a tenancy at will.[27] A tenancy at will is a tenancy which may continue indefinitely or may be determined by either party at any time. The tenant has no interest which he can alienate, for he has no definitive estate, merely bare tenure.

3.3.7 Licences

Genuine licences are not covered by the Agricultural Tenancies Act 1995. A non-exclusive licence was excluded from the protection of the Agricultural Holdings Act 1986.[28] Although a non-gratuitous exclusive licence did have protection under that Act, most such so-called licences would as a matter of law create a tenancy.[29]

---

[27] Agricultural Tenancies Act 1995, s 38(1).
[28] Agricultural Holdings Act 1986, s 2.
[29] *Street v Mountford* AC 809, [1985] 2 All ER 289.

Chapter 4

FORMALITIES

4.1 ESSENTIALS FOR A LEASE

A farm business tenancy must comply with the normal legal rules for the creation of a tenancy.

(1) The premises must be sufficiently defined.

(2) The tenant must be given exclusive possession of the premises during the term. If the occupier has not been granted exclusive possession then he will not have a tenancy. Whatever the intention of the parties or the terms of the agreement the courts in deciding whether a tenancy has been granted will look at the factual situation on the ground. In the immortal words of Lord Templeman:

> 'The manufacture of a five-pronged [*sic*] implement for manual digging results in a fork even if the manufacturer, unfamiliar with the English language, insists that he intended to make and has made a spade.'[1]

(3) The lease must be for a certain duration. It must therefore be for a fixed period of years or for a periodic term. A lease cannot be granted, for example, 'until such time as the landlord requires the land for road widening'.[2]

(4) The proper formalities must be observed.

4.2 LEASES AND TENANCIES UNDER THREE YEARS

A legal lease which takes effect in possession (ie at once), for a term not exceeding three years, whether or not the lessee is given power to extend the term, and is at the best rent reasonably obtainable without a fine can be created orally or in writing.[3] The lease will bind third parties.

A contract for a lease which fulfils the conditions in the previous paragraph can also be made orally.[4] To be enforceable against third parties, the contract will have to be registered as an estate contract[5] where the title is unregistered, or noted on the register where the title is registered.[6]

4.3 LEGAL LEASES AND TENANCIES OVER THREE YEARS

A deed is necessary to create a valid legal lease of more than three years.[7] Where the title is unregistered, such a lease will bind a third party whether he knows of it or not.

---

[1] *Street v Mountford* [1985] AC 809.
[2] *Prudential Assurance Co Ltd v London Residuary Body* [1992] 3 All ER 504, [1992] 3 WLR 279.
[3] Law of Property Act 1925, ss 52(1), (2)(d), 54(2).
[4] Law of Property (Miscellaneous Provisions) Act 1989, s 2(5)(a).
[5] Land Charges Act 1972, ss 2, 4.
[6] Land Registration Act 1925, ss 23, 48.
[7] Law of Property Act 1925, ss 52(1), 205(1)(ii),(xxiii).

On the other hand, if the title is registered, leases for more than 21 years must be registered with separate title in order to confer a legal estate on the lessee. Any subsequent assignments of such a lease must also be registered.[8] A lease for under 21 years, granted out of a registered title, is an overriding interest which is automatically binding on a transferee of the reversion.[9]

A contract to grant a legal lease must be made in writing, otherwise it will be void.[10] To bind third parties, the estate contract must be registered as a land charge where the title is unregistered[11] or noted on the title of the registered proprietor where the title is registered.[12]

4.4 EQUITABLE LEASES AND TENANCIES OVER THREE YEARS

If the agreement is made in writing, but not by deed, it is deemed to be a contract to grant a lease. The tenant will be treated for most purposes as if a lease had actually been granted.[13] He will, however, have an equitable lease only. This has some technical drawbacks.

4.4.1 Specific performance

The interest of the tenant under an equitable lease depends on the willingness of the court to grant specific performance. It will not grant this remedy if the tenant does not comply with the equitable maxims, such as coming to equity with clean hands.[14] The court will not therefore enforce the agreement against a tenant who is in breach of his obligations to the landlord. An arbitrator does not have power to order specific performance of a contract relating to land or an interest in land.[15] A lease is an interest in land.[16]

Where a tenant has gone into possession and paid rent by reference to a year or other period he will have acquired a periodic tenancy which will be enforceable in the courts.[17] Such a lease will be a legal lease and will bind third parties.

4.4.2 Easements

Another drawback is that certain easements and other rights are created where a lease is granted by deed but not where it arises from a contract.[18]

---

[8] Land Registration Act 1925, s 22 and s 123 (as amended by the Land Registration Act 1986, s 2(1)).
[9] Ibid, s 70(1)(k).
[10] Law of Property (Miscellaneous Provisions) Act 1989, s 2(1).
[11] Land Charges Act 1972, ss 2, 4.
[12] Land Registration Act 1925, ss 23, 48.
[13] *Walsh v Lonsdale* (1882) 21 ChD 9.
[14] *Coatsworth v Johnson* (1886) 55 LJQB 220.
[15] Arbitration Act 1950, s 15.
[16] Law of Property Act 1925, s 205(ix); Interpretation Act 1978, s 5, Sch 1.
[17] *Bell Street Investments Ltd v Wood* [1970] EGD 812.
[18] Law of Property Act 1925, s 62.

4.4.3 Burden of the covenants

There are also problems in enforcing covenants against third parties. The original parties to a contract for a lease will be bound by privity of contract on the benefits and burdens of the lease. The benefit of a contract can be assigned to a third party but not the burden. Where a leasehold estate is assigned, the covenants which touch and concern the land will pass to the new tenant under the doctrine of privity of estate.[19] If, however, no estate is assigned but merely the benefit of the contract there can be no privity of estate. On the other hand, if the tenant, by taking possession and paying rent, has become a legal periodic tenant, the burden of any covenants consistent with that interest will pass to the assignee.[20]

4.4.4 Third parties – unregistered title

If a lease is merely equitable, ie it has not been granted by deed, then, in order to bind third parties, it needs to be registered as a land charge under the Land Charges Act 1972.[21] Registration is deemed to be notice to the whole world.[22] Failure to register will make it void against a purchaser of the reversion for money or money's worth of a legal estate in the land.[23] This is so even if the purchaser has actual knowledge of the agreement.[24]

In practice, it is likely that the tenant will have a legal periodic tenancy which will be binding on a purchaser. However, a yearly tenancy may be terminated by notice of between one and two years. Under the agreement the tenant may have been entitled to a much longer term which will not be binding on the purchaser of the reversion unless registered.

4.4.5 Third parties – registered title

An equitable lease carved out of a registered title may be protected by a notice or caution on the registered title of the landlord.[25] However, even if this is not done, the tenant will have an overriding interest if he is in actual occupation or in receipt of the rents and profits.[26] An overriding interest will bind a purchaser of the reversion whether he knows of it or not.

4.5 ASSIGNMENTS

A deed is necessary for a legal assignment of a lease even if the original lease was created orally, for example a periodic tenancy.[27]

---

[19] *Spencer's Case* (1583) 5 Co Rep 16a.
[20] *Doe d. Thomson v Amey* (1840) 12 A&E 476.
[21] Land Charges Act 1972, ss 2, 4.
[22] Law of Property Act 1925, ss 198, 199.
[23] Land Charges Act 1972, s 4.
[24] *Midland Bank Trust Co Ltd v Green* [1981] AC 513.
[25] Land Registration Act 1925, ss 48, 54.
[26] Ibid, s 70(1)(g).
[27] Law of Property Act 1925, ss 52, 205(1)(ii).

If the assignment is merely in writing this will be an effective equitable assignment and will be binding between the assignor and assignee. There will be no privity of estate between the assignee tenant and the landlord, so the landlord may not be able to enforce the covenants in the lease. However, the assignee may be estopped[28] from denying liability and once there has been payment and acceptance of rent the assignee will become a periodic tenant and liable on the covenants applicable to such a tenancy.

Where the lease which has been assigned by deed has more than 21 years left to run, then it must be registered at the Land Registry if the assignee is to obtain legal title.[29] If the lease is already registered, then the assignment must be registered even if there are less than 21 years left to run.[30]

4.6 SOLICITORS ACT 1974

Under s 22 of the Solicitors Act 1974 an unqualified person who directly or indirectly:

'(a) draws or prepares any instrument of transfer or charge for the purposes of the Land Registration Act 1925, or makes any application or lodges any document for registration under that Act at the registry, or

(b) draws or prepares any other instrument relating to real or personal estate, or any legal proceeding'

in expectation of fee, gain or reward is guilty of an offence.

Instrument is defined to include a contract for sale or other disposition of land. Expressly excluded are leases of three years and under taking effect in possession and granted at the best rent without taking a fine. Contracts for such leases are also excluded. Qualified persons include solicitors, barristers, licensed conveyancers, notaries public, authorised practitioners and some public officers.

The Agricultural Tenancies Act 1995 amends the Solicitors Act 1974 by allowing accredited persons to draw or prepare any instrument:

'(i) which creates, or which he believes on reasonable grounds will create, a farm business tenancy (within the meaning of the Agricultural Tenancies Act 1995) or

(ii) which relates to an existing tenancy which is, or which he believes on reasonable grounds to be, such a tenancy.'

An accredited person

'means any person who is—

(a) a Full Member of the Central Association of Agricultural Valuers,

(b) an Associate or Fellow of the Incorporated Society of Valuers and Auctioneers, or

(c) an Associate or Fellow of the Royal Institution of Chartered Surveyors.'[31]

This means that accredited persons may draw up farm business tenancy agreements, assignments and surrenders of such tenancies even where they exceed three years.

---

[28] *Rodenhurst Estates Ltd v WH Barnes* [1936] 2 All ER 3.
[29] Land Registration Act 1925, s 123(1), as amended by the Land Registration Act 1986, s 2(1).
[30] Ibid, s 22.
[31] Agricultural Tenancies Act 1995, s 35.

4.7 STAMPING

An agreement for a lease is liable to stamp duty. Any duty paid must be denoted on the ensuing lease. If there is no prior agreement then the lease must be certified to that effect.[32]

Stamp duty is payable on agreements for leases, or leases, at a rent of over £500 per annum or for more than seven years. A document liable to stamp duty should be presented for payment within 30 days of its execution. Agreements may be presented within 30 days of the execution of the lease itself. There is a penalty for late payment. Counterpart leases will be assessed at 50p unless the duty charged on the counterpart is less than that amount.[33]

A lease for seven years or more and any transfer or sale of such a lease must be produced to the Commissioners of Inland Revenue and stamped with a separate stamp under the Finance Act 1931, s 28.

---

[32] Inland Revenue Direction, September 1994.
[33] Finance Act 1982, s 128.

Chapter 5

CONTRACTUAL TERMS

5.1 INTRODUCTION

In order for there to be a valid lease, minimum matters must be agreed. These are the parties, the property and the duration of the term. Although it is usual to agree a rent, an obligation to pay rent is not an essential term of a lease.[1] Where the basic terms are agreed, the law will imply certain obligations on the part of the landlord and tenant. Rather than spelling out all the terms of the agreement, the parties may agree to be bound by the 'usual covenants'. These are discussed below. However, the parties will more usually enter into a formal tenancy agreement which will contain express covenants and other terms.

The express covenants are subject to any overriding statutory provision. The Agricultural Holdings Act 1986 provides specifically for various terms in agricultural tenancies. Some of these statutory provisions will apply unless the parties agree to the contrary. Others will apply regardless of the agreement of the parties. In other words, it is not possible to contract out of those particular statutory provisions.

The approach for farm business tenancies under the Agricultural Tenancies Act 1995 is quite different. The fundamental principle underlying the legislation is freedom of contract. Statutory intervention is limited to six main areas. These are:

(1) definition of farm business tenancy;[2]
(2) notice required to terminate the tenancy;[3]
(3) tenant's right to remove fixtures;[4]
(4) rent review;[5]
(5) compensation;[6] and
(6) resolution of disputes.[7]

On all other matters the landlord and tenant are free to agree their own terms. They can negotiate contracts to suit their individual needs. Many of the terms are likely to be similar to those found in existing agricultural leases. However, as there are no provisions on freedom of cropping or cultivating according to the rules of good husbandry, it will be possible to have more effective environmental covenants than under the agricultural holdings legislation.

The scope of farm business tenancies is wider than that of traditional agricultural tenancies. The parties will have to consider, as with other business tenancies, what are the appropriate terms for a tenancy. They may wish to allow for future diversified enterprises.

---

[1] *Ashburn Anstalt v Arnold* [1989] Ch 1 Law of Property Act 1925, s 205(xxvii).
[2] Agricultural Tenancies Act 1995, ss 1–4.
[3] Ibid, ss 5–7.
[4] Ibid, s 8.
[5] Ibid, ss 9–14.
[6] Ibid, ss 15–27.
[7] Ibid, ss 28–30.

In particular, the parties will have to decide whether they want a periodic tenancy (yearly, half-yearly, quarterly or perhaps even monthly) or a tenancy for a fixed number of years. The legislation does not provide a minimum length of lease. For some purposes the parties may want long terms; for others shorter terms will be appropriate. For instance, a short-term tenancy may be needed to transfer milk quota. Tenants as well as landlords are contractually bound throughout the term; they may not always want to enter into long tenancies. The position is quite different from that under the Agricultural Holdings Act 1986. Although in practice the tenant has lifetime security, in law he has a yearly tenancy which he can terminate on giving between one and two years' notice to quit.[8]

Where there is provision in the tenancy agreement for a rent review, the landlord or the tenant might want to negotiate a break clause in the agreement which he could operate after a rent review. The parties might also want a break clause to enable the lease to be terminated on the death or incapacity of the tenant.

It should be noted that if the parties purport to create a tenancy for the life of the tenant, this will be converted automatically into a term of 90 years by s 149(6) of the Law of Property Act 1925. The wording of s 149(6) is:

> 'Any lease or underlease, at a rent, or in consideration of a fine, for a life or lives or for any term of years determinable with life or lives or on the marriage of the lessee ...'

It is not therefore considered that a lease granted for a fixed term with merely an option to determine the lease by serving a notice is caught by this provision.

5.2 MINIMUM EXPRESS TERMS

Where the parties have agreed on the property to be let and the duration of the lease, but nothing else, certain obligations are implied on behalf of the landlord and the tenant.

5.2.1 Landlord's implied obligations

There is an implied covenant by the landlord that the tenant will have quiet enjoyment of the demised premises.[9] This covenant has nothing to do with noise but means that the tenant will be free from disturbance by the landlord or by the lawful activities of those claiming under him. The landlord is not liable if the tenant is disturbed in his enjoyment by someone with title paramount, such as a superior landlord.[10] An example of breach of this covenant is where the land subsides due to the working of minerals.[11] There must be no substantial interference with the tenant's physical enjoyment of the land.[12]

The landlord must not derogate from his grant.[13] In layman's terms, he must not seek

---

8 Agricultural Holdings Act 1986, ss 2, 3, 25.
9 *Budd-Scott v Daniell* [1902] 2 KB 351.
10 *Baynes & Co v Lloyd & Sons* [1895] 2 QB 610.
11 *Markham v Paget* [1908] 1 Ch 697.
12 *Owen v Gadd* [1956] 2 QB 99.
13 *Palmer v Fletcher* (1663) 1 Lev 122.

to take away with one hand what he has given with the other. This obligation to some extent overlaps with the covenant of quiet enjoyment, but it can cover acts which do not amount to a breach of covenant. For example, if the land were let for the keeping of livestock and the landlord used adjoining land for some disturbing activity so that the animals did not flourish, then there might be liability under the principle of derogation from grant. The essence is that the act must make the premises substantially less fit for the purpose for which they were let.

5.2.2 Tenant's implied rights and obligations

The tenant is under an implied obligation to pay rent and all rates and taxes except those for which the landlord is liable. A tenant must not commit waste. His liability depends on the type of tenancy. A tenant for a fixed term of years is liable for both voluntary and permissive waste and must therefore keep the premises in proper repair.[14] Voluntary waste is a positive act:

> 'the committing of any spoil or destruction in houses, lands etc. by tenants, to the damage of the heir, or of him in reversion or remainder.'[15]

Examples of voluntary waste are opening and working a mine[16] or cutting timber on the demised land.[17] Permissive waste is an act of omission, rather than commission. The failure to do that which ought to be done. This would include failure to keep buildings in repair or to clean out a ditch.[18] Mere failure to cultivate land, however, has been held not to be permissive waste.[19]

A yearly tenant is liable for voluntary and permissive waste. His liability for permissive waste, though, is limited to keeping the premises wind and water tight.[20] A weekly tenant is not liable for permissive waste but he must use the premises in a tenant-like manner.[21] The same rules probably apply to quarterly and monthly tenants.

A yearly tenant or a tenant of a fixed-term tenancy determinable with lives was entitled at common law to emblements, provided the determination of the tenancy was not caused by his own act.[22] This right entitled the tenant to enter the land on the determination of the tenancy to reap the crops which he had sown.[23] This right applies only to annual crops such as corn, root crops and potatoes and not to fruit trees and timber. However, these rights are of historic interest as tenancies are no longer subject to sudden determination. A yearly tenant under the Agricultural Tenancies Act 1995 is entitled to notice of at least one year expiring at the completed year of his tenancy.[24]

---

14 *Yellowly v Gower* (1855) 11 Exch 274.
15 Bacon's Abridgement (7th edn) vol 8, p 379.
16 *Dashwood v Magniac* [1891] 3 Ch 306 at 360.
17 *Honywood v Honywood* (1874) LR 18 Eq 306.
18 *Powys v Blagrave* (1854) 4 De GM & G 488.
19 *Hutton v Warren* (1836) 1 M&W 466 at 472.
20 *Wedd v Porter* [1916] 2 KB 91.
21 *Warren v Keen* [1954] 1 QB 15.
22 Oland's Case (1602) 5 Co Rep 116a.
23 Co Litt 55b.
24 Agricultural Tenancies Act 1995, s 6. There is no specific provision as in the Agricultural Holdings Act 1986, s 21, stating that the notice of 12 months is in lieu of emblements, but as emblements relate to annual crops the same principle must apply.

A tenancy for life at a rent will be converted into a term of 90 years.[25] A tenancy granted by a life tenant under a strict settlement will not determine on the death of the life tenant.[26]

5.3 USUAL COVENANTS

Where a lease has actually been granted, the implied covenants set out above (see para 5.2) will apply, subject to any express agreement to the contrary. Sometimes, however, the parties will agree that a lease will be granted 'subject to the usual covenants'. Or, there may be merely an agreement for a lease. In the absence of any provision as to covenants, then it is implied that the usual covenants will apply.

5.3.1 Content of usual covenants

The following usual covenants[27] will always apply, in addition to, or in modification of, those implied covenants set out in para 5.2 above.

There will be a covenant on the part of the landlord for quiet enjoyment. The covenant extends only to the acts of the lessor and the rightful acts of those claiming from or under him.

On the part of the tenant the usual covenants are:

(1) to pay rent;
(2) to pay tenant's rates and taxes;
(3) to keep the premises in repair and deliver them up at the end of the term in this condition;
(4) to permit the landlord to enter and view the state of repair, if the tenant is liable to repair;
(5) to allow the landlord to re-enter for non-payment of rent and probably for breach of any other covenant.

5.3.2 Usual by custom or usage

In addition, there may be usual covenants which are particular to the trade or locality. If there is a dispute, the court will have to settle the matter taking into account the nature of the premises, their situation, the purpose for which they are being let and the length of the term, the evidence of conveyancers and the contents of books of precedents.[28] However, there is a distinction between covenants which are expressly and normally put in a lease and usual covenants in the technical sense.

5.4 EXPRESS COVENANTS

Clearly, express covenants depend on the negotiations between the parties and cannot be enumerated. However, certain covenants are usually found in all leases and these

---

[25] Law of Property Act 1925, s 149(6).
[26] Settled Land Act 1925, s 41. A tenant for life can grant a lease for a term not exceeding 50 years which will be binding on the successor in title.
[27] *Hampshire v Wickens* (1878) 7 ChD 555. *Chester v Buckingham Travel Ltd* [1981] 1 WLR 96.
[28] *Flexman v Corbett* [1930] 1 Ch 672.

are discussed below. Examples are also given of some of the express covenants the parties may want to include in farm business tenancies.

5.4.1 To pay rent

Under the implied and usual covenants, rent is paid in arrears.[29] An express covenant can provide that rent is to be paid in advance. At common law the rent continues to be payable even if the premises are destroyed, say by fire, or cannot be used for any external reason.[30] Express covenants can override this result and provide for the rent to be abated in specified circumstances.

A landlord may enforce payment of rent by an action for money, or distress, or by threat of forfeiture. The landlord who wants to rely on forfeiture should ensure that the lease contains a forfeiture clause and provides that the re-entry can occur when the rent is a stated number of days in arrears whether formally demanded or not.

The tenancy agreement may have specific provisions for review of the rent. The interaction of contractual and statutory provisions is discussed below. The important point to stress is that there will be a rent review unless there are contractual provisions to the contrary (see para 6.3).[31]

5.4.2 Not to assign, underlet or part with possession

Traditionally, tenancies of agricultural holdings have contained an absolute prohibition against assignment or underletting. Even if there is not a covenant to that effect, provided there is no agreement permitting assignment or underletting, the landlord under the Agricultural Holdings Act 1986 can serve a notice requiring a written tenancy, and once that notice has been served no assignment or underletting is valid until the conclusion of an agreement between the landlord and tenant or an arbitrator's award.[32]

At common law, assignments and underlettings are permitted unless there is a contrary provision in the tenancy agreement. Where there is an absolute prohibition against assignment or underletting, any such disposition will be valid but the landlord will be able to bring forfeiture proceedings or an action for damages.[33]

A lease may contain a covenant against assigning or sub-letting without the landlord's consent. In other words, there is not an absolute prohibition but a qualified prohibition. The Landlord and Tenant Act 1927[34] provides that where there is such a qualified covenant, there shall be implied by law, notwithstanding any agreement to the contrary, a proviso that the consent shall not be unreasonably withheld. This section, however, does not apply to agricultural holdings under the Agricultural Holdings Act 1986 or farm business tenancies under the Agricultural Tenancies Act 1995.[35]

---

[29] *Coomber v Howard* (1845) ICB 440.

[30] *Belfour v Weston* (1786) ITR 310.

[31] Agricultural Tenancies Act 1995, s 9.

[32] Agricultural Holdings Act 1986, s 6.

[33] *Old Grovebury Manor Farm Ltd v W Seymour Plant and Hire Ltd (No 2)* [1979] 1 WLR 1397.

[34] Landlord and Tenant Act 1927, s 19(1). The Landlord and Tenant (Covenants) Bill amends s 19 to allow the landlord to stipulate in the tenancy agreement the conditions on which he will allow assignment. See also Landlord and Tenant Act 1988. Duty of landlord to give consent or refusal within reasonable time and where consent is withheld reasons therefor.

[35] Ibid, s 19(4).

Where a long fixed-term lease is granted, it will be in the interests of the tenant to ensure that he will be able to assign the lease or that his landlord will accept a surrender. Alternatively, he should negotiate a break clause enabling the lease to be determined on his death. It should be noted, however, that where a tenant leaves his interest under the tenancy agreement by will, such a bequest does not amount to a breach of the covenant against assignment.[36] In general, there must be some voluntary dealing with the property *inter vivos* to constitute a breach. The involuntary vesting of the lease in the trustee in bankruptcy[37] or the compulsory sale of the lease under statutory provisions[38] would not amount to a breach.

5.4.3 To repair

It is a matter for negotiation whether the landlord or the tenant is liable for repairs. Often in long leases the tenant covenants to do all repairs. However, in short leases, the landlord frequently assumes liability for external and structural repairs. Under the Landlord and Tenant Act 1985,[39] if the lease is under seven years, the landlord is under a statutory duty to keep in repair the structure and exterior of the dwelling as well as the installations in the dwelling for the supply of water, gas and electricity and for sanitation. However, agricultural holdings under the Agricultural Holdings Act 1986 and farm business tenancies under the Agricultural Tenancies Act 1995 are expressly excluded from the 1985 Act.[40]

If no provision for repairs is made in a farm business tenancy, neither party is liable for them, apart from the implied provisions relating to waste (see para 5.2.2). There is nothing similar to the model clauses under the Agricultural Holdings Act 1986,[41] whereby in the absence of agreement to the contrary, responsibility is allocated between the parties.

The extent of the landlord's or tenant's repairing obligation under the lease depends on the particular wording. Where premises are out of repair when let, a covenant to keep them in good repair includes putting them into good repair.[42]

A covenant qualified by the words 'fair wear and tear excepted', excludes defects arising from normal use of the premises but not consequential damage. So for example a tenant with such a qualified covenant would not be liable for an unrepaired skylight but he would be liable for any damage caused by rain entering through the skylight.[43]

There is much case-law on the distinction between repair and renewal. It is really a question of degree[44] and so it is impossible to lay down general guidelines. Remedying an inherent defect may or may not be a repair. Replacing subsidiary parts of a building

---

[36] *Fox v Swann* (1655) Sty 482.
[37] *Re Riggs* [1901] 2 KB 16.
[38] *Slipper v Tottenham & Hampstead Junction Ry* (1867) LR 4 Eq 112.
[39] Landlord and Tenant Act 1985, s 11.
[40] Ibid, s 14(3). Agricultural Tenancies Act 1995, Sch, para 31.
[41] Agricultural Holdings Act 1986, s 7.
[42] *Proudfoot v Hart* (1890) 25 QBD 42 at 50.
[43] *Regis Property Co Ltd v Dudley* [1959] AC 370.
[44] *Ravenseft Properties Ltd v Davstone (Holdings) Ltd* [1980] QB 12.

such as rebuilding a wall,[45] replacing the roof,[46] replacing drain pipes have been held to be covered by the term repair. On the other hand, where substantial work is done then it may fall outside a repairing covenant.[47] In reaching a decision the court will take into account the terms of the lease, the type of building and its condition when let, the extent and nature of the repair, the nature, extent and costs of the works which need to be done, the value and life-span of the building and so on.[48]

The Leasehold Property (Repairs) Act 1938 does not apply to agricultural tenancies under the Agricultural Holdings Act 1986, nor to farm business tenancies under the Agricultural Tenancies Act 1995.[49]

5.4.4 To insure

There should be an express covenant to insure the property. Where there is such a covenant to insure by the landlord or tenant and the property is damaged by fire, the other party may, under s 83 of the Fires Prevention (Metropolitan) Act 1774, require that the insurance money be spent on reinstatement. Generally, the liability for insurance and reinstatement of the buildings will be undertaken by the landlord with the tenant insuring live and dead stock on the holding and all harvested crop and produce. Probably the tenant will also want to insure against his liability for repairs and against loss of profit which might flow from the destruction of the permanent equipment and the dislocation of his business.

5.4.5 Agricultural covenants for matters formerly covered by the Agricultural Holdings Act 1986

The parties may want to have express covenants to cover the matters for which there were statutory provisions under the Agricultural Holdings Act 1986. There are, for instance, no statutory provisions under the Agricultural Tenancies Act 1995 regarding good husbandry.[50] There is a duty at common law to cultivate land according to the custom of the country in a good and husbandlike manner.

In *Wedd v Porter*,[51] the Court of Appeal described the duty as follows:

'A tenant from year to year of a farm and buildings at a fixed rent, who has not entered into any other express covenant with the landlord than as to the amount of rent, is under an obligation implied by law to use and cultivate the lands in a husbandlike manner according to the custom of the country . . . and to keep the buildings wind and water tight.'

Since this is not a very onerous requirement and somewhat vague, the parties may want to agree to a more specific covenant. In particular, a landlord may want the tenant to covenant to deliver up the land on termination of the tenancy in a clean and proper condition.

---

[45] *Lurcott v Wakely* [1911] 1 KB 905.
[46] *Elite Investments Ltd v TI Bainbridge Silencers Ltd* [1986] 2 EGLR 43.
[47] *Brew Brothers Ltd v Snax (Ross) Ltd* [1970] 1 QB 612.
[48] *Holding and Management Ltd v Property Holdings PLC* [1990] 1 All ER 938 at 945.
[49] Leasehold Property (Repairs) Act 1938, s 7(1). Agricultural Tenancies Act 1995, Sch, para 8.
[50] cf Agricultural Holdings Act 1986 (eg ss 27(3)(a), 71, 72, 96(3)).
[51] *Wedd v Porter* [1916] 2 KB 91 at 100

If there is a breach of either the implied covenant at common law or express contractual provisions relating to good husbandry, the landlord will be able to bring a claim for damages. The good husbandry duties will also be enforceable by injunction. However, there is no statutory provision for general dilapidation and deterioration of the holding.[52] The remedies lie only if there are contractual provisions, imposing specific obligations or prohibitions on the tenant, or a covenant the effect of which is to prevent the deterioration of the holding generally.

Covenants may be imposed to prevent the tenant from ploughing permanent pasture, restricting the method of farming or restricting the tenant's right to dispose of crops or produce. Under a farm business tenancy, there are no statutory provisions allowing for the variation of terms relating to permanent pasture or providing for freedom of cropping.[53]

As there is no statutory provision for game damage[54] the tenant may want a contractual provision to reimburse him for damage which occurs where the shooting rights are reserved to the landlord or a third party. The contractual liability will be with the landlord not the third party. The landlord or the tenant may want a covenant for the making of a record of condition[55] of the holding in certain circumstances.

Tenants should ensure that they will be able to claim under the contract for standing crops, liming and other particular tenant right improvements.[56] Although the Agricultural Tenancies Act 1995 contains mandatory provisions for compensation, this is only payable where the landlord or the arbitrator, for improvements other than planning permission, has given consent to the improvement.[57] It is unlikely that individual consents will be given for normal farming operations which result in residual improvement to the land. A general consent given in the tenancy agreement to such operations will avoid any difficulty on the termination of the tenancy. A tenant might also want to make a specific contractual provision so that he could obtain compensation for hefted sheep on the termination of the tenancy.

5.4.6 General agricultural covenants

For a straightforward letting of land for agricultural purposes many of the standard reservations and covenants contained in existing agricultural tenancies will be relevant. Clearly, care will be needed not to repeat these verbatim. They will have been drafted against a background of yearly tenancies with security of tenure and other statutory interventions of the Agricultural Holdings Act 1986.

One covenant often found in agricultural tenancies is an obligation on the tenant to reside constantly at the farmhouse. The aim of such a clause is to ensure that the tenant personally supervises the farming and does not become an absentee tenant.

---

[52] As there are in the Agricultural Holdings Act 1986, ss 71 and 72.
[53] cf ibid, ss 14 and 15.
[54] cf ibid, s 20.
[55] cf ibid, s 22.
[56] cf ibid, ss 64, 65, Sch 8, Pt II.
[57] Agricultural Tenancies Act 1995, ss 15–20.

Other covenants which frequently appear in tenancy agreements, impose obligations on the tenant to maintain any quota on the land. A distinction has to be made between, for example milk quota, which is attached to land, and other quotas which the European Union has allocated to the producer.

Milk quota can be transferred by a tenant in two ways. First, the tenant can grant an underlease to the purchaser of the milk quota. Provided the sub-lease is for at least 10 months it will automatically transfer the quota to the sub-tenant.[58] If the purchaser does not use the quota on the land in the sub-tenancy, but on other land in which he has an interest, then on the termination of the tenancy there will be no quota attached to the let land and so no quota will revert to the mesne tenant. A covenant against assigning or underletting would mean that the milk quota could not be transferred without the consent of the landlord. However, it might be in the interests of both parties to allow assigning and sub-letting in some circumstances. In that event it would be better if the quota were to be protected by a positive obligation to maintain a certain stated number of litres on the land and to prohibit any transfer or charging of it.

Indeed, as the current dairy quota regulations provide for confiscation of milk quota by the Intervention Board where quota is not used or leased out in any quota year, there should be a covenant to maintain dairy production on the holding.[59] If the tenancy agreement merely prevents selling, leasing or otherwise dealing with quota then the tenant could sell his dairy herd and the quota might be lost.

Such clauses would also protect against 'massaging'. Where a tenant has other land in which he has a freehold or leasehold interest he can simply transfer his dairying activities to that other land thereby depriving the let land of milk quota. An appropriately drafted clause would prevent this.

Where quotas or premium rights are given to a producer and a tenant brings those rights to a tenancy, a contractual clause could ensure that the benefit remains with the let land during the currency of the agreement. However, any clause which purported to attach those rights to the land or to entitle the landlord to take over the rights at the end of the tenancy, without full compensation, would fall foul of European Union law and therefore be unenforceable.

A landlord might want a general covenant in the tenancy agreement that the tenant would not enter into any national or European Union support scheme without the landlord's previous written consent. He might also include in the agreement covenants by the tenant to supply Integrated Administration and Control System (IACS) information and to comply with specific requirements during the last year of the tenancy so that the landlord or incoming tenant does not lose the benefit of any payments.[60]

5.4.7 Environmental covenants

Landlords who are public bodies upon whom are imposed duties towards the environment, or wildlife trusts will want to include covenants in their tenancy

---

[58] EC Council Regulation 857/84, Art 7. Dairy Produce Quotas Regulations 1994, reg 7.
[59] Dairy Produce Quotas Regulations 1994, reg 33.
[60] See the Country Landowners Association publication *IACS: A Guide to Letting and Selling Land* Sept 1994 C1/94.

agreements to protect the environment. These will be much more effective than under the Agricultural Holdings Act 1986 where there is the concern that such covenants may be in conflict with the overriding principles of good husbandry.

These covenants could stipulate obligations for such work as ditch maintenance and hedge trimming or the control of burrowing animals on Scheduled Ancient Monuments. The covenants could regulate the type, frequency and timing of cropping. There is nothing equivalent to the freedom of cropping provision in the Agricultural Holdings Act 1986.[61] There could be covenants to abide by a particular grazing regime, including stocking density, types of animals and timing of grazing. Other covenants might prohibit the use of fertilisers or herbicides and contain positive obligations to control plants and weeds, for example grazing a hay meadow with sheep to control marsh ragwort. Activities such as feeding, burning and storing of specified articles could be regulated. In short, the landlord can offer the land on terms which fulfil particular environmental objectives. Naturally, if the requirements are onerous then this will be reflected in the rent and the readiness or otherwise of a prospective tenant to accept other terms of the tenancy.

5.4.8 Animal welfare

Some landlords are anxious to take a lead in protecting the welfare of animals on farms. Covenants may be imposed prohibiting the treatment of animals on the holding in such a manner as to cause unnecessary pain or distress. In many tenancy agreements the tenant undertakes to comply with provisions of any code or recommendations for the welfare of livestock issued under the authority of any statute relating to the welfare of livestock.

A landlord can apply for an injunction to prevent a breach of these covenants. Alternatively, he could start forfeiture proceedings. Although the tenant might obtain relief, he would do so only on condition that in the future he complied with his obligations.

5.4.9 Early resumption

A fixed-term contract is just that. In the absence of a contractual provision, it cannot be terminated at the whim of either party. In particular, if a landlord receives planning permission he has no right to determine the tenancy. The incontestable notice to quit on the Case B grounds which was available to a landlord of a yearly tenancy under the Agricultural Holdings Act 1986[62] has no application. Of course, if the farm business tenancy is a yearly tenancy, the landlord can terminate the tenancy by giving notice of at least 12 and less than 24 months expiring at the completed year of the tenancy.[63] The landlord does not have to rely on any ground for the notice to be effective.

---

[61] Agricultural Holdings Act 1986, s 15.
[62] Ibid, s 26, Sch 3, Pt I.
[63] Agricultural Tenancies Act 1995, s 5.

The parties may negotiate a break clause which will operate if the landlord obtains planning permission. However, a break clause in a tenancy of over two years will operate only if notice of at least 12 and less than 24 months has been served. There is nothing similar to s 25(2)(b) of the 1986 Act which allows the parties to agree a shorter notice for 'resumption of possession of the holding or some part of it for some specified purpose other than the use of the land for agriculture'.

If a landlord considers that one to two years' notice is too long, he can let the land for a fixed-term tenancy for any period of two years and under. No notice is required to terminate such a tenancy. Alternatively, he could let the land for a periodic tenancy less than a yearly tenancy. A monthly tenancy can be terminated by one month's notice, a quarterly tenancy by three months' notice and a six-month tenancy by six months' notice. Or, indeed, he could combine a short fixed term with a periodic letting. For instance, he could let for six months and then agree that the fixed-term tenancy will be followed by a monthly tenancy.

5.4.10 User clauses

Some of the most important clauses in farm business tenancy agreements will be user clauses. It is anticipated that the agreements will cover more than traditional agriculture but will not be totally open-ended. Clearly, a landlord will wish to exercise some control over his land. On the other hand, the closer the control the less rent a prospective tenant is likely to offer.

In order for the tenancy to remain a farm business tenancy under the Agricultural Tenancies Act 1995, it must comply with the business conditions.[64] These conditions stipulate that at least some of the land must be farmed (ie used for an agricultural activity) throughout the term. Any use of the land in breach of the terms of the tenancy is to be disregarded in determining whether at any time the tenancy meets the business conditions.[65] A landlord should ensure therefore that the tenant covenants to maintain some farming on the land during the term of the tenancy.

One of the concerns of landlords while the Bill was passing through Parliament, was the mandatory obligation to pay compensation to tenants for improvements which landlords thought they might not want and which might be inappropriate to the holding. However, no compensation is payable unless the landlord has given consent to the improvement.[66] Although a reference can be made to an arbitrator for consent, where the landlord refuses (other than where the improvement consists of planning permission) the arbitrator in deciding whether to give consent has to take into account the terms of the tenancy, and any other relevant circumstances.[67] Thus the user clause will be of prime importance. Only in exceptional circumstances, for instance in the interests of safety or to prevent pollution, would an arbitrator be justified in overriding a user clause.

---

[64] Ibid, s 1(2).
[65] Ibid, s 1(8).
[66] Ibid, ss 9, 17, 18.
[67] Ibid, s 19(5).

5.4.11 **Right of re-entry**

Most importantly, there should be a right of re-entry given to the landlord on breach of covenant. Since there is nothing equivalent to the incontestable notice to quit provisions of the Agricultural Holdings Act 1986,[68] the landlord will have to rely on the law of forfeiture if he wishes to bring a tenancy to an end for breach of covenant. Unless there is a proviso for re-entry, or observance of the covenant is a condition of the lease, he will not be able to obtain forfeiture.

The lease should also dispense with the need for a formal demand where forfeiture follows non-payment of rent.

It should be noted that the problem in *Parry v Million Pigs Ltd*[69] (where the forfeiture clause was invalid because it did not give the tenant sufficient time to claim compensation) will not occur in a forfeiture under the Agricultural Tenancies Act 1995. This is because there is no requirement that the tenant should give the landlord notice at least one month before the end of the tenancy in order for him to claim compensation. The tenant has to make his claim for compensation within two months from the termination of the tenancy, ie after, not before, the end of the tenancy.[70]

Although the tenant has to remove his fixtures during the continuance of his tenancy, it is not considered necessary that forfeiture should operate only on the expiration of a notice giving him sufficient time to do so. At common law, fixtures have to be removed on or before the termination of the tenancy, and if this does not occur before forfeiture, the right is lost.[71]

---

[68] Agricultural Holdings Act 1986, s 26, Sch 3, Pt I.
[69] *Parry v Million Pigs Ltd* (1980) 260 Estates Gazette 281.
[70] Agricultural Tenancies Act 1995, s 22(2).
[71] *Pugh v Arton* (1869) LR 8 Eq 626.

Chapter 6

RENT

6.1 INTRODUCTION

The underlying principle of the legislation, namely freedom of contract, is reflected in the provisions on rent.[1] The parties are free to agree the initial rent, whether or not this will be reviewable and, if so, the dates and frequency of any such reviews. However, if the contract makes provision for an upward only rent review then the tenant can demand that the matter be referred to arbitration. The arbitrator can determine the rent only on an open market basis.

The statutory provisions relating to the determination of rent are much less prescribed than the formula under the Agricultural Holdings Act 1986. They accord with the fundamental principle that rent is a payment for the right to occupy land. This sum will reflect supply and demand and is not directly related to the profit which a tenant might make from the land. Where there is security of tenure, as under the Agricultural Holdings Act 1986, then there is an argument that a tenant's security might be undermined if the rent could be raised to a level which was unaffordable. This is an outmoded notion and in the absence of security of tenure, there is no longer justification for artificially depressing the rent.

Where a tenancy agreement has a rent review clause, the landlord and tenant may settle the rent by negotiation. There is no mandatory requirement that the rent review be settled by arbitration.

It is possible in a written tenancy agreement to exclude the statutory rent review provision during the currency of the tenancy but not, it seems, during the period of a yearly tenancy which may arise on the expiration of a fixed term.

6.2 INITIAL RENT

Landlord and tenant will fix the initial rent. There is no statutory intervention on the amount of this rent, any more than there is for the initial rent under a tenancy governed by the Agricultural Holdings Act 1986.

The amount of initial rent will simply reflect the attractiveness or otherwise of the package which is on offer from the landowner. Thus if an owner puts on the market good quality land with first-class equipment and perhaps an attractive farmhouse, offering to make the property available for a long period, then it is to be expected that there will be strong competition from prospective tenants and a high rent will result. Conversely, if the property offered is of inferior land quality with a need for substantial expenditure by a tenant perhaps on drainage or renovation of the farm buildings, then a commensurate low rent will be forthcoming.

---

[1] Agricultural Tenancies Act 1995, ss 9–14.

The terms of the proposed tenancy as to the obligations for repair clearly will have a bearing on any rent offered. An impoverished landlord might seek to impose all repairing obligations on his tenant, as indeed might the landlord who had already equipped his farm to a high standard. The tenant being a shrewd man of business and well advised would determine his offer of rent reflecting the cost to him of the obligations which he was about to undertake.

Where the cost of repairing or indeed providing new farm buildings was onerous, the prospective tenant naturally would look for a length of lease within which to recover the benefit of his expenditure but it should be noted that in any event he will be entitled to compensation at the end of the lease.

Some leases will contain restrictions about the farming system to be practised, especially where a landlord is concerned about the appearance of the countryside or about particular environmental factors. Again, in these circumstances, the prudent tenant will adjust his offer of rent.

Under the existing legislation, since the grant of the tenancy confers lifetime security there has been intense competition on the rare occasions when tenancies have been offered and this has given rise to anxiety about open market rents. Under the new arrangements, whilst there will no doubt be competition given that farming is a prosperous industry in which there are many efficient operators seeking to expand their businesses, there is no reason to suppose that uneconomical rents will be offered. Tenants will be bidding for fixed terms and there will be no incentive to offer an artificially high rent simply to obtain a tenancy. This is, in part, because the landlord is not obliged to agree to a three-yearly rent review. He can agree that the rent should be reviewable at any specified interval or that it should not be varied at all.

6.3 FIXED RENT

The parties may agree that the rent shall remain the same throughout the term. This might be attractive to landlords or tenants who seek financial certainty in either return or liability. If they do so, it is essential that the contract expressly states that the rent is not to be reviewed during the tenancy.[2] Failure to do this will mean that the statutory rent review provisions will come into effect. Any agreement which is not set out in a written tenancy agreement will not be effective.

Professional advisers will need to be aware of this provision. It reverses the normal rule that a rent will remain the same throughout a fixed term unless there is a provision in the tenancy agreement that it is to be reviewed. Under the Agricultural Tenancies Act 1995, it is necessary to contract out of the rent review sections expressly.

6.4 PHASED RENTS

The parties may also agree that the rent will be increased at specified times to or by a specified amount.[3] For instance, where the tenant has agreed to provide expensive

---

[2] Ibid, s 9(a).
[3] Ibid, s 9(b)(i).

fixed equipment there may be a rent-free period for the first few years, or rather than having the expense and uncertainty of a rent review the parties might agree that the rent should be a stated amount for the first fixed period and a different specified figure for the remainder of the term. Provided it is clear from the document that apart from such specified changes, the rent is to remain fixed, then there will be no rent review. Any agreement not contained in a written tenancy agreement will not be effective.

6.5 OBJECTIVE CRITERIA

It is also possible for the parties to stipulate in the tenancy agreement that the rent shall be adjusted by reference to a formula which does not require or permit the exercise by any person of any judgement or discretion in relation to the determination of the rent of the holding. The formula must not be so drafted as to preclude a decrease in rent.[4] In other words, it will not be possible to have what is in effect an upwards only rent review. Again, it is necessary for the tenancy agreement to state clearly that apart from the specific terms for variation according to the agreed criteria, the rent is to remain fixed. This is to ensure that the statutory rent review provisions do not come into play.

The objective criteria might be a reference to an agreed percentage of annual turnover, or to the annual market price of wheat as published by a specified body such as the Home Grown Cereals Authority, or to the retail price index at pre-determined intervals. An assessment based on subjective judgement, for example a forecast of gross margins, would not qualify. It is important that the criteria are both certain and objective.

This form of rent assessment is not likely to have wide application but might be useful upon occasion where the use to which the property was to be put was unusual, so that there might be a dearth of market evidence at review. Surprising though it might seem, the difficulty can occur for example with recreational activity, such as rent determination for an equestrian gallop or even for a golf course. Whilst such land uses are commonplace, local market evidence can sometimes be sparse. In such circumstances a rent fixed by an agreed formula might well be appropriate.

Care must be taken in drafting any such clauses. Although the principle of rent fixed by reference to objective criteria is easy to state, it may be less easy to frame clauses which will work in practice.

6.6 REVIEWABLE RENTS

The parties can agree that the rent will be reviewed. This is likely to be the normal approach. They can stipulate their own formula for determining the rent at a review date. If they do so, the agreement will be binding unless either the landlord or the tenant serves on the other a statutory review notice of at least 12 but not more than 24 months before the contractual review date.[5] The procedure is discussed at para 6.12 below.

---

[4] Ibid, s 9(b)(ii).
[5] Ibid, s 10.

6.7 DATES OF RENT REVIEWS

Whether the rent is reviewed by reference to objective criteria or under contractual or statutory rent review provisions the parties can agree the dates for the rent reviews. The parties could specify the date and the years for such reviews, or that the rent should be reviewed at specified intervals on a given date.

If no dates are agreed for a rent review and a notice requiring a statutory rent review (see para 6.12.1) has been served, then the review date must be an anniversary of the beginning of the tenancy.

6.8 FREQUENCY OF REVIEWS

The parties can stipulate the frequency of rent reviews which may be more or less than the three years statutory fallback provision.[6] Where there is no contractual provision the statute gives the right for either party to demand a rent review every three years, but not at shorter intervals.[7]

The three-year period runs from either:

(i) the beginning of the tenancy; or

(ii) a date from which there took effect a previous direction of an arbitrator as to the amount of the rent; or

(iii) a date from which there took effect a previous determination as to the amount of rent made, otherwise than as arbitrator, by a person appointed under an agreement between the landlord and tenant;

(iv) a date from which there took effect a previous written agreement between the parties as to the amount of the rent, provided that such an agreement was entered into after the grant of the tenancy.[8]

This is a similar provision to that under the Agricultural Holdings Act 1986 which enables a rent review to be demanded as of right at not less than three-yearly intervals.[9] As under the 1986 Act there is no obligation to demand a rent review.

If the arbitrator directs, or the parties agree in writing that the rent is to remain unchanged, no rent review can be demanded for a further three years. It is slightly different from the corresponding provision in the Agricultural Holdings Act 1986. Under the 1986 Act, it is only a direction of an arbitrator that the rent shall remain unchanged that affects the three-year cycle. An agreement to that effect by the parties will not do so. On the other hand, if the parties agree that there shall be an increase or reduction of rent then that will prevent the rent being reviewed for another three years.

---

[6] Ibid, s 10(4), (5).
[7] Ibid, s 10(6)(a).
[8] Ibid, s 10(6)(b).
[9] Agricultural Holdings Act 1986, s 12, Sch 2, paras 4 and 5.

6.9 SEVERED REVERSION

Where the reversion is severed this has no effect on the tenancy which remains a single tenancy.[10] However, it is possible for the landlord to agree with the tenant that there should be separate tenancies of the land comprised in the severed parts of the reversion.

Provided that:

(i) the new landlord was immediately before the grant of the new tenancy entitled to a severed part of the reversionary interest in the original holding;

(ii) the tenant was the tenant of that original holding; and

(iii) the rent payable under the new tenancy in respect of the severed part is merely an appropriate portion of the rent payable for the entire holding immediately before the new tenancy began

then the minimum period of three years between statutory rent reviews is not affected by the creation of a new tenancy at a proportionate rent following severance of the reversion.[11] The parties do not therefore have to wait a further three years before a rent review. Once a rent review has taken place under the new tenancy, it will have its own three-yearly rent review cycle.

These are fallback provisions only. They will not apply where the parties have agreed in writing on the frequency of rent reviews.

6.10 AMOUNT OF RENT

The parties can contract that the rent:

(i) shall remain the same throughout the tenancy;

(ii) shall be increased to specified amounts at specified intervals; or

(iii) shall be increased or decreased by reference to objective criteria.[12]

They could also agree that the rent should be reviewed according to non-objective criteria but, in that event, it would be open to either party to require that the rent be determined by an arbitrator.

Under the Agricultural Holdings Act 1986 the rent has to be determined as at the date of reference.[13] The Agricultural Tenancies Act 1995, on the other hand, provides that the rent is to be determined at the review date. This is to avoid the rent being affected by different factors from those applicable at the review date.[14]

---

[10] *Jelly v Buckman* [1974] QB 488, [1973] 3 WLR 585, [1973] 3 All ER 853.
[11] Agricultural Tenancies Act 1995, s 11.
[12] Ibid, s 9.
[13] Agricultural Holdings Act 1986, s 12(2).
[14] Agricultural Tenancies Act 1995, s 10.

The arbitrator must determine the open market rent at which the holding might reasonably be expected to be let by a willing landlord to a willing tenant. He has to take into account all relevant factors including, in particular, the terms of the tenancy.[15] The respective obligations of the landlord and tenant in the tenancy clearly have a bearing on rental value as have provisions relating to the payment of rent, whether in advance or in arrears and the frequency of further reviews. However, any term of the tenancy regarding the manner in which a new rent is to be determined is overridden by the statutory requirement that the rent must be ascertained on the basis of the open market value.

In ascertaining the revised rent the arbitrator has to disregard the fact that the tenant is in occupation. He must also disregard any dilapidation, deterioration or damage to the buildings or land caused or permitted by the tenant.

Generally, rent will not be charged on any increase in the rental value of the holding which is attributable to the improvements made by the tenant. There are three exceptions when the increased value will not be so disregarded:

(1) Where there is an obligation on the tenant imposed by the tenancy agreement, or any previous tenancy agreement, to provide the improvement. The obligation must have been imposed on the tenant when the relevant tenancy was granted. The improvement is treated as a landlord's improvement which can be taken into account in ascertaining the rent.

(2) Where the landlord has made the tenant any allowance or given any benefit in respect of the improvement, the arbitrator must take into account the value of that allowance or benefit in determining the increase in rental value to the holding attributable to the improvement.

(3) Where the tenant has received compensation from the landlord for an improvement, the arbitrator must take into account that payment in determining the value to the holding attributable to the improvement.

These provisions are much simpler than the equivalent provisions in the Agricultural Holdings Act 1986. They are also less regulatory. The parties under a farm business tenancy have to be willing but are free to be imprudent if they so wish. In fact, it is doubtful if the word prudent, introduced by the Agricultural Holdings Act 1984, has added anything to the concept of willing parties. There is no reference in the Agricultural Tenancies Act 1995 to the character and situation of the holding nor to the productive capacity and its related earning capacity. Neither, for that matter, is there any reference to the rent for comparable holdings, although some, at least, of these factors many continue to be relevant.

In determining the rent, the arbitrator will take into account the residue of the unexpired term. He is not empowered to assess the rent on the basis of the original term even if there is a contractual provision to that effect. This is because the compensation provision is mandatory. In commercial leases the parties can stipulate that the rent be assessed as at the start of the term but, in the absence of such an

---

[15] Ibid, s 13.

agreement, rent is assessed on the length of the term left to run including provisions for break clauses.[16]

Broadly, determination of open market value is more a process of comparison than of calculation. The concept is a simple one and, as with anything else which might be bought and sold, the price to be paid for occupation whether weekly, monthly, quarterly, half-yearly or annually, whether in arrears or in advance is simply a reflection of what the market will pay. The task of the arbitrator will be that of weighing the evidence, likely to be mainly about comparable properties, so as to determine the rent at review. Initially and until there is a significant volume of letting under the new legislation, that task will not be easy. The burden of proof will rest with the party seeking change in rent, to justify the amount and to convince the arbitrator of the need for the appropriate rise or fall.

It should be noted that an arbitrator's award determining the rent of a property is inadmissible in evidence as a comparable property at another rent review. It is mere opinion based on evidence before him of the rent at which the premises could reasonably have been let and not evidence of what rent was really being obtained for properties in the market.[17] This is in contrast to the Agricultural Holdings Act 1986,[18] which provides specifically that the arbitrator should take into account rents fixed by arbitration under that Act.

6.11 OPENCAST COAL ACT 1958

Under the Opencast Coal Act 1958, as amended by the Coal Industry Act 1994, the Coal Authority has power, by a compulsory rights order, to acquire for the benefit of a licensed operator (within the meaning of the Coal Industry Act 1994), rights to occupy land for the purposes of carrying on opencast mining operations. Annual compensation is payable by the licensed operator to the person who would otherwise be entitled to occupy the land and compensation is payable to the owner of the freehold interest in the land when the period of occupation for mining has ended.

The Act has three provisions which impact on the rent review of a farm business tenancy. First, it directs an arbitrator to disregard any increase or decrease in the rental value which is attributable to the occupation of the holding or part of the holding by a person with the benefit of opencast planning permission for the purpose of carrying on any of the permitted activities.[19]

Secondly, where a tenant's improvements, for which he is entitled to compensation, are lost and replaced by other improvements, for which compensation is payable by the licensed operator, those improvements are not regarded as tenant's improvements. The arbitrator will therefore take them into account in determining the rental value of the holding.[20]

---

16 *Norwich Union Life Assurance Society v Trustee Savings Bank Central Board* [1986] 1 EGLR 136. *R & A Millet (Shops) Ltd v Legal and General Assurance Society Ltd* [1985] 1 EGLR 103.

17 *Land Securities PLC v Westminster City Council* [1993] 1 WLR 286, [1993] 4 All ER 124.

18 Agricultural Holdings Act 1986, s 12, Sch 2, para 1(3).

19 Opencast Coal Act 1958, s 14B(4); Agricultural Tenancies Act 1995, Sch, para 14.

20 Opencast Coal Act 1958, Sch 7, para 3A; Agricultural Tenancies Act 1995, Sch, para 20(5).

Thirdly, where a farm business tenancy is in existence before and continues after the end of a period of occupation by a licensed operator, the landlord or tenant may demand a reference to arbitration of the question whether there should be any variation in the terms of the tenancy agreement as a result of the occupation or use of the land for opencast mining activities. The variation may be of a term or condition relating to rent.[21]

6.12 PROCEDURE

6.12.1 Statutory review notice

Either the landlord or the tenant can serve a notice in writing on the other party requiring the rent for the holding to be referred to arbitration under the provisions of Pt II of the Agricultural Tenancies Act 1995.[22]

The notice must specify the date from which the rent review is to take effect and that date must be at least 12 but less than 24 months after the day on which the notice was given. The minimum of one year's notice required before a rent review may take effect, is the same period for which there is provision in s 12 of the Agricultural Holdings Act 1986. However, the rent review provisions of the 1986 Act operate, in effect, by determining an annual tenancy and creating a new one at the new rent. The length of the statutory notice which has to be given is the same as the length of notice needed to determine a yearly tenancy protected under the 1986 Act. It must be between one and two years terminating on the anniversary of the term date. There cannot therefore be a statutory rent review of a fixed-term tenancy under the 1986 Act. A fixed-term tenancy cannot, during that fixed term, be determined by a notice to quit except in accordance with any contractual provisions.

The review date must be in accordance with any written agreement between the parties. It is not necessary that the review date should be a term of the contract. It can be a separate agreement in writing. The parties may have agreed in writing that the rent can be varied as from a specified date or dates at specified intervals during the tenancy. They may have agreed that the rent review date is a specified date or dates.

Where there are no contractual agreements then the review date will be the anniversary of the tenancy. If the parties have not agreed on the frequency of reviews, then reviews cannot take place more frequently than every three years (see para 6.8).

6.12.2 Appointment of an arbitrator

Once the statutory review notice has been served the landlord and tenant may agree upon the rent or on an arbitrator or on some other person, to determine the rent. The arbitrator can determine the rent only on an open market basis.[23] On the other hand, a person appointed by agreement after the service of a statutory review notice who is

---

[21] Opencast Coal Act 1958, Sch 7, para 4A; Agricultural Tenancies Act 1995, Sch, para 20(7).
[22] Agricultural Tenancies Act 1995, s 10.
[23] Ibid, s 13.

not acting as an arbitrator can determine the rent on a basis agreed by the parties.[24] If neither an arbitrator nor any other person is agreed upon, then either party can apply to the President of the Royal Institution of Chartered Surveyors for the appointment by him of an arbitrator.[25]

Application to the President may be made at any time during the six months before the review date including the review date itself. No doubt the parties will negotiate between the giving of the statutory review notice and the date when they can apply for the appointment of an arbitrator. If no agreement as to the amount of rent has been achieved, and the parties have not appointed an arbitrator by six months before the review date, a unilateral application can then be made to the President. The application must be in writing and must be accompanied by such reasonable fee as the President may charge for the service.

If, after a statutory review notice has been given, the parties agree on an arbitrator or other person to determine the rent then an application cannot be made to the President for an appointment of an arbitrator by him. However, s 12 of the Agricultural Tenancies Act 1995 only precludes application to the President where agreement as to an arbitrator or other person has been reached after the service of a statutory rent review notice. It does not apply to an agreement made before such a notice.

---

[24] Ibid, s 12.
[25] Ibid, s 12.

Chapter 7

ENFORCEMENT OF COVENANTS

7.1 MEANING OF COVENANT

A covenant is an obligation in a deed or an enforceable agreement between landlord and tenant.[1] Covenants may be enforceable on the basis of privity of contract or estate or in equity as restrictive covenants. Alternatively, they may be enforced indirectly by bringing proceedings for forfeiture.

7.2 ENFORCEMENT BETWEEN ORIGINAL PARTIES

There is privity of contract between the original landlord and the original tenant. This means that the landlord can enforce all the covenants in the lease against the tenant throughout the term, even after the tenant has assigned the lease.[2] So if the tenant enters into a lease for 15 years and assigns that lease after only one year he will remain liable under the terms of the agreement for breaches committed by any assignee, until the end of the 15-year term. If there is an assignment of the reversion he will be liable to the new reversioner even though there has never been any privity of contract with that person. The landlord as the original contracting party remains liable throughout the term even though he may have assigned the reversion.[3]

Under the principle of privity of contract, if there is a rent review clause, the tenant will be liable for any increased rent under the clause, even though he was not a party to the rent review.[4] It is, of course, possible for the parties to limit the tenant's liability by a term in the tenancy agreement. A tenant may decide to sub-let rather than assign so as to be able to ensure that there is compliance with the covenants. There are legislative proposals, which would apply to tenancies granted after the commencement of the Act, for the abolition of the rule that the original parties have continuing liability on the covenants after assignment of their interests.[5]

7.3 POSITION OF ASSIGNEES

Covenants which touch and concern the land will bind the landlord for the time being and the tenant for the time being. A covenant will touch and concern the land (or, to use the modern phrase, have reference to the subject matter of the lease) if it affects the nature, quality, mode of user or value of the lease and is not expressed to be personal in nature.[6] Examples of covenants by the lessee which touch and concern the land are

---

[1] *Weg Motors Ltd v Hales* [1961] Ch 176, 193.

[2] *Thursby v Plant* (1670) 1 Wms Saund. z 30.

[3] *Stuart v Joy* [1904] 1 KB 368; Law of Property Act 1925, s 142(2).

[4] *Centrovincial Estate plc v Bulk Storage Ltd* (1983) 46 P&CR 393. *Selous Street Properties Ltd v Oronel Fabrics Ltd* (1984) 270 EG 643.

[5] See Law Com No 174 (1988). Lord Chancellor's Consultation Paper *Rights and Duties of Landlords and Tenants*, March 1995. Landlord and Tenant (Covenants) Bill 1995.

[6] *Spencer's Case* (1583) 5 Co Rep 16a. Law of Property Act 1925, ss 141(1), 142(2).

covenants to pay rent, to repair, to use for a particular purpose and not to assign the lease without the lessor's consent. Equivalent examples of covenants by the landlord which will bind on this basis are covenants to renew the lease, to supply the demised premises with water and not to build on certain parts of the adjoining land.

7.3.1 Assignment of lease

Where a tenant assigns his lease, the assignee is entitled to the benefit and subject to the burden of all the covenants and conditions touching and concerning the land.[7] This is known as the doctrine of privity of estate. For this doctrine to apply, there must be a legal assignment, ie by deed of the whole of the residue of the lease.[8] There is no privity of estate between a landlord and sub-tenant, and there is no privity of estate where there is an equitable assignment. However, the assignee may be estopped from denying liability on the covenants in the lease.[9]

An assignee, unlike the original tenant, is liable only for breaches committed while the lease is vested in him. He is under no liability for breaches committed before the lease was assigned to him[10] or after he has subsequently assigned it to someone else.[11] However, if a covenant is broken while the lease is vested in him, liability continues even after the assignment.[12]

7.3.2 Personal representatives

A personal representative of a deceased lessee or assignee, who takes possession will be personally liable on any covenants in the lease.[13] If he does not take possession he will not be personally liable but will have representative liability. This liability is limited to the extent of the assets vested in the personal representatives.[14]

Where the deceased was the original tenant, the personal representatives have a potential liability throughout the term of the lease. In order that the personal representatives may distribute the estate of the deceased, the Trustee Act 1925[15] protects them if:

(i) they satisfy any existing liabilities which have been claimed;

(ii) set aside any fixed sum agreed to be laid out on the premises; and

(iii) assign the lease to the person entitled under the will or intestacy or to a purchaser.

Where those conditions are fulfilled the personal representatives will cease to have representative liability although the assets may be claimed from the beneficiaries. The

---

[7] *Spencer's Case, supra.*
[8] Law of Property Act 1925, s 52(1).
[9] *Rodenhurst Estates Ltd v W H Barnes* [1936] 2 All ER 3.
[10] *Granada Theatres Ltd v Freehold Investments (Leytonstone) Ltd* [1959] Ch 592.
[11] *Paul v Nurse* (1828) 8 B&C 486.
[12] *Harley v King* (1835) 2 Cr M&R 18.
[13] *Tilney v Norris* (1700) 1 Ld Raym 553.
[14] *Helier v Casebert* (1665) 1 Lev 127.
[15] Trustee Act 1925, s 26.

personal representatives will continue to be personally liable if they have taken possession of the demised premises.

7.3.3 Indemnity of assignor

If a covenant is broken, the landlord can sue either the original tenant or the assignee in whom the lease was vested at the time of the breach. The landlord cannot sue both.[16] If the original tenant is sued he can claim indemnity against the defaulting assignee, whether or not he is the immediate assignee. This is an implied right which was established by common law.[17]

In addition, where there is an assignment it is usual for the assignor to obtain an express indemnity from his immediate assignee. Where the assignment is for value, there is an implied indemnity under the Law of Property Act 1925.[18] So if L grants T a lease which is assigned to A, and by A1 to A2, and by A2 to A3, and A3 is in breach, L can sue T (privity of contract) or A3 (privity of estate). T can claim by virtue of the implied indemnity against A3 or on an express indemnity against A1. A1 will then look to A2 under an express indemnity and A2 in turn, to A3. The decision against whom to claim, where the rules allow for alternatives, will depend on the solvency of the defendant and whether or not he can be traced.

7.3.4 Assignment of reversion

If the landlord assigns his reversion, subject to the lease, to a third party the benefit and burden of all covenants and provisions having reference to the subject matter of the lease will pass to that third party. The law is now contained in ss 141 and 142 of the Law of Property Act 1925 and covers leases granted by deed or in writing and probably even oral leases.

Where the reversion has been assigned, it is the assignee, not the assignor, who has the benefit of the covenants and so is entitled to sue the tenant for rent or for breaches of covenant, whether such rent accrued, or such breaches occurred, before or after the assignment.[19] Any rights of re-entry, which have not be waived, are enforceable by the new reversioner.[20] Waiver may be express or implied (see para 11.4.3). However, it will not be implied merely because the reversion is assigned 'subject to and with the benefit of' the lease.[21] This is because the acknowledgement of the lease is made to the new reversioner, not the tenant.

On the other hand, the liability of the original lessor remains throughout the whole term of the lease, even where he has assigned the reversion.[22] A tenant, even after he has assigned his lease, may sue the landlord for any breaches which occurred before that assignment.[23]

---

[16] *Brett v Cumberland* (1619) Cro Jac 521.
[17] The rule in *Moule v Garrett* (1872) LR 7 Ex 101.
[18] Law of Property Act 1925, s 77(1)(c), Sch 2, Pt IX.
[19] *Re King* [1963] Ch 459; *London and County (A&D) Ltd v Wilfred Sportsman Ltd* [1971] Ch 764.
[20] Law of Property Act 1925, s 141.
[21] *London and County (A&D) Ltd v Wilfred Sportsman Ltd, supra.*
[22] *Celsteel Ltd v Alton House Holdings Ltd (No 2)* [1987] 1 WLR 291 at 296.
[23] *City and Metropolitan Properties Ltd v Greycroft* (1987) 54 P&CR 266.

7.3.5 Severance of the reversion

A reversioner may assign part of his interest or part of his land. For example, where a fee simple reversioner grants a lease of his reversion to Y he has severed his interest. Y, the person entitled to the benefit of part of the reversionary interest will, as the immediate reversioner, obtain the benefit and burden of the covenants of the lease.[24]

On the other hand, the reversioner might assign the whole of his interest in part of his land. Under s 140 of the Law of Property Act 1925, all conditions and rights of re-entry become severable on the severance of the reversion. However, the tenancy continues as one tenancy.[25]

7.3.6 Equitable tenancies

Where a lease is equitable, for example where it is for a term exceeding three years and has been granted in writing but not by deed, there will be no privity of estate between the assignee of the lease and the landlord.

The original parties to the lease will be bound on the covenants by privity of contract. But when the equitable lease is assigned, the assignee will not be liable on the covenants to the landlord except possibly on the principles of estoppel.[26] Under the normal contractual rules, the burden of a contract cannot be assigned to a third party, however, the benefit can be assigned. Thus, the assignee can enforce the covenants, the benefit of which has been assigned to him, against the landlord.

The statutory provisions for the passing of the benefit and burden of the covenants on an assignment of the reversion apply to equitable tenancies in the same way as they apply to legal tenancies.[27]

7.4 RESTRICTIVE COVENANTS

At common law, in the absence of privity of contract or estate, covenants are unenforceable. Therefore, a landlord cannot enforce any covenants against a sub-tenant. Similarly, a sub-tenant cannot enforce any covenants against a head landlord. However, equity allows negative covenants, ie those which do not involve the covenantor in the expenditure of money, to be enforced if certain conditions are fulfilled.[28]

In order for the burden of a restrictive covenant to pass from the original contracting party, four conditions must be fulfilled. First, the covenant must be negative in nature, however expressed, secondly, the covenant must have been intended to run with the land and not be personal to the covenantor,[29] thirdly, at the date of the covenant, the

---

[24] *Wright v Burroughes* (1846) 3 CB 685.
[25] *Jelley v Buckman* [1974] QB 488.
[26] *Austerberry v Corporation of Oldham* (1885) 29 ChD 750.
[27] Law of Property Act 1925, ss 141, 142.
[28] *Tulk v Moxhay* (1848) 2 Ph 774.
[29] Law of Property Act 1925, s 79(1). Covenants post-1925 are deemed to be made by the convenantor on behalf of himself, his successors in title and the persons deriving title under him unless there is a contrary intention.

covenantee must own land that will benefit from the covenant. A landlord's reversion has been held to be a sufficient interest to entitle him to enforce a covenant against a sub-tenant, even though he has no other adjoining land.[30] Finally, the successor must have notice of the covenant. A sub-tenant is entitled to call for his immediate landlord's title and, even if he does not do so, he will be deemed to have constructive notice of all matters such as a restrictive covenant, which an inspection would have revealed.[31] Covenants in leases cannot be registered under the Land Charges Act 1972.[32]

7.5 REMEDIES

7.5.1 Breach of covenant

Before deciding whether to bring an action for breach of covenant, it will be necessary to decide whether what the tenant has done, does amount to a breach. In the case of user clauses, this may not always be clear-cut. So far as opencast mining is concerned, there is a statutory provision that nothing done or omitted by the landlord or tenant in allowing opencast mining activities, for which planning permission has been granted, will be taken to be a breach of any term or condition of the tenancy.[33]

7.5.2 Damages

The common law remedy for breach of covenant is damages. Where the breach is of the tenant's covenant to repair, damages are limited by statute to the amount of diminution in the value of the landlord's reversion. No damages are recoverable if the premises are to be demolished, or structurally altered in such a way as to make the repairs valueless on the determination of the lease.[34] If there is a covenant not to make improvements and improvements nevertheless are made, the value of the landlord's reversion may be enhanced. In that situation, assuming that he does not obtain an injunction to reinstate, the landlord may be entitled to the cost of restoring the premises to their original state plus any loss of rent incurred while the necessary works are carried out.[35]

A tenant can also bring an action against his landlord for breach of the landlord's repairing covenants. The amount of damages will be the amount of loss caused to the tenant, the object being to put the tenant in the same position as if the breach had not occurred. A tenant who does repairs for which the landlord is liable is entitled to deduct the cost from the present or future rent.[36] He should give notification to the landlord before doing so and, as a precaution, obtain at least two estimates for the cost of the work.

---

[30] *Regent Oil Co Ltd v JA Gregory (Hatch End) Ltd* [1966] Ch 402 at 433.
[31] *Patman v Harland* (1881) 17 ChD 353.
[32] Land Charges Act 1972, s 2(5)(ii).
[33] Opencast Coal Act 1958, s 14B(3); Agricultural Tenancies Act 1995, Sch, para 14.
[34] Landlord and Tenant Act 1927, s 18.
[35] *Duke of Westminster v Swinton* [1948] 1 KB 524.
[36] *Lee Parker v Izzet* [1971] 1 WLR 1688.

The Leasehold Property (Repairs) Act 1938 protects tenants of property let for a term certain of not less than seven years which has at least three years left unexpired. A special notice has to be served and the tenant has a right to serve a counter-notice. Where he does so, the landlord cannot proceed without leave of the court. However, specifically excluded from the Act are agricultural holdings governed by the Agricultural Holdings Act 1986, and farm business tenancies under the Agricultural Tenancies Act 1995.[37]

7.5.3 Injunction

Injunctions are orders by the court to put right a breach of covenant (mandatory) or prevent a breach occurring (negative). An injunction might be awarded to compel a tenant or sub-tenant to comply with a restrictive covenant in a lease. Injunctions are appropriate for enforcing a landlord's covenant for quiet enjoyment and preventing a landlord from derogating from his grant. A landlord might seek an injunction to enforce a tenant's user covenant or a covenant against assigning or sub-letting. Injunctions are not automatic and lie in the discretion of the court. Being an equitable remedy, the applicant must comply with the maxims of equity.

7.5.4 Specific performance

Another equitable remedy is an action for specific performance. This is an order of the court compelling the defendant to perform his obligations under a contract. This again is a discretionary remedy and the court will take into account, among other things, the conduct of the plaintiff and the hardship which would be caused to the defendants. A tenant, although not a landlord, may obtain an order for specific performance. This will compel a landlord to do specific work where the landlord is in breach of a repairing covenant.[38]

7.5.5 Forfeiture

Where there is a forfeiture clause and the tenant has failed to comply with a s 146 notice (see para 11.4.6 on forfeiture), a landlord may forfeit the lease. This remedy may be useful in enforcing covenants between a landlord and sub-tenant, between whom, as explained, there is neither privity of contract nor estate, or between a landlord and an assignee who has taken only an equitable assignment. If the landlord brings forfeiture proceedings, the sub-tenant or assignee may decide to comply with the covenants in the lease in order to avoid losing their interests. Although the sub-tenant and assignee could apply to the court for relief, it might be better to perform the covenant than have the uncertainty and cost of seeking relief.[39]

7.5.6 Distress

In some circumstances where a tenant has failed to pay rent the landlord may, without a court order, enter the premises and enforce payment by seizing and selling sufficient

---

[37] The Leasehold Property (Repairs) Act 1938, s 7(i), as amended by the Agricultural Tenancies Act 1995, Sch, para 8.
[38] *Jeune v Queens Cross Properties Ltd* [1974] Ch 97.
[39] Law of Property Act 1925, s 146(2).

goods which he finds on the premises so as to meet the rent. The law relating to distress is ancient and archaic. Some goods such as perishables, are privileged and cannot be seized. Others, such as tools of the trade, can be seized only if sufficient other distress is not available.

It is possible that some of the goods found on the premises will belong not to a tenant but to a third party. The Law of Distress Amendment Act 1908 enables the third party to serve a declaration on the landlord stating that the tenant has no right of property or beneficial interest in the goods which are being distrained.

There are no special rules relating to distress for farm business tenancies under the Agricultural Tenancies Act 1995. This is in contrast to the provisions in the Agricultural Holdings Act 1986.

Under s 18(2) of the Agricultural Holdings Act 1986, agisted livestock (ie under a contract of agistment by which stock are taken in by a tenant to be fed at a fair price) cannot be distrained for rent where there is other sufficient distress available. If there is insufficient distress the sum recovered by distress may not exceed the sum the owner of the livestock has agreed to pay the owner for their feeding. The owner can redeem the livestock by paying that sum to the distrainer. In contrast, agisted livestock taken in by a tenant under a farm business tenancy will be dealt with in the same way as other goods and chattels belonging to third parties.

The Agricultural Holdings Act 1986 provides that distress is limited to one year's unpaid rent. Under the general law, which will apply to farm business tenancies, distress can be levied for up to six years' arrears.[40]

7.6 DIRECTIVE 93/13/EC

EC Directive 93/13 applies to unfair terms in consumer contracts. It has been implemented by the Unfair Terms in Consumer Contracts Regulations 1994, SI 1994/3159 which came into force on 1 July 1995.

The full scope of this Directive is far from certain. However, it is generally considered that it does apply to tenancy agreements where the landlord is running a business connected with property. The Directive should not apply to a farm business tenancy as the tenant is not a private individual consumer, but a businessman. If the regulations apply, they will do so to any term which has not been individually negotiated.

An unfair term is defined in the regulation as any term which:

> 'contrary to the requirements of good faith causes a significant imbalance in the parties' rights and obligations under the contract to the detriment of the consumer.'

If a term is held to be unfair then it will not be binding on the consumer. The contract itself will continue to bind the parties if the unfair term can be severed without undermining the rest of the contract.

---

[40] Limitation Act 1980, s 19.

Chapter 8

FIXTURES AND COMPENSATION

8.1 INTRODUCTION

One of the purposes of the Agricultural Tenancies Act 1995 is to ensure that a tenant is encouraged to invest in his businesses and thereby reinvigorate the wider rural economy. It provides that, on the termination of the tenancy, he will receive proper compensation for the letting value of improvements which remain attached to the holding. However, a landlord shall not be burdened by making compensation for improvements which are inappropriate to the holding. Compensation is payable only where consent of the landlord is obtained before the improvement is carried out.[1] Where consent is not obtained, generally, the tenant will be entitled to remove buildings and fixtures under s 8 of the 1995 Act. Even where consent is obtained, the tenant may opt to remove the improvement as a fixture (unless it was a condition of the landlord's consent agreed to by the tenant that the fixture or building should be left on the holding) rather than claiming compensation.

8.2 FIXTURES

8.2.1 What are fixtures?

Land includes not only the estate in land itself and interests in or over it, but also includes, among other things, buildings and objects attached to such buildings.[2] The term fixtures means anything which has become so attached to land as to form, in law, part of that land.

An object may not be a fixture; it may remain a chattel. In deciding whether or not it is a fixture, there are two main tests. The first is the degree of annexation. Generally, there must be some substantial annexation to the land for the object to become a fixture. A poultry shed which rests on timber laid on the ground is not a fixture.[3] It is not attached but merely stands on the ground by its own weight.

If an article is securely fixed then prima facie it is a fixture. If it is not securely fixed then prima facie it remains a chattel. However, the second test, the purpose of annexation, is the decisive factor. Was the chattel fixed for the purpose of enjoying it as a chattel or was it fixed to improve the land or buildings? Statues, even though resting on their own weight and not attached to the land, have been held to be fixtures where they were part of a landscaped garden,[4] whilst tapestries, attached by tacks to wooden strips fastened to the wall by two-inch nails, have been held to remain chattels.[5]

---

[1] Agricultural Tenancies Act 1995, ss 17 and 18.
[2] Law of Property Act 1925, s 205(1)(ix).
[3] *Culling v Tufnal* (1694) Bull NP 34 (Dutch barn, the supports of which rested in sockets let into the ground not a fixture). *Wiltshear v Cottrell* (1853) 1 E&B 674.
[4] *D'Eyncourt v Gregory* (1866) LR 3 EQ 382.
[5] *Leigh v Taylor* [1902] AC 157, *Berkley v Poulett* [1977] EGD 754.

8.2.2　Removal of fixtures at common law

If an article remains a chattel, it can be removed by the person who owns the chattel. However, if it is a fixture then it becomes part of the land and will, subject to important exceptions, belong to the fee simple owner and cannot be removed.[6]

Fixtures attached by a tenant, therefore, are landlord's fixtures unless they can be removed under the exceptions, when they are known as tenant's fixtures. Tenant's fixtures can be removed while the tenancy continues and even after it has ended if the tenant remains in possession as a tenant or under some other right.[7] If a tenancy is terminated by a notice which does not allow enough time to remove the fixtures, the tenant is allowed a reasonable time after the end of the tenancy to remove them.

Before the Agricultural Tenancies Act 1995, the fixtures which a tenant has been entitled to remove are trade fixtures, ornamental fixtures and, under the Agricultural Holdings Act 1986, agricultural fixtures.

Trade fixtures are those fixtures attached by the tenant for the purpose of his trade or business.[8] Examples are vats, boilers, petrol pumps and the fixed beer pumps of a public house.

The exception for ornamental and domestic fixtures is more limited than trade fixtures. In order for the tenant to be able to remove such a fixture the chattel must be complete in itself and removable without causing substantial injury to the building.[9] So a conservatory on brick foundations has been held not to be removable but stoves and kitchen ranges have been held to be capable of removal.

8.2.3　Fixtures under the Agricultural Holdings Act 1986

At common law, agricultural fixtures were not regarded as trade fixtures and so could not be removed.[10] Statute provided that agricultural fixtures could be removed. The rules are now set out in s 10 of the Agricultural Holdings Act 1986. A tenant may remove agricultural and other fixtures before or within two months of the determination of the tenancy provided:

 (i)　one month's written notice is given to the landlord;

 (ii)　all rent due is paid and all the tenant's obligations under the tenancy have been performed;

(iii)　no avoidable damage is done in the removal;

(iv)　any damage done is made good; and

 (v)　the landlord is given an option to buy the fixtures at a fair price.

A tenant of an agricultural holding is also entitled to remove fixtures which are trade, ornamental or domestic fixtures according to the common law rules.

---

[6]　*Quicquid solo plantatur, solo cedit.*
[7]　*New Zealand Government Property Corporation v HM&S Ltd* [1982] QB 1145.
[8]　*Poole's Case* (1703) 1 Salk 368.
[9]　*Martin v Roe* (1875) 7 E&B 237, 244.
[10]　*Elwes v Maw* (1802) 3 East 38.

8.2.4 Fixtures under the Agricultural Tenancies Act 1995

The rules for the removal of such fixtures are set out in s 8 of the Agricultural Tenancies Act 1995. They are simpler than those contained in s 10 of the Agricultural Holdings Act 1986 and are exhaustive so far as removal by the tenant is concerned. There is no additional right to remove trade or ornamental fixtures.[11] Common law rules conferring rights on third parties in relation to the removal of fixtures will continue to apply. The tenant's right to remove fixtures and buildings overrides any provision in a tenancy agreement or local custom to the contrary.[12] There is an exception, however, where a landlord imposes a condition on giving his consent to an improvement, that the tenant will not remove the building or fixture on the termination of the tenancy.[13] It enables the landlord to ensure that a particular facility will be available for the use of an incoming tenant, but gives the outgoing tenant the certainty that compensation will be payable.

A farm business tenant has the right to remove any fixture, not just agricultural fixtures, which the tenant has affixed to the holding under the current tenancy or previous tenancies.[14] He is also entitled to remove buildings and any part of a building.[15] At common law, a tenant cannot remove substantial buildings.[16]

The right of removal may be exercised at any time during the course of the tenancy. It may also be exercised after the tenancy has ended provided that the tenant has not actually quit the holding but remains in possession as tenant. Under s 10 of the Agricultural Holdings Act 1986, the tenant had two months after the end of the tenancy in which to remove the fixture. However, this is not the position at common law for trade and ornamental fixtures. At Committee stage in the House of Lords, the Government resisted an amendment to allow a two-month removal period. Lord Howe, Parliamentary Secretary for Agriculture, Fisheries and Food, said:

> 'The Committee should bear in mind the fact that the notice provisions of the Bill ensure that both parties know at least a year in advance that a tenancy is due to end. I believe that that period gives every opportunity to settle arrangements over fixtures and buildings which a departing tenant wishes to remove. Therefore, a further two months from the end of the tenancy is, I suggest, simply not necessary in those circumstances.'[17]

The tenant must not cause any avoidable damage to the holding during the removal of the building or fixture.[18] Any damage done must be made good immediately.[19] This accords with the common law rules for the removal of trade fixtures. Farm business tenants have the right to remove fixtures and buildings, regardless of whether substantial damage is caused in the process. For example, it may be necessary to demolish a wall of a building in order to remove intact some fixed machinery which

---

[11] Agricultural Tenancies Act 1995, s 8(7).
[12] Ibid, s 8(6).
[13] Ibid, s 8(2)(d).
[14] Ibid, s 8(i).
[15] Ibid, ss 8(i)(b) and 38(i).
[16] *Pole-Carew v Western Counties General Manure Co* [1920] 2 Ch 97.
[17] HL Committee Stage, col 1170, 12 December 1994.
[18] Agricultural Tenancies Act 1995, s 8(3).
[19] Ibid, s 8(4).

was assembled within that building. However, the tenant would then have to rebuild the wall.

The tenant has the right to remove fixtures or buildings acquired by him as well as those affixed or erected by the tenant himself.[20] This situation could arise where an incoming tenant pays the outgoing tenant for a fixture which is left behind on the holding. When the tenancy of the incomer ends, he may wish to remove it. The tenant will not be able to claim compensation from the landlord for an improvement because the landlord will not have given his consent to the improvement but the tenant will be able to remove the fixture for which he paid.

The tenant cannot remove buildings or fixtures in the following circumstances:[21]

 (i) where the tenant was required, either by the tenancy agreement or otherwise to affix a fixture to the holding or to erect a building. Where, for instance, pollution control regulations made it necessary for certain buildings to be improved, it would not be appropriate if those buildings were removed at the end of the tenancy. The tenant in such circumstances would be entitled to compensation provided he had obtained the consent of the landlord or the arbitrator;[22]

 (ii) where a tenant substitutes a fixture or building for one belonging to the landlord. This accords with the common law position;[23]

(iii) where compensation has already been paid to the tenant for an improvement made to the holding. This might be statutory compensation under s 16 of the Agricultural Tenancies Act 1995 or compensation agreed on a voluntary basis between the parties.

(iv) where the landlord has given consent under s 17 of the 1995 Act to the tenant making the improvement on the condition that the improvement is not removed and the tenant has agreed to that condition. This provision overrides the normal presumption that a tenant can choose whether to remove a fixture or building or leave it behind and claim compensation. A landlord is likely to want the tenant to agree to such a condition where the retention on the property of a particular fixture may be useful to him or to an incoming tenant.

8.3 COMPENSATION

8.3.1 Summary

Part III, the most substantial part of the 1995 Act, contains the mandatory provisions which entitle the tenant to compensation for improvements at the end of his tenancy.

---

[20] Ibid, s 8(5).

[21] Ibid, s 8(2).

[22] See, ibid, ss 17, 19.

[23] Presumably he could remove his own fixture provided that he replaced the landlord's fixture, or one of at least equal value, and made good any damage caused by the substitution. Wrongful removal of a fixture is an act of waste but where there has been a substitution of the original or equivalent fixture the landlord would not be able to show any loss to his reversion.

The provisions apply to both written and oral tenancy agreements notwithstanding any agreement to the contrary. In order to obtain compensation, four conditions must be fulfilled:

  (i) the tenant must obtain the landlord's written consent to the improvement;

 (ii) the improvement must have been made at the expense, whole or partial, of the tenant;

(iii) the improvement must not be removed from the holding at the end of the tenancy; and

(iv) the improvement must add to the letting value of the holding.

A statutory right to independent arbitration is given to either party in respect of both the landlord's consent (except where the improvement is planning permission) and the amount of compensation to be paid when the tenancy ends.

8.3.2 What is an improvement

A tenant's improvement is defined in s 15 of the Agricultural Tenancies Act 1995 as either:

(a) a physical improvement made on the holding by the tenant by his own effort or wholly or partly at his own expense; or

(b) an intangible advantage which (i) is obtained for the holding by the tenant by his own effort or wholly or partly at his own expense, and (ii) becomes attached to the holding.

The 1995 Act has nothing similar to the Schedules of long and short-term improvements which are contained in the Agricultural Holdings Act 1986. Not only would such Schedules run counter to the aim of deregulation in the statute, but it would be impossible to anticipate the range of improvements which might be made in a tenant's diversified business. So far as intangible advantages and, in particular, quotas are concerned, it would be even more difficult to specify these for they may quickly become out of date. This is especially so for agricultural quotas which are subject to frequent changes in the Common Agricultural Policy of the European Union.

Intangible improvements include planning permission and production quotas, such as milk quotas, which are attached to land by operation of the relevant legislation. However, quotas, for example livestock premium quotas, which are allocated to producers as a personal right and can be sold or removed to another holding by tenants, will not be covered.

Goodwill may amount to an intangible improvement where it remains with the holding on the termination of the tenancy. This is sometimes referred to as 'cat goodwill' as contrasted with 'dog goodwill' which goes with the departing tenant. Where consent is given for, say a golf course, compensation could include the goodwill which follows from the establishment of a successful business. There will be no compensation for goodwill which does not survive the tenancy.

The benefit of management agreements entered into by the tenant with the Government or a statutory body could amount to an intangible improvement. Compensation would be payable if the agreements had been entered into with the approval of the landlord and survive the termination of the tenancy, provided that they add to the tenanted value.

8.3.3 Routine improvements

A routine improvement is defined by s 19(10) of the Agricultural Tenancies Act 1995 as follows:

> '"routine improvement", in relation to a farm business tenancy, means any tenant's improvement which—
>
> (a) is a physical improvement made in the normal course of farming the holding or any part of the holding, and
>
> (b) does not consist of fixed equipment or an improvement to fixed equipment,
>
> but does not include any improvement whose provision is prohibited by the terms of the tenancy.'

The definition of fixed equipment is derived from s 96(1) of the Agricultural Holdings Act 1986:

> '"fixed equipment" includes any building, or structure affixed to land and any works constructed on, in, over or under land, and also includes anything grown on land for a purpose other than use after severance from the land, consumption of the thing grown or its produce, or amenity.'

The purpose of the definition is to cover many of the tenant right matters for which compensation was obtainable under Sch 8, Pt II of the Agricultural Holdings Act 1986. The term tenant right could not be used as it was not susceptible of legal definition. Nor was it considered acceptable to have a Schedule with a list of tenant-right matters which might quickly grow out of date. The main examples of routine improvements are likely to be growing crops, liming, residual manurial values and acts of husbandry.

The rules relating to compensation for routine improvements are, with one exception, the same as the rules relating to other improvements. Before compensation can be claimed, the written consent of the landlord or that of the arbitrator must be obtained to the making of the improvements. It is hoped that in most cases there will be a general consent given by the landlord in the tenancy agreement to the making of routine improvements.

Where a landlord gives consent to an improvement he can do so before or after the improvement is made. However, where the landlord refuses consent the tenant can only apply to the arbitrator if he has not begun to provide the improvement. During the passage of the Bill through the House of Commons it was argued that tenants carrying out routine agricultural operations would not consider applying for consent before so doing. An exception has therefore been made for routine improvements. An application may be made to the arbitrator for consent to a routine improvement after the tenant has begun to provide the improvement.

The amount of compensation for a routine improvement is assessed in the same way as other improvements. The value is an amount equal to the increase attributable to the improvement in the value of the holding at the termination of the tenancy as land comprised in a tenancy (see para 8.3.9). It is not the value to an incoming tenant.

It is possible for an application to an arbitrator in respect of consent for a routine improvement and the settlement of a claim relating to compensation for a routine improvement to be made at the same time. Section 22(4) of the Agricultural Tenancies Act 1995 provides that where this happens the President of the Royal Institution of Chartered Surveyors must appoint the same arbitrator on both applications. Where the applications are made by the same person only one fee is payable in respect of the costs of making the appointment.

It should be noted that some of the tenant-right matters referred to in the Agricultural Holdings Act 1986 will not count as improvements under the Agricultural Tenancies Act 1995. Severed or harvested crops are chattels and not an improvement to the holding. Normally, the tenant will have a right to sell or remove them from the holding. Where there is a contractual provision that they must remain on the holding, the tenant should ensure that under the terms of the contract he obtains adequate payment for leaving them behind.

Acclimatised or hefted sheep are not an improvement to the holding. If a landlord or incoming tenant is to take over such sheep, the outgoing tenant should ensure that there is a written agreement for him to be paid not only for the sheep but the additional value which has resulted from the hefting.

8.3.4 Right to compensation

Provided certain conditions are fulfilled, a farm business tenant has the statutory right to obtain from his landlord compensation for any improvement made to a holding by him or at his expense. That entitlement arises at the end of the tenancy when the tenant quits the holding. The parties cannot contract out of the compensation provisions.[24]

In order to be eligible for compensation the tenant must have obtained the written consent of the landlord or that of the arbitrator to make the improvement. Where he does not receive such consent, he may remove the improvement in accordance with s 8 of the Agricultural Tenancies Act 1995.

The tenant will not receive compensation for any physical improvement which is removed from the holding or any intangible advantage which does not remain attached to the holding.[25] So, for example, if a tenant opts to remove, in accordance with s 8 of the 1995 Act, any fixtures or building erected by him, he will not be entitled to compensation.

---

[24] Agricultural Tenancies Act, 1995 s 26(1).
[25] Ibid, s 16(2).

Another example where the tenant would not be entitled to compensation, is where he has 'massaged' milk quota away from the land which is the subject of the tenancy agreement. It is possible for a tenant who occupies other land to transfer the quota to that other land. On quitting the land held under a farm business tenancy, compensation is payable by the landlord only in respect of the quota which remains attached to that land.

Section 16(3) of the Agricultural Tenancies Act 1995 provides that any claim for milk quota compensation shall be made under that Act and not under the complex provisions of the Agriculture Act 1986. The 1986 Act provides that where, on the termination of the tenancy of any land, the tenant has milk quota registered as his in relation to a holding, he will be entitled on quitting to obtain from his landlord compensation if the tenant had milk quota allocated to him or was in occupation of the land as tenant on 2 April 1984 and had milk quota transferred to him, the cost of which was borne wholly or partly by him.[26]

A tenant who acquired quota under other circumstances would not be eligible for compensation under the 1986 Act. However, where he acquires quota after the commencement of a farm business tenancy and that quota remains with the land on the termination of the tenancy, then he can claim compensation for the intangible advantage. The Statute does not allow him to carry forward any entitlement he had to compensation under the Agriculture Act 1986 if he surrenders his old tenancy under the Agricultural Holdings Act 1986 and enters into a new farm business tenancy. The tenant should therefore ensure that compensation for milk quota is settled at the time the tenancy under the Agricultural Holdings Act 1986 ends and before the farm business tenancy is granted.

8.3.5 Landlord's consent for improvement other than planning permission

A tenant's statutory right to compensation for improvements made to a holding is conditional upon the landlord giving consent in writing to the provision of the improvement.[27] This is so that landlords are required to pay compensation only for those improvements which they knew their tenant was intending to make and which they consider reasonable in accordance with the particular tenancy agreement.

The consent may be given in a separate document or in the tenancy agreement itself.[28] It may be particular, for example for the erection of a building. On the other hand, a landlord might give a general consent in the tenancy agreement. An example might be a general consent for the laying of field drains or water pipes or for routine improvements.

---

[26] Agriculture Act 1986, s 13, Sch 1, Pt I.
[27] Agricultural Tenancies Act 1995, ss 17 and 18. The Landlord and Tenant Act 1927, s 19, which provides that where there is a contractual provision against making an improvement without the landlord's consent the consent shall not be unreasonably withheld, does not apply to farm business tenancies. Similarly, the provision that no fine shall be payable for the alteration or the user of the demised premises does not apply. See, ibid, s 19(4).
[28] Ibid, s 17(2).

The consent does not have to be given before the improvement is made. This should be contrasted with the tenant's right to go to arbitration on refusal of consent.[29] The reference to arbitration has to be made before the tenant has begun to provide the improvement except for routine improvements.

The consent may be given conditionally or unconditionally. Where the consent is given conditionally, the conditions must relate to the improvement and not to the amount of compensation.[30] The method of assessment of compensation is mandatory and cannot be altered by agreement. The value of the improvement cannot be written down. This is in contrast to s 67(2) of the Agricultural Holdings Act 1986 which enables the landlord to give consent to an improvement 'upon such terms as to compensation or otherwise as may be agreed upon in writing between the landlord and the tenant'.

Examples of relevant conditions are that a building should not exceed a particular size or that it be constructed from local materials. The landlord might give consent on condition that the tenant agrees to give up his right to remove the improvement as a tenant's fixture under s 8 of the Agricultural Tenancies Act 1995 (see para 8.2.4).

8.3.6 Landlord's consent for planning permission

Where the improvement consists of planning permission there are more detailed provisions as to the landlord's consent. Under the Agricultural Holdings Act 1986 and the Landlord and Tenant Act 1927 (for business tenancies), compensation is not payable for planning permission. One of the terms of the Joint Industry Statement (see Appendix III) was that compensation should be payable in respect of planning permission gained by a tenant which related to activities on a holding and which were not prohibited by the tenancy agreement. It was not intended by the Joint Industry Statement that the tenant should obtain a share of the development potential by being compensated for planning permission enabling any development within a given use class. The compensation is limited to the development for the specified purpose for which consent of the landlord was given and the legislation reflects this. Development potential is a proper incident of the freehold reversion not of the leasehold interest.

In order for the tenant to obtain compensation for any planning permission which he has secured, the following conditions must be satisfied:[31]

(a) the landlord must have given consent in writing to the tenant making an application for planning permission; and

(b) such consent must be expressed to be given for the purpose of either:

    (i) enabling a specified physical improvement lawfully to be made on the holding by the tenant; or

    (ii) enabling the tenant lawfully to undertake a specified change of use; and

(c) at the end of the tenancy, the physical improvement must not have been completed or the change of use must not have been brought into effect.

---

[29] Ibid, s 17(3).
[30] Ibid, s 17(4).
[31] Ibid, s 17(4).

Where the works are completed by the end of the tenancy, compensation is payable in respect of the value to the holding of the improvement itself. This value will be enhanced because of the planning permission but the tenant cannot claim separate compensation for securing planning permission.[32]

The landlord may, as with consent for other improvements both physical and intangible, give his consent in respect of planning permission either unconditionally or on condition that the tenant agrees to a specified variation in the tenancy agreement.[33] But there is a major difference here in that there is no appeal to an arbitrator, as there is for other improvements, against the landlord's refusal to give consent to an application for planning permission.[34] The effect of the refusal will be that the tenant will not be entitled to compensation. The tenant could, however, proceed with his application for planning permission, provided he is not prevented from doing so by a term in his tenancy agreement. If he obtains planning permission and consent is given either by the landlord or the arbitrator to the physical improvement or change of use carried out on the basis of the planning permission, then the tenant will be entitled to compensation for any improvement which is actually carried out. The value attributable to the planning permission will be taken into account in assessing the compensation.[35] This is normal valuation practice.

8.3.7 Application to arbitrator on refusal or failure to give consent or unacceptable conditions

A tenant may give to his landlord a notice in writing demanding arbitration where he is aggrieved because his landlord:

(a) has refused to give consent to an improvement; or

(b) has failed to give consent to the improvement within two months of the tenant's written request for such consent; or

(c) has required the tenant to agree a variation in the terms of the tenancy as a condition of giving such consent.

A tenant cannot, however, demand a reference to arbitration where he is aggrieved by a refusal, or failure, or imposition, of unacceptable conditions relating to planning permission.[36]

The position for agricultural holdings under the Agricultural Holdings Act 1986 is slightly different. Section 67 and Sch 7, Pt II of the 1986 Act enable a tenant, whose landlord refuses consent to specified long-term improvements, to apply to the Agricultural Land Tribunal for consent. The tenant may also apply to the Tribunal where the landlord has imposed unacceptable conditions to his consent. Section 67 does not, however, deal with unreasonable delay by a landlord in giving his consent.

---

[32] Ibid, s 20(4).
[33] Ibid, s 18(2) and (3).
[34] Ibid, s 19(1)(a).
[35] Ibid, s 20(4).
[36] Ibid, s 19.

Section 19 of the Agricultural Tenancies Act 1995 provides that a tenant may demand arbitration where his landlord has failed to give consent to an improvement within two months of a written request by the tenant for such consent. This prevents the tenant suffering from undue delay by the landlord and may be important where, for instance, a tenant needs to undertake urgent works to deal with pollution from a livestock unit or to provide additional facilities in advance of a holiday season.

The section applies in respect of non-routine improvements which the tenant has not yet begun to provide.[37] This is in contrast to the provision under s 17(1) of the 1995 Act where the landlord's consent, as distinct from the reference to an arbitration, can be sought after the improvement has been made. The arbitrator's consent for routine improvements can be requested after the improvement has been made.

In order to give landlords a degree of certainty, s 19(2) of the 1995 Act sets reasonable time-limits for a tenant to exercise the statutory right to demand arbitration in respect of a proposed improvement. There are no such time-limits under the Agricultural Holdings Act 1986 within which application to the Tribunal must be made.

Under s 19 of the Agricultural Tenancies Act 1995 where a landlord has refused consent, or imposed conditions on his consent, notice requiring arbitration must be given within two months beginning with the day on which notice from the landlord, refusing consent or requiring the variation of the tenancy as a condition of consent, was given to the tenant.

Where a landlord has failed to give a requested consent within two months of the tenant's written request to the landlord for such consent, notice requiring arbitration must be given within a further two months.

8.3.8 Appointment of arbitrator

Once a tenant has given notice, the parties may agree whom should be appointed an arbitrator. Where no agreement is reached, either party may apply to the President of the Royal Institution of Chartered Surveyors for the appointment of an arbitrator by him.[38]

8.3.9 Powers and duties of arbitrator

An arbitrator who is appointed under s 19 of the Agricultural Tenancies Act 1995 must consider whether it is reasonable for the tenant to provide the proposed improvement. In answering this question the arbitrator must have regard to the terms of the tenancy.[39] The length of the term left to run as well as any user clauses would be relevant. A tenancy agreement may restrict the activities which the tenant may carry out on the let land. There may be specified permitted uses or there may be a requirement that all tenant's improvements must be related to agricultural use. There could even be a term that no improvement of any kind will be permitted on the holding. Such a restriction would have a bearing on the other terms of the tenancy, especially on the amount of rent which could be obtained for the land. The tenancy

---

[37] Ibid, s 19(1).
[38] Ibid, s 19(4).
[39] Ibid, s 19(5).

agreement might also contain other relevant conditions. There might, for instance, be a covenant by the tenant that he would use traditional local materials in any new buildings erected by him.

In determining whether it is reasonable for a tenant to provide a proposed improvement, the arbitrator may only override a contractual term of the tenancy where other factors in a particular case outweigh the express conditions of the contract. A possible example might be where the parties have agreed that there will be no tenant's improvements whatsoever on the holding, but urgent works are necessary to prevent the occurrence of a serious pollution incident.

The arbitrator is also directed to take into account all other relevant circumstances including the circumstances of the landlord and tenant. So the financial resources of the parties could be relevant considerations. For example, a wealthy tenant might want to carry out an improvement towards the end of a tenancy, which would be of benefit to his own business, but for which a less affluent landlord might be unable to pay current value compensation if the tenancy were to end on the agreed term date.

The Agricultural Holdings Act 1986[40] gives a landlord, where the Tribunal has granted consent to a long-term improvement, the right to serve notice in writing on the Tribunal and the tenant, that the landlord proposes himself to carry out the improvement. There is no similar provision in the 1995 Act. However, an offer by the landlord to make the improvement himself could be a relevant circumstance which the arbitrator would take into account. For greater certainty, a landlord who wishes to mitigate any end of tenancy compensation, should consider negotiating a term in the tenancy agreement which would give him the option of making any improvements which the tenant might propose.

The arbitrator may give approval to the tenant's improvement. If he does so, then that approval takes effect for the purposes of compensation and the farm business tenancy as if it were the consent of the landlord.[41] The arbitrator may also withhold approval. What he cannot do, however, is to give approval subject to conditions, whether his own or those of the landlord. Nor can he vary any conditions required by the landlord in respect of the landlord's consent.[42]

So if the landlord refuses consent, the arbitrator could either uphold the landlord's refusal or grant consent. If the landlord consents, but subject to conditions which are unacceptable to the tenant, the arbitrator can either refuse consent to the improvement or give consent unconditionally. The effect in both cases is that the landlord will be deemed to have given consent. If the landlord gives a conditional consent but the arbitrator refuses consent, the landlord's consent will stand subject to the conditions imposed by the landlord. On the other hand, if the arbitrator gives consent, it is necessarily unconditional. Thus, the landlord's conditions will not be valid.

For tenancies under the Agricultural Holdings Act 1986, the Agricultural Land Tribunal is empowered under s 67(4) of that Act to approve an improvement either

---

[40] Section 67(5).
[41] Agricultural Tenancies Act 1995, s 19(7).
[42] Ibid, s 19(6).

unconditionally or on such conditions as it considers to be just. The section specifically enables the Tribunal to give approval subject to a reduction in the amount of compensation payable for the tenant's improvement. An amendment in the Agricultural Tenancies Bill to allow the arbitrator to give approval to an improvement 'either conditionally or subject to such conditions as he may think fit' was rejected at Committee stage in the House of Lords. Lord Howe stated:

> '...I am not convinced that in this instance flexibility is desirable. Landlords may be nervous about the type of conditions which arbitrators might attach when giving consent. In any case, we would have to prohibit what might be the most obvious condition; namely, a reduced amount of compensation for the improvement. ... one of the key provisions in the Bill is that a tenant should receive full compensation for improvements, made with the landlord's, or an arbitrator's, consent. I would like to suggest ... that if the parties know that the arbitrator is limited in what he can do, they will endeavour to reach agreement.

> Arbitration is, after all, a last resort. We believe that a single test of whether it is reasonable for the tenant to proceed with the improvement, either conditionally or subject to the landlord's conditions, will encourage compromise between the parties and reduce the temptation to take up extreme positions and rely on the arbitrator to "split the difference" as it were.'[43]

8.3.10 Amount of compensation for improvement other than planning permission

The amount of compensation payable to a tenant for a tenant's improvement (other than for any planning permission obtained by the tenant), is an amount equal to the increase attributable to the improvement in the value of the holding at the termination of the tenancy as land comprised in a tenancy.[44] Thus the measure of value is not the increase in the value of the landlord's reversion but the increase in the tenanted value.

Section 20 of the Agricultural Tenancies Act 1995 is simpler and more flexible than the provisions on compensation in s 66(1) of the Agricultural Holdings Act 1986. Those provisions specify that compensation is to be an amount equal to the increase in the value of the holding as a holding which is attributable to the improvement, having regard to the character and situation of the holding and the average requirements of tenants reasonably skilled in husbandry. The 1995 Act, as in other matters, takes a less prescriptive approach. Compensation is not limited to agricultural improvements. It is not, however, totally open ended. There are three main safeguards for the landlord. First, to qualify for compensation the landlord's consent, or that of the arbitrator, has to be given for the improvement. Secondly, where the question of consent is referred to arbitration, the arbitrator is directed to take into account not only the terms of the tenancy, which would include the length of the term left to run and any user clauses, but also any other relevant circumstances, including the circumstances of the tenant and the landlord. Thirdly, the improvement must add to the letting value of the holding. A specialised improvement which is of no use to anyone other than that particular tenant would not add to the letting value of the holding.

[43] HL Committee Stage, col 1235, 13 December 1994.
[44] Agricultural Tenancies Act 1995, s 20(1).

Deductions from the amount of compensation payable will be made, subject to the detailed rules explained below, where the tenant has been given an allowance or benefit for the improvement or a grant has been made from public money.

Where the parties have agreed in writing that the landlord will make a financial or material contribution towards the provision of the improvement, the compensation payable at the end of the tenancy is reduced by the proportion in terms of value that the landlord's contribution represented of the total cost of providing the improvement.[45] Although the value of the improvement will decrease during the life of the tenancy, the proportion by which the compensation is reduced remains the same throughout. So if a landlord had contributed 25 per cent of the cost of a building, the tenant will receive three-quarters of the compensation to which he would have been entitled had he met the total cost of the building.

This is a much wider provision than s 66(3) of the Agricultural Holdings Act 1986. That section provides for a benefit given, or allowed, to the tenant pursuant to a written agreement to be taken into account in assessing compensation for those six improvements listed in Sch 8, Pt I to the 1986 Act, which do not require the landlord's consent.

Where a grant is made out of public money for a tenant's improvement, the amount of compensation which a landlord is required to pay at the end of the tenancy is reduced in proportion to the amount of grant received by the tenant.[46] If the tenant fails to apply for a grant then the landlord will have to pay full compensation. He should, therefore, make sure that the tenancy agreement imposes an obligation on the tenant to apply for any grants for which he might be eligible.

Section 20(3) of the Agricultural Tenancies Act 1995 is similar to s 66(5) of the Agricultural Holdings Act 1986. However, s 66 applies only to money provided by Parliament or from Local Government funds whilst s 20(3) of the 1995 Act applies to grants of money provided from any public money and this would include the European Union.

An element in the compensation for a physical improvement which has been carried out or a change of use which has been effected, pursuant to a planning permission, will be the value of the planning permission which was needed for the particular improvement.[47]

A landlord may refuse consent to a tenant's application for planning permission. This will preclude the tenant from obtaining compensation at the end of his tenancy for an unimplemented planning permission. However, if the tenant nevertheless obtains planning permission for a physical improvement or change of use and the arbitrator gives consent enabling the improvement authorised by the planning permission to be effected, the landlord will have to pay compensation reflecting not only the improvement itself but the planning permission which was necessary for the improvement to be made.

---

[45] Ibid, s 20(2).
[46] Ibid, s 20(3).
[47] Ibid, s 20(4).

8.3.11 Compensation for planning permission

Where a tenant obtains planning permission but by the end of the tenancy the tenant has not made the physical improvement or effected the change of use, specified by the landlord when giving his consent to the tenant applying for planning permission, compensation will be payable to the tenant under s 21 of the Agricultural Tenancies Act 1995. Compensation is based on the increase in value at the end of the tenancy as land comprised in a tenancy which is attributable to the fact that the specified physical improvement or change of use is authorised by planning permission. This means that the value is to be calculated at the termination of the tenancy on the basis that the holding is re-let. The compensation will not cover any development, which could take place by virtue of the permission, wider than the specified purpose for which the consent of the landlord was given. In assessing compensation, it will be necessary to value the land in the absence of the grant of planning permission but with the potential for obtaining such permission, and deduct that value from the increased value.

If the parties have agreed in writing that the landlord will make a financial or material contribution towards the obtaining of planning permission, any compensation otherwise payable at the end of the tenancy in respect of the permission will be reduced proportionately.[48]

8.3.12 Settlement of claims

If the parties are unable to agree on the amount of compensation, then the tenant can within two months from the end of his tenancy give notice in writing to his landlord of his intention to make a claim. The notice must comply strictly with the statutory time-limit and must specify the nature of the claim.[49] The time-limit is the same as that under s 83(1) of the Agricultural Holdings Act 1986.

After a notice has been given, the parties may still settle the claim by agreement in writing or they may appoint an arbitrator. Upon failure to do either of these things, either party may apply to the President of the Royal Institution of Chartered Surveyors for the appointment of an arbitrator. The application must be in writing and must be accompanied by such reasonable fee as the President may prescribe.[50]

An application cannot be made earlier than four months from the date on which the tenancy ended. In contrast, s 83(4) of the Agricultural Holdings Act 1986 provides that a period of eight months must elapse before an arbitrator can be appointed. In practice, this has proved to be too long, where parties find at an early stage that they cannot reach agreement.

Where a tenant remains in occupation of part of a holding, either under a new tenancy or as a tenant at sufferance (ie he holds over on the determination of his fixed-term tenancy, without the landlord's assent or dissent) and the tenant has a claim for compensation relating to that part of the holding, the two-month (for the notice of

---

48 Ibid, s 21(3).
49 Ibid, s 22(1), (2).
50 Ibid, ss 22(3), 30.

claim) and four-month (application for an arbitrator) time-limits do not start to run until the termination of the occupation.[51]

8.3.13 Successive tenancies

The statutory right to compensation for improvements is drafted on the assumption that, when a tenancy comes to an end, the tenant will quit the holding. In practice, he may often be granted a further tenancy. Where this happens, the right of the tenant to compensation for improvements made during the earlier tenancy or tenancies is preserved. The new tenancy does not have to be on the same terms as the tenancy under which the improvements were made, although the tenant and the holding must be the same.[52] This is a similar provision to s 69(1) of the Agricultural Holdings Act 1986.

The parties could agree, however, that the compensation should be paid at the end of a farm business tenancy even though the tenant will remain in occupation of the holding under a new tenancy. He is then specifically precluded from claiming compensation later for those improvements made during this earlier tenancy. He can claim for improvements made in later tenancies for which he has not received compensation.[53]

8.3.14 Resumption of part of the holding

At common law, a landlord cannot obtain possession of part of a holding unless there is a contractual provision allowing him to do so. Section 140 of the Law of Property Act 1925 allows a landlord of a severed reversion to serve a notice to quit part if, under the terms of the tenancy agreement or by statutory provision, the landlord could give notice to quit the whole. Section 140 does not confer a right to serve a notice to quit. It merely provides that where such a right exists and there has been a severance of the reversion, each landlord can give a notice in respect of his severed interest.

There is no statutory equivalent in the Agricultural Tenancies Act 1995 to s 31 of the Agricultural Holdings Act 1986 enabling a landlord to give notice to quit relating to part of the holding. Therefore, a landlord of a farm business tenancy can give such a notice only where the tenancy agreement permits it or s 140 of the Law of Property Act 1925 applies.

Where the landlord does resume possession of part of a holding, that part of the holding is deemed to be a separate holding. Compensation is calculated as at the date on which possession is taken.[54] The basis on which the compensation is assessed is the increase in value of the entire original holding which is attributable to improvements made on the part of the holding which is taken from the tenant. Original holding means the land comprised in the farm business tenancy on the date that the landlord gave his consent to the improvement or the date when an arbitrator gave his approval to the improvement.[55] This ensures that the tenant is no worse off in respect of

51 Ibid, s 22(5).
52 Ibid, s 23(1).
53 Ibid, s 23(2), (3).
54 Ibid, s 24(2), (3), (5).
55 Ibid, s 24(5).

compensation for improvements made on the part taken from his tenancy than he would have been if the tenancy of the entire holding had come to an end. This would be particularly important where a tenant received notice to quit that part on which improvements central to the tenant's business were situated. Where there is a contractual provision enabling the landlord to regain possession of part of the holding, a tenant will no doubt take this into account in planning his improvements. However, where a notice to quit part follows a severance of the reversion, the position is different. The tenant has no control over whether there is a severance or not and may not have anticipated a notice to quit part.

It may be, however, that the improvements are not on the land taken but on the land retained. Again, compensation is calculated on the value which the improvement had to the entire original holding, not just the part retained. The date for ascertaining the value, though, is different. It is not the date on which part of the land was repossessed by the landlord, but the date of the termination of the tenancy.[56]

It is important, therefore, that a landlord who has served notice to quit part, should bear in mind the contingent liability for improvements made on the retained land which enhanced the value, not only of that land, but also the land already taken out of the tenancy. Where a landlord is contemplating severance he should apportion any future potential liability for compensation. On a severance, all rights of re-entry become severable. One landlord will not, therefore, be able to control the service of any notice to quit given by the other landlord in accordance with the tenancy agreement.

It should be noted that the ability to give notice to quit part is not the same thing as an early resumption clause. Section 140 of the Law of Property Act 1925 will come into play only where a landlord has the right to serve a notice to quit the whole. Therefore, a landlord could not serve a notice to quit part to take effect before the end of a fixed-term tenancy. It may be that a tenancy agreement does contain a specific break clause. However, this contractual provision will not entitle the tenant to claim compensation for disturbance. This is because the tenancy has not been brought to an end prematurely. It has been brought to an end because of an express contractual condition. There are no provisions under the Agricultural Tenancies Act 1995 entitling a landlord to terminate a tenancy otherwise than in accordance with the tenancy agreement. Thus, there is no statutory provision for compensation for disturbance.[57]

Compensation for improvements on the land regained by the landlord, or on termination of the tenancy for improvements on the land retained, will be reduced where the landlord has given a benefit or allowance to the tenant in respect of the improvement.[58] A reduction will also be made where a tenant has been or will be given a grant from public funds in connection with the improvement.[59] The value of planning

---

[56] Ibid, ss 20, 21, 24(4).
[57] The disturbance compensation provisions under ss 60–63 of the Agricultural Holdings Act 1986 are needed because: (a) of the lifetime security given to tenants under that Act; and (b) the early resumption notice provisions under s 25. Under the Agricultural Tenancies Act 1995, 1–2 years' notice is needed for the operation of a break clause.
[58] Agricultural Tenancies Act 1995, ss 20(2), 21(3), 24(4).
[59] Ibid, ss 20(3), 24(4).

permission obtained by the tenant may be taken into account in determining the amount of compensation payable for the improvement (see para 8.3.9).[60]

Section 24(3) of the Agricultural Tenancies Act 1995 deals with compensation in respect of planning permission which has not been implemented where the landlord has regained possession of part. The amount of compensation is equal to the increase in value of the original holding as land comprised in a tenancy (ie the increase in tenanted value) attributable to the fact that the planning permission authorises the physical improvement or change of use specified by the landlord when he gave his consent to the tenant's application for planning permission. Original holding is defined as the land comprised in the farm business tenancy when the landlord or arbitrator gave consent or approval to the tenant's improvements. The value is calculated at the date on which the landlord regained possession of part.

Where the planning permission relates to the land retained then compensation is calculated on the value of the permission at the date of the termination of the tenancy to the original holding.[61]

Where the parties have agreed in writing that the landlord will give or allow a benefit in consideration of the tenant securing planning permission, the amount of compensation otherwise payable in respect of the permission is reduced. The reduction will be in proportion to the amount which the benefit already given bears to the total cost of obtaining planning permission.[62]

8.3.15 Compensation where reversion severed

Even though the reversion may be severed, the tenant, on quitting the entire holding, can require that he be paid compensation as if there were a single landlord.[63] This provision is similar to s 75 of the Agricultural Holdings Act 1986. It ensures that a tenant is not disadvantaged by the fragmentation of the reversionary interest in the holding by providing that claims for compensation are settled in relation to the entire holding which the tenant has quit. Section 25(1) of the Agricultural Tenancies Act 1995, however, applies only in respect of the compensation to which the tenant is entitled for improvements under s 16 of that Act. It will not apply to any additional contractual compensation which the parties may have agreed.

Where there has been a severance and the compensation is determined at arbitration, rather than by agreement, the arbitrator must apportion the liability for compensation between the persons in whom the reversionary interest is vested. Any additional costs to which such an apportionment gives rise are to be paid by such persons in such proportions as the arbitrator directs.[64] A similar provision is found in s 75(2) of the Agricultural Holdings Act 1986.

---

[60] Ibid, ss 20(4), 24(4).
[61] Ibid, ss 21, 24(4).
[62] Ibid, s 21(3).
[63] Ibid, s 25(1). The tenancy continues as one tenancy after the severance, *Jelley v Buckman* [1974] QB 488.
[64] Agricultural Tenancies Act 1995, s 25(2).

8.3.16 Contractual provisions on compensation

It is not possible to contract out of the mandatory statutory provisions of the Agricultural Tenancies Act 1995.[65] These provisions override any contractual agreement or local custom. However, the parties can agree that additional compensation should be paid for matters not covered by Pt III of that Act.[66]

For example, the parties may agree that compensation will be paid for any damage caused to a tenant's crops during the exercise of sporting rights reserved to the landlord. There is no statutory provision for game damage as there is under s 20 of the Agricultural Holdings Act 1986.

There might also be a contractual provision for additional compensation of a specified amount to be paid to the tenant should the landlord operate a contractual break clause in a fixed-term tenancy.

8.3.17 Allotments, smallholdings and market gardens

Provision is made for compensation for improvements payable to tenants of smallholdings and allotments under the Smallholdings and Allotments Act 1908, and of market gardens and allotments under the Allotments Act 1922. Where smallholdings, allotments and market gardens are let under a farm business tenancy, any compensation payable to a tenant will be in accordance with Pt III of the Agricultural Tenancies Act 1995 and not under the Allotment Acts.[67] Similarly, the special provisions in s 28 of the Opencast Coal Act 1958 relating to market gardens do not apply if the tenancy is a farm business tenancy.[68]

8.3.18 Business tenancies

Compensation for improvements for business tenancies is governed by the Landlord and Tenant Act 1927. Agricultural holdings under the Agricultural Holdings Act 1986 and farm business tenancies under the Agricultural Tenancies Act 1995 are specifically excluded from the 1927 Act.[69]

8.3.19 Compensation where compulsory purchase powers

Additional compensation is payable, as explained below, by an acquiring authority exercising compulsory powers where the land acquired is used for agriculture by way of a trade or business. A farm business tenant is entitled to this statutory compensation for all land, whether agricultural or not, comprised in his farm business tenancy. Non-agricultural business tenants and residential tenants, whilst they may have a right to compensation for disturbance under the general law, do not have a statutory right to additional compensation.

---

[65] Ibid, s 26(1).
[66] Ibid, s 26(2).
[67] Small Holdings and Allotments Act 1908, s 47. Allotments Act 1922, s 3(7) as amended by the Agricultural Tenancies Act 1995, Sch, paras 1 and 3.
[68] Ibid, Sch, para 17.
[69] Landlord and Tenant Act 1954, s 17(1) as amended by the Agricultural Tenancies Act 1995, para 5.

The acquiring authority has power to pay the displaced person such reasonable allowance as it thinks fit towards his removal expenses and the loss which he will sustain by reason of the disturbance to his trade or business. In estimating the loss, the authority must have regard to the period for which the land might reasonably have been expected to be available for the purpose of the trade or business and to the availability of other land suitable for that purpose.[70]

A farm business tenant is not entitled to the equivalent of the additional disturbance compensation on termination of his tenancy which is given to a tenant of an agricultural holding under the Agricultural Holdings Act 1986. Therefore, s 12 of the Agriculture (Miscellaneous Provisions) Act 1968 which provides for additional compensation to be paid under the 1986 Act, in consequence of the compulsory acquisition of an agricultural holding, will not apply to land held under a farm business tenancy.[71] In addition, s 48 of the Land Compensation Act 1973, which provides for certain disregards in relation to compensation following compulsory purchase of an interest in land let under the Agricultural Holdings Act 1986, will not be relevant.[72] The disregards relate to matters specific to that Act, in particular security of tenure.

8.3.20 Compensation under the Opencast Coal Act 1958

The Coal Authority has power to acquire compulsorily for the benefit of a licensed operator (within the meaning of the Coal Industry Act 1994), rights to occupy land for the purposes of carrying on opencast mining operations. Such operations may mean that improvements made by the tenant on land within the farm business tenancy are lost. Therefore, the Agricultural Tenancies Act 1995 has made amendments to the Opencast Coal Act 1958 to deal with three situations. First, where the tenancy or a successor tenancy continues after the mining operations cease; secondly, where the tenancy terminates before the mining operations ceased; thirdly, where the tenant's improvements are replaced by others.

Paragraph 16 of the 1995 Act inserts a new section, s 25A, into the Opencast Coal Act 1958. The section applies where:

(a) some part of the land comprised in a compulsory rights order is held, when the period of opencast mining begins, under a farm business tenancy;

(b) tenant's improvements have been made before those activities started which give the tenant a prospective right to compensation under s 16 of the 1995 Act;

(c) the benefit of some of those improvements has been lost; and

(d) the tenancy or a successor tenancy continues after the period of occupation for opencast mining activities has ended.

If the above conditions are fulfilled then the compensation provisions of Pt III of the 1995 Act apply as if no mining activities had taken place and the tenant quitted the

---

[70] Agriculture (Miscellaneous Provisions) Act 1963, s 22 as amended by the Agricultural Tenancies Act 1995, Sch, para 21.
[71] Ibid, Sch, para 23.
[72] Ibid, Sch, para 24.

holding immediately before those activities ended. However, the notice which must be served under s 22(2) of the Agricultural Tenancies Act 1995 before a claim for compensation can be enforced is not required for the purposes of s 25A of the Opencast Coal Act 1958. This is because the new section is concerned with prospective, not immediate, rights of compensation.

Where the tenant has lost the benefit of some only of the improvements which give him a prospective right to compensation, the 1995 Act compensation provisions apply as though the improvements, of which the tenant's land has not lost the benefit, were not tenant's improvements. The effect is that the tenant will not obtain immediate compensation from his landlord for those improvements, the benefit of which has not been lost. However, he will get compensation for them when eventually he quits the holding.

Paragraph 20 of the Sch to the 1995 Act inserts a new paragraph, 1A, into Sch 7 to the Opencast Coal Act 1958. This new paragraph provides that if, before opencast mining activities have ended, the tenant of a farm business tenancy quits the holding, he is entitled to be paid by the landlord compensation for improvements on quitting the holding even though the improvements may have been lost. The land is deemed to be in the state which subsisted immediately before the date of entry for the mining activities. The tenant is entitled to compensation if he quits before the termination of his tenancy, provided that the tenancy terminates before the end of the period of mining occupation without being succeeded by another tenancy.

Paragraph 20 also introduces a new paragraph, 2A, into Sch 7 to the 1958 Act. Where improvements have been lost as a result of opencast mining activities and replaced, the replaced improvements are to be treated as tenant's improvements even though not provided by the tenant. This ensures that the tenant, on quitting the holding, is paid compensation by the landlord for the replaced improvements.

Paragraphs 1A and 2A operate only if conditions (a) and (b) in s 25A of the 1958 Act are fulfilled. That is, the farm business tenancy must predate the date of entry for the mining activities and the tenant must have made improvements which gave him, immediately before that date, a prospective right to compensation under s 16 of the Agricultural Tenancies Act 1995.

8.3.21 Compensation for subsidence

Under the Coal Mining Subsidence Act 1991 as amended by the Coal Industry Act 1994, compensation may be payable for diminution in value of the land caused by subsidence. The compensation is known as depreciation payments and is paid to the owner of the land. Where agricultural land is let otherwise than for building purposes, the owner will be the landlord. However, where a farm business tenant (or a tenant of an agricultural holding under the Agricultural Holdings Act 1986) is liable under the terms of the tenancy to make good the damage, the depreciation payments will be paid to the tenant. Even if the tenant is not liable to make good the damage, where he is entitled to compensation for improvements then the depreciation payments may be paid to him provided that the landlord and tenant have agreed that the tenant is entitled to compensation. This will also apply where entitlement has been established on arbitration under the Agricultural Tenancies Act 1995, for farm business tenants, or the Agricultural Holdings Act 1986 for tenants of agricultural holdings governed by that Act.[73]

Any question as to whether or not the tenant is a tenant of a farm business tenancy will be referred to arbitration under s 28 of the 1995 Act. Questions on the amount of compensation will also be referred to arbitration under that section.

8.3.22 Agricultural charges on compensation

Section 5 of the Agricultural Credits Act 1928 enables a farmer to create, in favour of a bank, an agricultural charge on any of his farming stock and other agricultural assets as security for sums advanced to him or paid on his behalf under any guarantee by the bank, and interest, commission and charges thereon. 'Other agricultural assets' include a tenant's right to compensation under the Agricultural Holdings Act 1986 and his right to compensation under Pt III of the Agricultural Tenancies Act 1995.[74]

---

[73] Ibid, Sch, paras 36, 37.
[74] Ibid, Sch, para 7.

Chapter 9

SPECIAL CATEGORIES OF LANDLORD

9.1 INTRODUCTION

This chapter looks at the special provisions in the Agricultural Tenancies Act 1995 where the landlord is the tenant for life of a strict settlement or the trustees of a trust for sale. It also deals with the position where the Crown or specified universities and schools are the landlord. Finally, the position of the mortgagor landlord is considered.

9.2 POWER OF LIMITED OWNER TO CONSENT

A landlord of a farm business tenancy, whatever his estate or interest in the holding, may for the purposes of the Act give any consent, make any agreements or enter into any transaction as if he were a fee simple owner, or, where his interest is a leasehold interest, as if he were absolutely entitled to that lease.[1] This is a similar provision to that under the Agricultural Holdings Act 1986.[2]

9.3 APPLICATION OF CAPITAL MONEY

9.3.1 Agricultural Tenancies Act 1995

Capital money under a strict settlement or trust for sale may be expended upon:

(i) improvements made by the landlord;

(ii) compensation paid to the tenant for improvements made by him;

(iii) the cost, charges and expenses incurred by the landlord of any reference to arbitration on disputes regarding consents to, or compensation for, improvements.[3]

The tenant for life or trustee has the right to require the sum payable as compensation and any costs, charges and expenses incurred by him in connection with the tenant's claim, to be paid out of capital money.[4]

Both of these sections are based on the compensation provisions for improvements made by business tenants.[5]

No distinction is made, either in the Agricultural Tenancies Act 1995 or in the Landlord and Tenant Act 1927, between long- and short-term improvements. Although a tenant for life is permitted to insist that all improvements, however

---

[1] Agricultural Tenancies Act 1995, s 32.
[2] Agricultural Holdings Act 1986, s 88.
[3] Agricultural Tenancies Act 1995, s 33(1).
[4] Ibid, s 33(3).
[5] Landlord and Tenant Act 1927, s 13.

short-lived, should be borne by capital he may not consider it right to do so. The sections are permissive not mandatory. They do not state that all improvements must be defrayed out of capital. The tenant for life under a strict settlement is in the dual position of beneficiary and trustee. He should, consider therefore, what is in the best interests of the trust estate and of the other beneficiaries.

9.3.2 The Universities College Estates Act 1925

The Universities College Estates Act 1925 applies to the Universities of Oxford, Cambridge and Durham and to Winchester and Eton Colleges. The permitted investments for capital money under the Act include money spent on improvements, compensation and arbitration costs and expenses as set out in para 9.3.1 above.[6]

9.3.3 Agricultural Holdings Act 1986

The Settled Land Act 1925 enables capital money to be paid to the tenant for life for money expended and costs incurred by him as landlord 'in or about the execution of any improvements comprised in Schedule 7 to ... the Agricultural Holdings Act [1986]'.[7] This has been held not to cover compensation paid by the landlord to the outgoing tenant because the payment is not an execution of any improvements.[8] However, where money is paid as compensation to a tenant, the tenant for life landlord can obtain from the Minister of State at the Ministry of Agriculture, Fisheries and Food (MAFF), or, in Wales, the Secretary of State, an order charging the holding with repayment of compensation.[9] Charges which relate to improvements may be redeemed out of capital.[10]

Even where this occurs (and MAFF states that a charging order has been made only twice in the last 20 years), the trustees subsequently should make some accounting adjustments between the tenant for life and the remainderman. This is because it would be inequitable if those improvements which are likely to be exhausted within a short time were allowed to become a permanent burden on capital.[11] This contrasts with the position where the tenant for life executes the improvements. Whatever the life expectancy of those improvements, he can insist that payment for them be made out of capital.

Although capital money cannot be used to pay compensation to the tenant for improvements, it can be used to meet the cost of current repairs undertaken by the tenant for life. This is because the improvements are those specified in Sch 7 to the Agricultural Holdings Act 1986, and the Schedule includes repairs to fixed equipment. Moreover, this has been held to be so where the landlord carried out repairs for which the tenant was contractually liable and where the landlord was not a landlord at all within the meaning of the agricultural legislation.[12]

---

6 Universities and College Estates Act 1925, s 26.
7 Settled Land Act 1925, s 73(1)(iv).
8 *Re Duke of Wellington's Estate* [1972] Ch 374.
9 Agricultural Holdings Act 1986, s 86.
10 Settled Land Act 1925, s 73(1)(ii).
11 *Re Duke of Manchester's Settlement* [1910] 1 Ch 106.
12 Agricultural Holdings Act 1986, s 89. *Re Duke of Northumberland* [1951] Ch 202; *Re Lord Brougham and Vaux's Settled Estates* [1953] 2 All ER 655.

9.3.4 Comment

A general principle of trust law is that trustees should hold a balance between the interests of the life tenant and the remainderman. Therefore, capital money should be spent on permanent improvements which will benefit the remainderman as well as the life tenant, but repairs should be paid out of income. The Settled Land Act 1925 for strict settlements, applied by the Law of Property Act 1925 to trusts for sale, has specific rules to give effect to this principle.

The Agricultural Holdings Act 1948 and subsequent Acts, as interpreted by the courts, upsets this careful accounting process. The cases have been criticised by writers[13] and judges.[14]

It is also wrong that the tenant for life should not be allowed to pay compensation for tenant's improvements out of capital. However, this may not be too much of a problem because of the practice of writing down the value of improvements.

For future tenancies, the Agricultural Tenancies Act 1995 has restored the correct accounting principles. Capital money is payable both for the execution of improvements and for the payment of compensation where the tenant effects the improvements. Repairs will not be chargeable to capital. The Agricultural Tenancies Act 1995 has no Schedule of improvements and there are no specific provisions dealing with repairs. This means that the normal trust rules will apply; the tenant for life will be responsible for the costs of repairs.

9.4 POWER TO RAISE MONEY BY MORTGAGE

Section 71 of the Settled Land Act 1925 enables the tenant for life to raise money by mortgage for the purposes set out in the section. The same provisions are extended to trusts for sale by s 28 of the Law of Property Act 1925. Section 33(2) of the Agricultural Tenancies Act 1995 enables money to be raised by mortgage for the purpose of paying compensation to tenants for improvements.

9.5 LEASES AT BEST RENT

Sometimes, statutory provisions stipulate that leases may be granted provided that the best rent is obtained. Examples of special category landlords who may do so are mortgagors and mortgagees in possession and a tenant for life of a strict settlement. Section 34 of the 1995 Act provides that in calculating the best rent or reservation in the nature of rent, it shall not be necessary to take into account against the tenant any

---

[13] See eg Megarry and Wade *Law of Real Property* 5th edn (Stevens, 1984).

[14] Harman J in *Re Sutherland Settlement Trusts* [1953] 2 All ER 27 declined to follow *Re Duke of Northumberland* [1951] Ch 202 where expenditure had been incurred on repairs before the coming into force of the Agricultural Holdings Act 1984. In *Re Wynn* [1955] 3 All ER 865, Harman J refused to extend the principle in *Re Duke of Northumberland* to a life tenant under a trust for sale. In *Re Boston's Will Trusts* [1956] 1 All ER 593, Vaisey J, the judge in *Re Duke of Northumberland* and *Re Lord Brougham and Vaux's Settled Estates* [1953] 2 All ER 655, seemed uneasy about his earlier decisions.

increase in the value of the holding arising from any improvements made or paid for by him. This is consistent with the disregard for tenant's improvements on a rent review. Section 34 is similar to s 90 of the Agricultural Holdings Act 1986.

9.6 THE CROWN

The Agricultural Tenancies Act 1995 applies to an interest which belongs to the following:

(i) the Crown;

(ii) the Duchy of Lancaster;

(iii) the Duchy of Cornwall;

(iv) a government department or is held on trust for Her Majesty for the purposes of a government department. [15]

Compensation payable by the Chancellor of the Duchy of Lancaster for tenant's improvements may be raised and paid under s 25 of the Duchy of Lancaster Act 1817, as an expense incurred in improvements of land belonging to Her Majesty in right of the Duchy. [16] In the corresponding provision of the Agricultural Holdings Act 1986, compensation for long-term improvements had to be paid under s 25 while short-term improvements defined in Pts I and II of Sch 8 to the Act, had to be paid out of the annual revenues of the Duchy. [17]

Where land belongs to the Duchy of Cornwall, the purposes authorised by s 8 of the Duchy of Cornwall Management Act 1863 include the payment of compensation for tenant's improvements. [18]

9.7 THE MORTGAGOR LANDLORD

Under the Law of Property Act 1925, s 99, a mortgagor in possession may grant agricultural or occupation leases for any term not exceeding 50 years. This is subject to any contrary intention expressed by the mortgagor and mortgagee in the mortgage deed or by a separate document in writing. [19] However, under the Agricultural Holdings Act 1986, there was no power to prevent such leasing where the mortgage was made after 1 March 1948 and related to agricultural land. [20] This provision of the 1986 Act has been superseded by an amendment to s 99 of the Law of Property Act 1925. A new sub-section to that section provides that any power to grant a lease cannot be excluded in relation to any mortgage of agricultural land made after 1 March 1948

---

[15] Agricultural Tenancies Act 1995, s 37.

[16] Ibid, s 37(5).

[17] Agricultural Holdings Act 1986, s 95(4).

[18] Agricultural Tenancies Act 1995, s 37(6).

[19] Law of Property Act 1925, s 99(13).

[20] Agricultural Holdings Act 1986, s 100, Sch 14, para 12. See also Landlord and Tenant Act 1954, Pt II, s 36(4).

but before 1 September 1995. Similarly, where a mortgage of agricultural land is made on or after 1 September 1995, it is not possible to exclude the power to grant a lease of an agricultural holding which, by virtue of s 4 of the Agricultural Tenancies Act 1995, continues to be governed by the Agricultural Holdings Act 1986. It will, however, be possible to prevent, by a contractual provision in the mortgage deed or other written document, a mortgagor of land subject to a mortgage granted on or after 1 September 1995 from granting a farm business tenancy.[21]

---

[21] Agricultural Tenancies Act 1995, s 31.

Chapter 10
HOUSING

10.1 THE FARM BUSINESS TENANT

A farm business tenant is given no residential security on the termination of his tenancy under any of the Acts set out below.

10.1.1 The Agricultural Tenancies Act 1995

There are no provisions on residential security in the Agricultural Tenancies Act 1995. Amendments to the Bill to provide such security were put down in the Committee Stage in the House of Lords but were withdrawn. Lord Howe expressed the reasons for opposing security as follows:

> 'The effect of the amendment would be that all land agents, advisers and landowners would look for ways of avoiding its restrictive provisions. Depending on circumstances, they might opt for share-farming arrangements or contract farming. Alternatively, they could split the house and the land, letting the land on a farm business tenancy but letting the house on an assured shorthold tenancy so that they could regain possession at the appropriate time. Some might simply sell their farmhouses and let the bare land to neighbouring farmers. That is just what we see happening at present. Given the fears that have been expressed about fragmentation of farms, I wonder whether Members of the Committee opposite really believe that to be desirable.

> We and the main industry organisations representing tenants as well as landlords take the view that tenants are businessmen who are capable of making important decisions. The conditions under which they occupy their homes are clearly of prime importance to them. It is not something insignificant that they are likely to overlook. Farmers managing on Gladstone v Bower tenancies and other such short-term, insecure arrangements are in that position at present – or in a worse position. In the Bill we have ensured that they will have at least 12 months' notice when a tenancy is to end. That will give them time to make alternative arrangements – much more time than the two months which assured shorthold tenants in the private residential rented sector are entitled to, and possibly more than they need.'[1]

10.1.2 The Reserve and Auxiliary Forces (Protection of Civil Interests) Act 1951

Section 27 of the Reserve and Auxiliary Forces (Protection of Civil Interests) Act 1951 protects servicemen in respect of business and professional premises. Excluded from the protection are tenants of agricultural holdings within the meaning of the Agricultural Holdings Act 1986 and farm business tenants under the Agricultural Tenancies Act 1995. However, farm business tenants are protected if the tenancy includes a dwelling-house occupied by a person responsible for the control (whether as tenant or servant or agent of the tenant) of the management of the holding. Provided certain conditions are fulfilled, the court has a discretion to grant a new tenancy where the old

---

[1] Hansard, HL Committee Stage, col 1130, 12 December 1994.

tenancy would terminate by the effluxion of time or the service of a notice to quit by the landlord before, or within 2 months, of the ending of a period of relevant service.

10.1.3 The Leasehold Reform Act 1967

The Leasehold Reform Act 1967 enables a tenant of a house, occupied as his residence and held on a long lease at a low rent, to acquire the freehold or an extended lease. This right of enfranchisement does not apply to agricultural tenancies under the Agricultural Holdings Act 1986, nor to farm business tenants under the Agricultural Tenancies Act 1995.[2]

10.1.4 Rent (Agriculture) Act 1976

The Rent (Agriculture) Act 1976 gives security of tenure to 'qualifying workers' who have a 'relevant licence or tenancy' which is in 'qualifying ownership'. A qualifying worker is one who has worked full time in agriculture for 91 out of the previous 104 weeks. A relevant licence or tenancy is one which is excluded from the protection of the Rent Acts because the occupant pays a low rent or no rent. A dwelling is in qualifying ownership if the occupier is employed in agriculture and his employer either owns the dwelling-house as the immediate landlord or licensor, or has made arrangements with another person to provide the accommodation. Such occupants have the status of 'protected occupiers' with much the same protection as under the Rent Acts, but with a number of variations. When a protected occupier dies, there is one succession. His spouse or a member of his family may succeed to the occupancy.

On the determination of the protected occupancy the occupier becomes a statutory tenant. The landlord can obtain possession only in limited circumstances. The grounds for possession are similar to those under the Rent Act 1977. There are, however, special re-housing provisions. If the landlord requires vacant possession for another agricultural worker, who is needed in the interests of efficient agriculture and he cannot reasonably provide suitable alternative accommodation for the occupier himself, the housing authority must use its best endeavours to re-house the displaced occupier.

On 15 January 1989, the Rent (Agriculture) Act 1976 was superseded by the Housing Act 1988. It will, however, continue to apply to old tenancies and to new tenancies in limited circumstances. For instance, the 1976 Act will continue to apply to a tenancy in succession to an old tenancy which has terminated and to a tenancy of a dwelling-house which is alternative accommodation for the tenant of a 1976 Act tenancy where the landlord has regained possession.

The protection afforded by the Act is conferred on a person who has a 'relevant tenancy', if he is a 'qualifying worker' and the dwelling-house is in 'qualifying ownership'. Agricultural tenancies under the Agricultural Holdings Act 1986 and farm business tenancies are excluded from the definition of relevant tenancies.[3]

---

[2] Leasehold Reform Act, s 1(3)(b)(i), (ii), as amended by the Agricultural Tenancies Act 1995, Sch, para 22.

[3] Rent (Agriculture) Act 1976, s 9(3), (4), Sch 2, as amended by the Agricultural Tenancies Act 1995, Sch, para 26.

10.1.5 The Rent Act 1977

The Rent Act 1977 confers security of tenure on residential tenants who fulfil certain conditions. The Act has been replaced by the Housing Act 1988 for most tenancies entered into on, or after, 15 January 1989. Section 10 of the 1977 Act provides that a tenancy is not a protected tenancy if the dwelling-house is comprised in an agricultural holding under the Agricultural Holdings Act 1986 and is so occupied by the person responsible for the control (whether as tenant or as servant or agent of the tenant) of the farming of the holding. Also excluded from the status of a protected tenancy is a dwelling-house under a farm business tenancy which is occupied by the person responsible for the control (whether as tenant or as servant or agent of the tenant) of the management of the holding.[4]

10.1.6 The Protection From Eviction Act 1977

Section 3 of the Protection From Eviction Act 1977 applies where any premises have been let as a dwelling under a tenancy which is not a statutorily protected tenancy or an excluded tenancy. If the occupier continues to reside in the premises after the end of the tenancy, the owner must not, other than by court proceedings, enforce against the occupier his right to recover possession.

A statutorily protected tenancy is defined to include both tenancies under the Agricultural Holdings Act 1986 and farm business tenancies under the Agricultural Tenancies Act 1995. This means that court proceedings are not necessary to regain possession of the farmhouse or other accommodation occupied by the tenant after the termination of his tenancy.[5]

10.1.7 The Housing Act 1985

Part IV of the Housing Act 1985 relates to secure tenancies of dwelling-houses let as separate dwellings by landlords in the public sector. The Act confers various rights on secure tenants including security of tenure. A tenancy is not a secure tenancy if the dwelling-house is comprised in:

(1) an agricultural holding (within the meaning of the Agricultural Holdings Act 1986) and is occupied by the person responsible for the control (whether as tenant or servant or agent of the tenant) of the farming of the holding; or

(2) a farm business tenancy and is occupied by the person responsible for the control of the management of the holding.[6]

10.1.8 The Housing Act 1988

The Housing Act 1988 superseded the Rent Act 1977 with effect from 15 January 1989. Tenancies of dwelling-houses, subject to some limited exceptions, entered into on or after that date are no longer protected under the 1977 Act. They are either assured tenancies or assured shorthold tenancies under the Housing Act 1988.

[4] Rent Act 1977, s 10(1), (2); Agricultural Tenancies Act 1995, Sch, para 27.
[5] Protection From Eviction Act 1977, s 8(i)(d), (g); Agricultural Tenancies Act 1995, Sch, para 29.
[6] Housing Act 1985, Sch, para 8; Agricultural Tenancies Act 1985, Sch, para 30.

Certain types of tenancies cannot be assured tenancies under the 1988 Act. These include a tenancy of a dwelling-house which is comprised in:

(1) an agricultural holding under the Agricultural Holdings Act 1986, and is occupied by the person responsible for the control (whether as tenant or a servant or agent of the tenant) of the farming of the holding; or

(2) a farm business tenancy and is occupied by the person responsible for the control (whether as tenant or servant or agent of the tenant) of the management of the holding. Tied cottage protection (the assured agricultural occupancy) is only applicable to an agricultural worker who does *not* have control of the farming or management of the holding.[7]

Under Pt IV of the Housing Act 1988, it is possible for duly authorised persons to acquire the freehold of dwelling-houses from a public sector landlord. Certain tenancies, including farm business tenancies, granted after an application to exercise the right to buy has been served by the prospective purchaser, will be determinable by four weeks' notice, regardless of any contractual fixed term.[8] This is to ensure that the public sector landlord does not defeat the right to buy provisions of the Housing Act 1988.

10.2 FARM MANAGER

A farm manager is not to be within the provisions of the Rent Act 1977 or the Housing Act 1988 and so will not acquire any statutory protection against a landlord who has granted a farm business tenancy to the employer of the manager. He may, however, as an agricultural worker, be entitled to protection against the farm business tenant either as a sub-tenant or licensee. Should the mesne tenancy be determined, he will then, in some circumstances, be entitled to protection against the head landlord. These provisions are discussed below.[9]

10.3 FARM WORKERS

Where a farm business tenant sub-lets a dwelling-house to an employee, the employee may be protected both against his immediate landlord, the farm business tenant, and, in certain circumstances, against the head landlord. At common law the sub-tenancy would fall with the head tenancy unless the mesne tenant surrendered his tenancy. A farm worker will also be protected if he has a relevant licence, rather than a tenancy, under the Rent (Agriculture) Act 1976 or an assured agricultural occupancy under the Housing Act 1988.

10.3.1 The Rent (Agriculture) Act 1976

If the mesne tenancy is a farm business tenancy or tenancy under the Agricultural Holdings Act 1986, and the tenant sub-lets a dwelling-house to an agricultural

---

[7] Housing Act 1988, Sch 1, para 7; Agricultural Tenancies Act 1995, Sch, para 34.

[8] Housing Act 1988, s 101(2); Agricultural Tenancies Act 1995, Sch, para 33.

[9] For an excellent exposition of tied agricultural accommodation, see C P Rodgers, *Agricultural Law*, Ch 11 (Butterworths, 1991).

employee at a low rent before 15 January 1989, then the sub-tenant will be protected under the Rent (Agriculture) Act 1976.

Section 9 of the Act ensures that:

> 'where a dwelling-house forms part of premises which have been let as a whole on a superior tenancy but which do not constitute a dwelling-house let on a statutorily protected tenancy'

then, if the sub-tenancy is itself a protected occupancy or statutory tenancy, there will be protection. This is achieved by deeming the dwelling-house to have been let under a separate superior tenancy. Sub-section (2) gives a sub-tenant protection where the mesne tenancy of a statutorily protected tenancy of a dwelling-house is determined. It provides that the sub-tenant shall become the tenant of the landlord on the same terms as if the tenant's statutorily protected tenancy had continued.

In order to be protected, the sub-letting must be lawful and not in breach of any covenant in the lease against sub-letting. The sub-tenant must himself be protected as an agricultural worker under the 1976 Act.

10.3.2 The Rent Act 1977

Where the sub-tenants are agricultural workers but are not occupying tied accommodation under low rents, they may be protected under s 137(3) of the Rent Act 1977.

The Act provides that where the sub-letting is of a dwelling-house on part of the property comprised in the head lease then, when the head tenancy comes to an end, there will be deemed separate lettings of the dwelling-house and the remainder of the property. The sub-tenant will be deemed to become the tenant of the landlord on the same terms as if the statutorily protected tenancy had continued. It is necessary, as under the 1976 Act, that the sub-tenancy is a protected tenancy and is a lawful sub-letting. Moreover, the sub-tenant will be protected only if he is an agricultural worker who would have been protected under the Rent (Agriculture) Act 1976 had the rent not been too high.[10] It should be noted that s 137(3) of the Rent Act 1977 specifically defines premises to include an agricultural holding within the Agricultural Holdings Act 1986 or land comprised in a farm business tenancy under the Agricultural Tenancies Act 1995.[11] In other cases, the superior tenancy must be of a dwelling-house. Therefore, no protection was given under the 1977 Act to a residential sub-tenant of a tenancy, which was protected as a business tenancy under the Landlord and Tenant Act 1954, Pt II.[12]

10.3.3 The Housing Act 1988

If a sub-tenancy is created after 15 January 1989, the Housing Act 1988 will apply and not the Rent (Agriculture) Act 1976 or the Rent Act 1977.

---

[10] Rent Act 1977, ss 99, 137(3).

[11] Ibid, sub-s 137(3). The section was amended to reverse (in part) the decision in *Maunsell v Olins* [1975] AC 373. This case held that 'premises' did not include an agricultural holding.

[12] *Pittalis v Grant* [1989] 2 All ER 622, CA

Where the sub-letting is an assured tenancy, it will continue on the determination of the mesne tenancy.[13] The former sub-tenant will hold directly from the head landlord on the terms of the old tenancy. If the sub-tenant has not an assured tenancy but is an agricultural employer occupying tied accommodation as an assured agricultural occupant, he will also be protected.[14] Sub-tenancies which include more than two acres of agricultural land with the dwelling-house cannot be assured tenancies.[15] Similarly, illegal sub-tenancies will not be protected. Farm business tenancies may have a contractual prohibition against assigning or sub-letting.

Although tenancies of dwelling-houses comprised in an agricultural tenancy under the Agricultural Holdings Act 1986 or a farm business tenancy under the Agricultural Tenancies Act 1995 and occupied by the person responsible for the farming or management of the land, cannot be assured tenancies if the occupation of such a dwelling-house is instead by an agricultural employee, it can give rise to an assured agricultural occupancy.[16] On the other hand, although the mesne tenancy does not have to be an assured tenancy itself, the head landlord will not be bound by the sub-tenancy if he could not grant an assured tenancy. An example would be where the head landlord is the Crown or local authority.[17]

It is possible for the tenant to grant his farm worker an assured shorthold tenancy rather than an assured tenancy or an assured agricultural occupancy.[18] However, the sub-letting cannot be an assured shorthold tenancy if the rent is £250 or under per annum or if more than two acres of agricultural land are let with the dwelling. Provided the prescribed notices are served before the grant of the tenancy and before its determination, the tenant will not be entitled to any security of tenure beyond the contractual term.[19]

It is important that the letting is genuinely separate from the contract of employment. The maximum amount which can be deducted from wages by way of rent is currently £1.50 per week.[20] Therefore, it is not possible to deduct sufficient rent to satisfy the assured shorthold provisions. There is always a danger that additional wages paid to cover the rent will be seen by the courts as a sham to avoid giving the worker security as an assured agricultural occupant.

10.3.4 The Protection From Eviction Act 1977

A farm worker who is unable to satisfy the agricultural worker condition contained in either the Housing Act 1988 or the Rent (Agriculture) Act 1976 and who is unable to claim the protection of the Rent Act 1977 or the protection given to tenants of assured tenancies under the Housing Act 1988, will enjoy the protection provided by the Protection From Eviction Act 1977. Section 4 of the Act provides that a farm worker

---

[13] Housing Act 1988, s 18(1).
[14] Ibid, s 24(3).
[15] Ibid, Sch 1, para 6.
[16] Ibid, s 24(2).
[17] Ibid, s 18(2).
[18] Ibid, s 20.
[19] Ibid, s 21.
[20] Agricultural Wages Act 1948, ss 3 and 7, Sch 4. Agricultural Wages Order 1995.

who has occupied premises under the terms of his employment in agriculture has six months' security of tenure as from the date when his contractual right to occupy the dwelling under the service agreement ceases.[21] That will usually be the date when his contract of employment terminates. However, the owner can apply to the county court for possession within that six-month period and the court can make a possession order. But if he does so, the court must suspend the order for the remainder of the six-month period unless it is satisfied that:

(1) other suitable accommodation is, or will within that period, be made available to the occupier; or

(2) the efficient management of any agricultural land or the efficient carrying on of any agricultural operations would be seriously prejudiced unless the premises are available for occupation by a person to be employed by the landlord; or

(3) greater hardship would be caused by the suspension of the order than by its execution; or

(4) the occupier of the dwelling or anyone residing with him has been causing damage to the premises or has been guilty of misconduct which is a nuisance or annoyance to persons occupying other premises;

and being satisfied in one or other of these points, the court considers it would be reasonable not to suspend the execution of the order for the remainder of that period.

---

[21] Section 30(3) of the Housing Act 1988 extended s 4 of the Protection From Eviction Act 1977 to cover licences as well as tenancies.

Chapter 11

TERMINATION OF TENANCIES

11.1 NOTICE TO QUIT

11.1.1 Fixed term

At common law, a fixed-term tenancy expires automatically at the end of the fixed term. The common law rule is preserved in the Agricultural Tenancies Act 1995 for fixed-term tenancies of two years or less. For tenancies over two years, a written notice of at least 12 but less than 24 months must be served expiring on the contractual termination date. If no notice is served then the tenancy will continue as a yearly tenancy on the terms of the original tenancy so far as are applicable to a tenancy from year to year.[1] The yearly tenancy can be terminated by a written notice of at least 12 but less than 24 months expiring at the end of the completed year.[2] The notice can be served during the last year of the fixed term so that the tenancy is terminated at the end of the following year.[3] It is not possible to contract out of this provision.[4]

The death of either the landlord or tenant will not terminate the tenancy. However, parties could provide in the tenancy agreement that, after the death of either party, a notice of between one and two years could be served.

11.1.2 Yearly tenancies

In order to terminate a yearly tenancy a written notice of at least 12 but less than 24 months taking effect at the end of a year of the tenancy must be served. It is not possible to contract out of this provision.[5] A yearly tenancy will continue after the death of either party until notice of between one to two years is served.

11.1.3 Other periodic tenancies

A tenancy from week to week, month to month, quarter to quarter or other periods, such as successive periods of 364 days,[6] must be terminated by a notice of a full period expiring at the end of the completed period unless the parties agree otherwise.[7] There is no provision in the Agricultural Tenancies Act 1995 dealing with periodic tenancies other than those from year to year.

Where there is a dwelling-house comprised in the letting then at least four weeks' notice must be given, even though the tenancy may be a weekly tenancy.[8]

---

[1] Agricultural Tenancies Act 1995, s 5.
[2] Ibid, s 6(1).
[3] Ibid, s 6(2).
[4] Ibid, s 5(4).
[5] Ibid, s 6(2).
[6] *Land Settlement Association Ltd v Carr* [1944] KB 657.
[7] *Queen's Club Gardens Estate Ltd v Bignell* [1924] 1 KB 117.
[8] Protection From Eviction Act 1977, s 5, as amended by the Housing Act 1988, ss 25–32.

11.1.4 Break clauses

A farm business tenancy may contain a break clause giving either the landlord or the tenant the option of terminating the tenancy of the holding or part of the holding. Where the tenancy is for more than two years this option can be exercised only where a notice has been served of at least 12 but less than 24 months before the date when it is to take effect. It is not possible to contract out of this statutory requirement.[9]

11.1.5 Contrast with the Agricultural Holdings Act 1986

Under the Agricultural Holdings Act 1986, a notice to quit an agricultural holding is invalid if it purports to terminate the tenancy before the expiry of 12 months from the end of the then current year of the tenancy. However, the rule does not apply where a notice is given:

> 'in pursuance of a provision in the contract of tenancy authorising the resumption of possession of the holding or some part of it for some specified purpose other than the use of the land for agriculture.'[10]

This provision has to be understood against the lifetime security of tenure given to tenants under the 1986 Act. There is no similar provision in the Agricultural Tenancies Act 1995. A landlord who is contemplating letting land will need to consider what future uses might arise for the land in question. He will take this into account when deciding the length of term which he is willing to offer to a prospective tenant. The tenant also needs to plan his business; he cannot do so efficiently if he is to be subject to an early resumption clause at the whim of the landlord.

Section 31 of the Agricultural Holdings Act 1986 allows for a notice to quit part of a holding for specified purposes. If a landlord of a farm business tenancy wants to resume possession of part then he will have to negotiate a contractual term to that effect. There is no statutory equivalent to s 31. Any contractual provision allowing resumption of part will be subject to the statutory requirement that notice of between one and two years must be served. Except in the cases where an incontestable notice to quit can be served, the 1986 Act enables the tenant to refer to the Agricultural Land Tribunal any notice to quit served on him by the landlord. If the tenant does this, the notice to quit will not take effect unless the Tribunal consents to its operation.[11] The Agricultural Tenancies Act 1995 has no similar provision. A notice to quit of the correct length properly served will have the effect of terminating the tenancy.

11.1.6 Severed reversion

Where there is a right to serve a notice to quit and the landlord has assigned part of the reversion, any landlord of the severed part can serve a notice to quit relating to that part.[12] However, the tenant is given the option of quitting the entire holding by serving a counter-notice within one month upon the reversioner(s) of the rest of the land.[13]

---

[9] Agricultural Tenancies Act 1995, s 7(1).
[10] Agricultural Holdings Act 1986, s 25(2)(b).
[11] Ibid, s 26.
[12] Law of Property Act 1925, s 140(1).
[13] Ibid, s 140(2).

The notice given by the landlord of the severed reversion will have to comply with the notice rules relating to a fixed-term tenancy or a tenancy from year to year, or to the exercise of an option to terminate the tenancy or resume possession of part. In all three situations the notice must be given between 12 and 24 months before the date on which it is to take effect. On the other hand, the counter-notices served by a tenant in response do not have to comply with the statutory rules in the 1995 Act for notices terminating yearly tenancies and exercising break clauses.[14]

11.1.7 Lease for lives

A lease at a rent granted for life or lives or for a term of years determinable with a life or lives or on the marriage of the lessee is converted into a term of 90 years. The lease continues after the death or marriage but can then be determined by either party serving on the other one month's written notice expiring on one of the quarter days applicable to the tenancy, or, if there are no special quarter days on one of the usual quarter days.[15] Such leases are extremely rare today. But the 1995 Act provides that the one to two-year notice provision will not apply.[16] There was a similar exception under the Agricultural Holdings Act 1986.[17]

11.1.8 Joint landlords or tenants

Where there is a periodic tenancy, a notice will be valid even if given by one of the joint landlords or joint tenants.[18] This is because periodic tenancies expire at the end of each period unless all the parties agree to the continuation. If one of those jointly entitled gives notice to quit, it shows that he has not agreed to the continuation of the tenancy.

However, a notice operating a break clause,[19] or a statutory notice,[20] must be given by all joint owners of the interest. One landlord or tenant alone cannot deal with the estate because the whole estate is not vested in him.

11.1.9 Sub-tenancies

Where a landlord serves a notice to quit on a tenant then once the notice has taken effect the sub-tenancy will also determine. This is the position at common law. No statutory protection is given to the sub-tenant against the head landlord under either the Agricultural Holdings Act 1986 or the Agricultural Tenancies Act 1995.

Similarly, where the tenant gives a notice to quit to his landlord, the sub-tenancy will also determine.[21] If the tenancy out of which the sub-tenancy was carved determines,

---

14 Agricultural Tenancies Act 1995, ss 6(1), (2), 7(1), (2).
15 Law of Property Act 1925, s 149(6).
16 Agricultural Tenancies Act 1995, s 7(3).
17 Agricultural Holdings Act 1986, s 25(2)(d).
18 *Hammersmith and Fulham LBC v Monk* [1992] 1 AC 478.
19 *Leek and Moorlands BS v Clark* [1952] 2 QB 788.
20 *Newman v Keedwell* (1978) 35 P&CR 393.
21 *Pennell v Payne* [1995] 2 All ER 592. The Court of Appeal bases the decision on policy grounds. The main argument is that a landlord should not have a sub-tenant forced upon him as a direct tenant. However, the decision could have been based on straightforward property principles, *nemo dat quod non habet*.

it is difficult to see on what basis the sub-tenancy can continue. The tenant has not made a disposition of his interest, as he does on a surrender, he has simply brought it to an end.

The tenant could not have granted to his sub-tenant an interest greater than he himself had, ie a periodic tenancy determinable by notice. Although, surprisingly, a periodic tenant can grant a fixed-term tenancy, that tenancy would determine when the head tenancy is terminated following a notice to quit.[22] However, until recently, authority suggested that the sub-tenancy would continue.[23] The reasoning was that the tenant by his voluntary act should not be able to prejudice the interest of a third party, that is his sub-tenant.

If a tenant exercises a break clause under a fixed-term tenancy the sub-tenancy will also determine. Where a sub-tenancy determines because the tenant serves a notice to quit on his landlord or exercises a break clause, he may be liable to the sub-tenant under the covenants for title.[24]

11.2 SURRENDER

Although there is no express saving under the Agricultural Tenancies Act 1995 for a tenancy to be terminated by surrender (or forfeiture) as there is in s 24(2) of the Landlord and Tenant Act 1954, there is no restriction on the parties agreeing to terminate a tenancy in this way. An agreement to surrender in the future might be void if it were held to be a way of avoiding the requirement to give a minimum of 12 months' notice before operating a break clause.

The effect of a surrender by a tenant to his immediate landlord is to merge and extinguish the lease in the landlord's reversion. A joint tenancy cannot be surrendered without the concurrence of both joint tenants.[25] Where the surrender is made by the assignee, not only will it release him from all liabilities but it will also release earlier tenants even if liable under direct covenant with the landlord.[26] Third party rights existing at the time of the surrender will continue to be binding in the hands of the landlord for as long as they would have lasted.[27]

An express surrender must be made by deed,[28] although a surrender in writing made for value may be effective in equity. Surrender may take place by operation of law where the parties act in such a way as to indicate their intention to surrender the lease. An example is where a tenant accepts a new lease from his immediate landlord even though the new lease is for a shorter term than the old.[29] A variation of an existing

---

[22] *MacKay v Mackreth* (1785) 4 Doug KB 213. Tenancy from year to year is treated as continuing until it is in fact determined. Therefore, it is potentially longer than, say, an underlease of 99 years.
[23] *Brown v Wilson* (1949) 208 LT 144.
[24] *Cohen v Tanner* [1900] 2 QB 609.
[25] *Hounslow LBC v Piling* [1994] 1 All ER 432.
[26] *Deanplan Ltd v Mahmoud* [1992] 3 WLR 467.
[27] *ES Schwab & Co v McCarthy* (1975) 31 P&CR 196.
[28] Law of Property Act 1927, s 52.
[29] *Ive's Case* (1597) 5 Co Rep 11a.

lease may operate as a surrender and regrant.[30] There will be a surrender where the tenant gives up possession of the premises and the landlord accepts the position.

During the Second Reading in the House of Commons of the Agricultural Tenancies Bill, Mr Martyn Jones, Opposition Spokesman on Agriculture, expressed concern that existing tenants would be forced to surrender their tenancies. He said:

> 'One of the strong points persuading the NFU and the Tenant Farmers Association to accept the package was that existing agricultural lettings would not be affected by the introduction of farm business tenancies. In our opinion, however, they should not be too complacent. On the face of it, existing tenants are safe from threat, but as the Bill becomes law, the landowner will have an even greater incentive to engineer the termination of old arrangements, or – in the case of pre 1986 agreements to persuade the tenant's children to give up their rights of succession. Cash bribes are an obvious approach, but the tenant must also watch for the stealthy move – for example, sending a farm business tenancy agreement for the son or daughter to sign when the father is on his deathbed, in the knowledge that, for succession to operate, the successor must apply to the Agricultural Land Tribunal to have the tenancy assigned to him or her. A tenant might be moved to a larger or more productive farm on the estate, on the condition that he or she entered into a farm business tenancy. The landlord might even accompany the transfer with an unenforceable verbal promise that the tenant's son would succeed him to the tenancy when the time came.'[31]

Landlords who have agreed with their tenants for the surrender of existing tenancies, should ensure that those tenants are advised in writing to seek independent legal advice. Landlords should also spell out in writing the legal effect of the surrender of an Agricultural Holdings Act 1986 tenancy and the grant of a new tenancy under the Agricultural Tenancies Act 1995. This should avoid a claim by the tenant being upheld in court that he has been subject to undue pressure by his landlord or that he did not know the consequences of the surrender.

11.2.1 Joint landlords and tenants

A surrender has to be agreed by all the parties.[32] One joint landlord or one joint tenant cannot effect a valid surrender. The estate or interest is one estate or interest vested in all the landlords, or all the tenants, in an undivided whole.

11.2.2 Sub-tenancies

When a tenant surrenders his tenancy, this does not determine the sub-tenancy. The statutory effect of the surrender is to assign the tenant's reversion on the sub-tenancy to the freeholder.[33] The sub-tenant is promoted and will become the tenant of the head landlord. The tenant's reversion is incumbered by the sub-tenancy so that he cannot dispose of the reversion free of the incumbrance. He cannot give what he has not got (*nemo dat quod non habet*).

---

[30] *Baker v Merckel* [1960] 1 QB 657.
[31] HC Second Reading, col 102, 6 February 1995.
[32] *Leek and Moorlands BS v Clark* [1952] 2 QB 788. *Greenwich London Borough Council v McGrady* (1982) 81 LGR 288.
[33] Law of Property Act 1925, s 139.

11.3 MERGER

A lease may terminate by merger. This occurs where the tenant acquires the interest of the landlord or where a third party acquires both the lease and the reversion.

11.4 FORFEITURE

11.4.1 The Agricultural Holdings Act 1986

Forfeiture is seldom relied on under the Agricultural Holdings Act 1986. This is because, in most cases, the provisions for serving an incontestable notice to quit are, in some respects, more clearly defined than the rules for forfeiture and because of the right to relief in forfeiture proceedings given to tenants. At common law the interest of a tenant from year to year could be terminated by six months' notice. The Agricultural Holdings Act 1986, and its statutory predecessors, requires a notice of between one and two years expiring on the anniversary of the tenancy.[34] Although the tenant has only a yearly tenancy he has in effect lifetime security because, with limited exceptions, he is able to refer any notice to quit to the Agricultural Land Tribunal. In the absence of consent from the Tribunal to the operation of the notice, it will be inoperative.[35] It is against this background of security of tenure that it was just to allow a landlord to serve an incontestable notice to quit for certain breaches of covenant by the tenant.

Under the Agricultural Tenancies Act 1995, there is no security of tenure other than that conferred by the contract itself. In these different circumstances, it is entirely proper that landlords should, like their counterparts in the commercial and residential sectors, be required to rely on the normal forfeiture rules.

The Law Commission has proposed radical reform of the law of forfeiture. It has produced a report with a draft termination of tenancies bill.[36] At the time of writing, the Government has not implemented the proposals.

11.4.2 Availability of forfeiture

The Agricultural Tenancies Act 1995 does not preclude a tenancy being terminated by forfeiture. However, a landlord has no automatic right to forfeit a lease. In order to do so, there must be a forfeiture clause in the lease,[37] or the observance of the covenant must be a condition of the lease (eg the lease is granted on condition, or provided that, the covenants are performed).[38] Any well-drawn lease will contain a proviso for re-entry on breach of covenant. The only other exception to the need for a forfeiture clause is where the tenant denies his landlord's title to the land which is leased. In that situation the landlord is entitled to forfeit the tenancy forthwith. It seems that there is no need to serve any notice before forfeiture nor will the tenant be entitled to relief.[39]

---

[34] Agricultural Holdings Act 1986, s 25.
[35] Ibid, s 26.
[36] Law Com No 221 (1994).
[37] *Doe d. Wilson v Philips* (1824) 2 Bing 13. See Morris J in *Kent v Conniff* [1953] 1 QB 361 at 375.
[38] *Doe d. Lockwood v Clarke* (1807) 8 East 185.
[39] *W G Clark (Properties) Ltd v Dupre Properties* [1992] Ch 297 *Warner v Sampson* [1959] 1 QB 297.

11.4.3 Waiver of breach

If a landlord waives a breach of covenant, he will not be able to forfeit the lease. Waiver may be express or implied. It will be implied where the landlord is aware of the breach of covenant which gives the right to forfeiture and does some unequivocal act recognising the continued existence of the lease.[40]

Any knowledge acquired by the landlord's agent will be imputed to the landlord.[41] Waiver will be implied where a landlord with knowledge of the breach distrains for rent due before or after the breach,[42] demands, sues for or accepts rent due after the breach.[43] This is so even where rent is mistakenly accepted by a lowly subordinate of the landlord's agent or 'without prejudice'.[44] Waiver is a matter of law. It does not depend on intention.

On the other hand, waiver covers the particular breach only and does not operate as a waiver of all future breaches.[45] Moreover, it is still possible to sue for damages for breach of covenant.[46]

11.4.4 Method of forfeiture

Forfeiture can be effected by issuing and serving a writ. The writ usually contains a demand for possession, so the service of the writ will determine the lease.[47] The landlord can forfeit by peaceable entry on the land unless the premises include a dwelling and someone is lawfully residing in it or part of it.[48] It is, however, an offence if any violence is used or threatened and the landlord knows that there is someone on the premises who is opposed to the entry.[49]

There are preliminary steps which must be taken before the lease can be forfeited. These depend on whether the forfeiture is for non-payment or rent or breach of other covenant or conditions.

11.4.5 Forfeiture for non-payment of rent

If forfeiture is to be available to the landlord, there must either be a forfeiture clause or the payment of rent must be a condition of the lease. In addition, the landlord must have made a formal demand for rent, unless the lease exempts him from doing so or one half year's rent is in arrears and there is not sufficient distress on the premises to satisfy the arrears.[50] The formal demand is an onerous requirement. The landlord or his authorised agent must demand the exact sum due on the day when it falls due at

---

[40] *Matthews v Smallwood* [1910] 1 Ch 777.
[41] *Metropolitan Properties Co Ltd v Cordery* (1979) 39 P&CR 10.
[42] *Ward v Day* (1863) 4 B&S 337.
[43] *David Blackstone v Burnetts (West End) Ltd* [1973] 1 WLR 1487.
[44] *Segal Securities Ltd v Thoseby* [1963] 1 QB 887. *Central Estate (Belgravia) Ltd v Woolgar (No 2)* [1972] 1 WLR 1048.
[45] Law of Property Act 1925, s 148.
[46] *Stephens v Junior Army and Navy Stores Ltd* [1914] 2 Ch 516.
[47] *Canas Property Co Ltd v K L Television Services Ltd* [1970] 1 QB 433.
[48] Protection From Eviction Act 1977, s 2.
[49] Criminal Law Act 1977, s 6.
[50] Common Law Procedure Act 1852, s 210.

such covenient hour before sunset as will give time to count out the money, the demand being made on the premises and continued until sunset.[51] It is for this reason that leases should provide that the lease may be forfeited if the rent is a specified number of days in arrears whether lawfully demanded or not.

Forfeiture was seen by equity as being merely security for the payment of rent. Therefore, if the tenant paid the rent due, and the landlord's expenses, equity would grant relief provided it was just and equitable to do so. Originally, as long as there was no delay, equity imposed no time-limit on an application for relief.[52] The Common Law Procedure Act 1852[53] provides, however, that if forfeiture is by High Court proceedings the Court must stay proceedings if the tenant pays arrears and costs before the trial. The right applies only if rent is six months in arrears.

Where the landlord has procured a court order for possession, an application for relief must be made within six months of the order.[54] Where forfeiture is not by High Court proceedings the statute does not apply, but the Court tends to adopt roughly the same time-limits.[55] Relief is discretionary but is usually granted. If relief is granted the old lease is revived.[56]

The tenant can also apply for relief in a county court action. If he pays into court not less than five clear days before the return date all the arrears of rent and the costs, the action will be discontinued. Where this is not done and the court orders possession of the land to be given to the landlord at the expiration of a period, being not less than four weeks, the tenant can obtain relief by paying into court within that time all the rent, arrears and costs. After the landlord has regained possession the tenant has a discretionary right to relief for a further six months. Where relief is granted the tenant holds under the old lease.[57]

11.4.6 Forfeiture for the breach of other covenants and conditions

If forfeiture is to be available, there must be a forfeiture clause or observance of the covenant must be a condition of the lease. Before forfeiting, the landlord must serve a statutory notice in writing.[58]

The notice must:

(i)   specify the breach;

(ii) require it to be remedied if possible;

(iii) demand compensation if the landlord so requires.

---

[51] *1 Wims Saund* (1871) 434.
[52] *Hill v Barclay* (1811) 18 Ves 56.
[53] Common Law Procedure Act 1852, s 212.
[54] Ibid, s 210.
[55] *Thatcher v C H Pearle & Sons (Contractors) Ltd* [1968] 1 WLR 748.
[56] Common Law Procedure Act 1852, s 212.
[57] County Courts Act 1984, ss 138, 139.
[58] Law of Property Act 1925, s 146. A break clause which operates on the default of the tenant will be treated as a forfeiture clause and so will be subject to a s 146 notice and the tenant will be entitled to apply to the court for relief.

Most breaches of positive covenants, such as to carry out work or repairs[59] are capable of remedy. Most, though not all, negative covenants are not so capable.[60]

For instance, a breach of covenant against assigning or sub-letting has been held to be incapable of remedy.[61] The actual assignment is valid, however, so that the notice specifying the breach must be served on the assignee.[62] If there is any doubt as to whether the breach is capable of remedy, then the notice should require the specified breach to be remedied, if capable of remedy.[63]

The landlord must give the tenant reasonable time to comply with the notice. A reasonable time will depend on all the circumstances, for example how long it will take to do the repair work or terminate the breach. Even where the breach is irremediable, a reasonable time must be given to allow the tenant to consider his position.[64]

After a reasonable time, the landlord may proceed with the forfeiture if there is no compliance with the notice. The tenant has the right to apply for relief either in any action by the landlord to enforce the covenant or by a separate application.[65] Where the forfeiture is enforced by action, the right to apply for relief is available at any time before the landlord has taken possession following a judgment in his favour.[66] After that, he can claim no relief. On the other hand, where the landlord takes possession without a court action the right to relief continues without time-limit. Delay may, however, be taken into account by the court in deciding whether or not to grant relief.[67]

The court has an absolute discretion as to the terms on which it will grant relief.[68] Once relief is granted the lease is treated as if it had never been forfeited.[69] Relief is likely to be granted where a breach has been remedied unless the tenant's personal qualifications are important and he is an unsatisfactory tenant.[70] Where, after forfeiture, a landlord has granted a legal lease to a lessee without knowledge of the tenant's right to seek relief, then any relief will be subject to the new lease.[71]

11.4.7 Bankruptcy or the taking of the lease in execution

Where there has been a breach of a condition against the tenant's bankruptcy, or, in the case of a company, winding up, or the taking of the lease in execution, and the tenancy is of agricultural or pastoral land, the lease can be forfeited at once. A notice does not have to be served and the tenant does not have a right to claim relief.[72]

---

[59] *Expert Clothing Service & Sales Ltd v Hillgate House Ltd* [1986] Ch 340.
[60] *Rugby School (Governors) v Tannahill* [1934] 1 KB 695.
[61] *Scala House & District Property Col Ltd v Forbes* [1974] QB 575.
[62] *Old Grovebury Manor Farm Ltd v W Seymour Plant Sales and Hire Ltd* [1979] 1 WLR 1397.
[63] *Glass v Kencakses Ltd* [1966] 1 QB 611.
[64] *Horsey Estate Ltd v Steiger* [1899] 2 QB 79. *Scala House & District Property Co Ltd v Forbes, supra.*
[65] Law of Property Act 1925, s 146(2).
[66] *Billson v Residential Apartments Ltd* [1992] 1 AC 494.
[67] Ibid.
[68] Law of Property Act 1925, s 146(2).
[69] *Dendy v Evans* [1909] 2 KB 894.
[70] *Bathurst (Earl) v Fine* [1974] 1 WCR 905.
[71] *Fuller v Judy Properties Ltd* [1992] 14 EG 106.
[72] Law of Property Act 1925, s 146(9).

These special provisions also apply to leases of property where the personal qualifications of the tenant are of importance for the preservation of the value of the character of the property or on the ground of neighbourhood to the lessor or any person holding under him. In addition, they apply where the lease is of mines or minerals, a public house or beershop or a furnished house.

In other cases, the position on bankruptcy or execution is complex. During the year following the bankruptcy or execution the landlord must serve a statutory notice and the tenant can apply for relief. If the lease is sold during the year, s 146 of the Law of Property Act 1925 will continue to apply. Otherwise the trustee in bankruptcy might not be able to dispose of the lease at a reasonable price. But, if the lease is not sold within the year, the protection of s 146 is lost.[73] The landlord can forfeit the lease and the tenant will have no right to relief.

11.4.8 Sub-tenancies

If a head tenancy is forfeited any sub-tenancy will automatically determine. However, the sub-tenant can apply for relief against forfeiture for non-payment of rent, breach of other covenants, or bankruptcy of the head tenant. He has this right even if it is not available to the head tenant. If he obtains relief, the court will grant him a lease no longer than his sub-lease. A sub-tenant will usually enter into a direct lease with the landlord of the tenant, whose lease has been forfeited, on terms similar to his former sub-lease.[74]

---

[73] Ibid, s 146(10).
[74] Ibid, s 146(4).

Chapter 12

DISPUTE RESOLUTION

12.1 PURPOSE OF THE PROVISIONS

The purpose of the dispute resolution provisions is to give the landlord and tenant the option of specifying their own dispute resolution procedures except for the determination of rent in pursuance of a statutory review notice, consent to improvements and compensation, when arbitration is compulsory. In addition to the statutory measures for settling disputes the parties can agree to some form of alternative dispute resolution procedure. The essence of such procedures is that it is open to the parties during the negotiations to decide to go to arbitration, or where arbitration is not compulsory, the courts.

12.2 COMPULSORY ARBITRATION

12.2.1 Determination of rent

The landlord or tenant under a farm business tenancy may give the other a statutory review notice requiring that the determination of the rent from the review date should be referred to arbitration.[1] This is discussed in Chapter 6.

The parties can then appoint an arbitrator by agreement or a third party, who is not acting as arbitrator, to determine the rent. If this is not done then either party can, during the period of six months ending with the review date, apply to the President of the Royal Institution of Chartered Surveyors for the appointment by him of an arbitrator.[2]

There is no provision dispensing with the time-limits. Time is therefore of the essence. Although the High Court has power under s 27 of the Arbitration Act 1950 to extend the time for commencing arbitration proceedings, s 31(2) of that Act excludes the power where arbitration arises under statute.

12.2.2 Consent to improvements

In order for a tenant to be entitled to compensation for improvements at the end of his lease, he needs to have obtained the prior consent of his landlord.[3] Where the landlord refuses, or fails to give consent, or imposes variations in the terms of the tenancy as a condition of giving his consent which are unacceptable to the tenant, the tenant may, by notice in writing given to the landlord, demand that the question should be referred to arbitration.[4]

There are no time-limits imposed by s 19. If the landlord refuses consent or gives it

---

[1] Agricultural Tenancies Act 1995, s 10.
[2] Ibid, s 12.
[3] Ibid, s 17.
[4] Ibid, s 19.

subject to unsatisfactory conditions, the tenant must serve his notice within two months of receiving the landlord's refusal or conditions to consent.[5] Where the landlord fails to give consent within two months of the tenant's request, the tenant must serve his notice within four months from his original request.[6]

If after a notice has been given the parties do not agree on an arbitrator then either the landlord or tenant can apply to the President of the Royal Institution of Chartered Surveyors for an appointment of an arbitrator by him.[7]

12.2.3 Compensation

Part III of the Agricultural Tenancies Act 1995 sets out the conditions which must be fulfilled before the tenant is entitled to compensation (see Chapter 8). Claims for compensation have to be made in writing by the tenant within two months of the determination of the tenancy.[8] If the parties do not settle the claim and have not appointed an arbitrator by agreement since the tenant has given notice in writing of his claim, then either party may, after four months from the termination of the tenancy, apply to the President of the Royal Institution of Chartered Surveyors for the appointment of an arbitrator.[9]

12.3 VOLUNTARY ARBITRATION

For any other dispute, other than those discussed above, there are fall back provisions providing for arbitration. The parties can stipulate in the contract for a third party, other than an arbitrator, to resolve disputes by a decision which is binding on both parties, or may instead go to court.[10] Arbitration, or a decision by an expert, is particularly suitable for valuation matters, hence the compulsory provisions for arbitration over rent and compensation for improvements, but may not be appropriate for settling complicated legal issues, unless the arbitrator is also a lawyer.

Where the parties do not opt for the court or an independent third party, disputes concerning rights and obligations under the Agricultural Tenancies Act 1995, under the terms of the tenancy or under any custom, are determined by arbitration.[11]

Where a dispute has arisen, either the landlord or tenant may give the other notice in writing specifying the dispute and stating that, unless an arbitrator is appointed by agreement within two months, an application will be made to the President of the Royal Institution of Chartered Surveyors for an appointment of an arbitrator by him. Once the two-month time-limit, specified in the notice, has elapsed either party may apply to the President of the Royal Institution of Chartered Surveyors.[12]

---

[5] Ibid, s 19(3)(a).
[6] Ibid, s 19(3)(b).
[7] Ibid, s 19(4).
[8] Ibid, s 22(2).
[9] Ibid, s 22(3).
[10] Ibid, ss 28(4), 29.
[11] Ibid, s 28.
[12] Ibid, s 28(2), (3).

12.4 ARBITRATION UNDER THE AGRICULTURAL TENANCIES ACT 1995

The Agricultural Tenancies Act 1995 provides that a sole arbitrator shall determine any matters which are required to be settled by arbitration.[13] The parties may appoint an arbitrator by agreement or apply to the Royal Institution of Chartered Surveyors for appointment of an arbitrator. Application for an appointment of an arbitrator by the President of the Royal Institution of Chartered of Surveyors must to be made to him in writing. The President has power to charge a reasonable fee and this must accompany the application.[14]

Where an arbitrator who has been appointed dies or is incapable of acting, the parties can appoint a new arbitrator by agreement. In default of agreement, either party may apply to the President of the Royal Institution of Chartered Surveyors for an appointment of an arbitrator by him.[15] There is no specific provision dealing with an arbitrator who refuses to act. In such circumstances the court, under s 10 of the Arbitration Act 1950, can appoint another arbitrator if one is not appointed by the parties or the arbitrator.

Sections 10 (rent review disputes), 19(1) (consent for improvements) and 22 (claims for compensation) contain their own regulations and time-limits for referring the matters to arbitration.

Apart from these specific provisions, the rules and procedures on arbitration are governed by the Arbitration Acts 1950–1979.

12.5 ARBITRATION UNDER THE ARBITRATION ACTS 1950–1979

12.5.1 General principles

If a dispute is referred to arbitration under the compulsory provisions or under s 28 of the Agricultural Tenancies Act 1995 then the procedure and practice is governed by the Arbitration Acts 1950–1979 on those matters which are not specifically set out in the relevant sections of the Agricultural Tenancies Act 1995. There is nothing in the 1995 Act corresponding to the detailed arbitration code provided in Sch 11 to the Agricultural Holdings Act 1986. There are, however, specific provisions dealing with the appointment of an arbitrator (see para 12.4).

12.5.2 Removal of an arbitrator

The High Court may give leave to remove an arbitrator.[16] It may exercise such power where the arbitrator has misconducted himself or the proceedings or shown bias.[17] An

---

[13] Ibid, s 30(1).
[14] Ibid, s 30(2).
[15] Ibid, s 30(3).
[16] Arbitration Act 1950, s 23(1).
[17] Ibid, s 24(1).

arbitrator may also be removed where he has delayed in dealing with the reference or in making his award.[18]

12.5.3　Remuneration

The parties may agree in advance the remuneration of the arbitrator. If no agreement is made the arbitrator is entitled to a reasonable remuneration.[19] When the reference is completed and a valid award made, in the absence of a contrary agreement, the arbitration may assess the amount of his remuneration and either tax it in his award[20] or leave the taxation to the High Court.[21] If the arbitrator fixes an excessive amount by way of remuneration and a party has paid in order to obtain the award, he can bring an action to recover anything above that which is fair and reasonable. However, if the amount is included in the award itself which would be unusual, then he will have to apply to have that part of the award set aside.[22]

12.5.4　Conduct of the arbitration

The arbitration must be conducted according to legal principles.[23] Therefore, unless the parties agree to the contrary, each party must be notified of the hearing,[24] given a reasonable opportunity to attend,[25] and adduce evidence,[26] and argue his case.[27]

The procedure is not laid down in the Agricultural Tenancies Act 1995. In all probability, arbitrators will tend to follow the practices which have grown up in dealing with disputes under the Agricultural Holdings Act 1986. Failure to do so would not be a cause for setting aside the award unless the procedure was contrary to natural justice.

The arbitrator is generally bound by the rules governing the admissibility of evidence.[28] However, the parties may agree that the strict rules of admissibility need not be followed by the arbitrator.[29] The arbitrator has power to examine the parties and witnesses on oath or affirmation.

There are no time-limits imposed on an arbitrator for the making of his award.[30] However, when an award is remitted by the court the arbitrator must make his award within three months after the date of the order.[31]

---

[18]　Ibid, s 13(3).
[19]　*Crampton and Holt v Ridley & Co* (1887) 20 QBD 48. *Willis v Wakeley Bros* (1891) 7 TLR 604.
[20]　Arbitration Act 1950, s 18(1).
[21]　Ibid, s 18(2).
[22]　*Llandrindod Wells Water Co v Hawksley* (1904) 68 JP 242.
[23]　*Ritchie v W Jacks & Co* (1922) 10 LLL Rep 519.
[24]　*Oswald v Earl Grey* (1855) 24 LJQB 69.
[25]　*Fetherstone v Cooper* (1803) 9 Ves 67.
[26]　*Carey and Brown v Henderson and Liddell* (1920) 2 LLL Rep 479.
[27]　*Ritchie v W Jacks & Co, supra.*
[28]　*A-G Davison* (1825) M'Cle & Yo 160, but see *Buxton* (1993) 58 Arbitration 229.
[29]　*Macpherson Train & Co Ltd v J Milhem & Sons* [1955] 2 Lloyd's Rep 59.
[30]　Arbitration Act 1950, s 13(1).
[31]　Ibid, s 22(2).

12.5.5 Powers of the court

The High Court has no general supervisory powers over the reference to arbitration.[32] It can, however, make orders in respect of the following matters *inter alia*:

 (i) security for costs;[33]

 (ii) the giving of evidence by affidavit;[34]

(iii) the examination on oath of any witness before an officer of the High Court or any other person;[35]

(iv) the preservation, detention or inspection of any property or thing which is the subject of the reference;[36]

 (v) interim injunctions and the appointment of a receiver.[37]

These powers can be invoked during the course of the reference and are without prejudice to any powers which might be vested in the arbitrator.[38]

Where a party fails to comply with an order made by an arbitrator, the arbitrator can apply to the High Court for an extension of his powers.[39] The court may give him power to continue with the reference in default of appearance or any other act of one of the parties.[40]

12.5.6 Preliminary point of law

Either of the parties, with the consent of the arbitrator, can apply to the High Court to determine a point of law.[41] The court must be satisfied that the determination of the application might produce substantial savings in costs to the parties and the point of law is one in respect of which leave to appeal from the award would likely to be given by the court.[42] The court has taken a very restrictive approach to applications on preliminary points of law. Unless the High Court gives leave, no appeal to the Court of Appeal is allowed from the High Court's decision on whether or not to entertain the application.[43] If all the parties agree to make an application to the High Court on a preliminary point of law, then these restrictions on the jurisdiction of the High Court do not apply.[44]

12.5.7 The award

The award must determine all the disputes between the parties which have been referred to arbitration but not ones which have not been so referred. Where the award

---

[32] *Exormisis Shipping SA v Oonsoo, the Democratic People's Republic of Korea and the Korean Foreign Transportation Corporation* [1975] 1 Lloyd's Rep 402 at 343.

[33] Arbitration Act 1950, s 12(6)(a).

[34] Ibid, s 12(6)(c).

[35] Ibid, s 12(6)(d).

[36] Ibid, s 12(6)(g).

[37] Ibid, s 12(6)(h).

[38] Supreme Court Act 1981, s 43A.

[39] Arbitration Act 1979, s 5(1).

[40] Ibid, s 5(2).

[41] Ibid, s 2(1).

[42] Ibid, s 2(2).

[43] Ibid, s 2(2A).

[44] Ibid, s 2(1).

has these omissions or additions, it will be invalid and unenforceable unless the good can be severed from the bad.[45] The award must be expressed in clear and unambiguous language[46] and must be final unless it is specifically an interim award.[47]

There is no specific form for the award unless the agreement of reference prescribes the form.[48] The arbitrator need not give reasons unless one of the parties gave notice that a reasoned award was required, or there was a special reason why such notice was not given.[49]

Once an award has been made, the arbitrator has no further jurisdiction. However, under the slip rule the arbitrator has power to correct clerical errors.[50] This rule does not enable the arbitrator to correct errors of fact or law.[51] If the award is only an interim award, the arbitrator's authority is determined only in respect of the matters dealt with in the interim award.[52]

In the absence of an agreement to the contrary, made on the reference, an arbitration award is final and binding on the parties and any persons claiming under them.[53] The parties are under an obligation to comply with the terms of the award. The matters covered by the award are *res judicata* and so the parties cannot bring fresh proceedings on the same cause of action.[54] However, this rule will not apply on a later arbitration where there are new circumstances, for example on the next rent review.

12.5.8 Remedies

The arbitrator has power to order payment of money from one party to the other by way of debt or damages. He can also make a declaration as to the rights of the parties including the entitlement to an indemnity in respect of a liability or expenditure. He can also direct that interest be paid on any sum due.[55] Once the award has been made, interest accrues on the sum awarded from the date of the award at the same rate as a judgment debt.

The arbitrator has no power to order specific performance of a contract relating to land or an interest in land.[56] This would include a tenancy agreement.

12.5.9 Costs

The costs of the reference and award are at the discretion of the arbitrator. Any costs are taxable in the High Court unless the award directs otherwise. Where an award makes no provision for costs, either party to the award may, within 14 days of its publication, apply to the arbitrator for a direction as to costs.[57]

---

[45] *Duke of Buccleuch v Metropolitan Board of Works* (1870) LR 5 Exch 221.
[46] *River Plate Products Netherlands BV v Establissement Coargrain* [1982] 1 Lloyd's Rep 628.
[47] *Stockport Metropolitan Borough Council v O'Reilly* [1978] 1 Lloyd's Rep 595.
[48] *Everard v Paterson* (1816) 6 Taunt 25.
[49] Arbitration Act 1979, s 1(6).
[50] Arbitration Act 1950, s 17.
[51] *Mutual Shopping Corporation of New York v Bayshore Shipping Co of Monrovia. The Montan* [1985] 1 All ER 520.
[52] *Fidelitas Shipping Co Ltd v V/O Exportchleb* [1966] 1 QB 630, [1965] 2 All ER 4.
[53] Arbitration Act 1950, s 16.
[54] *Whitehead v Tattershall* (1839) 1 Ad & EL 491.
[55] Arbitration Act 1950, s 19A.
[56] Ibid, s 15.
[57] Ibid, s 18.

The parties should always consider making a *Calderbank* offer,[58] ie an offer without prejudice save as to costs, linked to asking for an interim award only on the substantive issue. The final award on costs will then be made in the light of the *Calderbank* offer.

12.5.10 Remission or setting aside of an award

The High Court has power to remit an award for the reconsideration of the arbitrator. Where the arbitrator has misconducted himself or the proceedings, the High Court may set aside the award.[59] However, it should be noted that the time-limits are very short. An application by originating motion[60] must be made within 21 days after the award has been made and published to the parties.[61]

Remission or setting aside takes place where:

(1) the arbitrator has misconducted himself or the proceedings;

(2) there is some defect or error patent on the face of the award;

(3) the arbitrator has admitted a mistake which he wishes be corrected;

(4) material evidence, which could not with reasonable diligence have been discovered before the award was made, has since been obtained;

(5) for reasons other than misconduct the arbitration was not considered fully and it would be inequitable to allow the award to stand without further deliberations.[62]

Mistakes of fact or law are not a ground for remission but may enable an appeal.[63]

The court has a discretion whether it will set aside rather than remit an award.[64] It will usually do so where there has been a serious miscarriage of justice, or where it is likely that the arbitrator could not fairly determine the issue.[65] Remission is appropriate where an arbitrator admits his mistake or where further findings of fact are needed.

Where a matter is remitted, the jurisdiction of the arbitrator is revived.[66] The court has power to remit the whole or part of the award.

Where an award is set aside, then it ceases to exist. Normally, there will be a reference to a new arbitrator.

A defective award may be void or voidable. If the arbitrator has exceeded his jurisdiction[67] or failed to make a decision, his award will be void.[68] Where it is void, a party may apply to the court for a declaration that he is not bound by the award.[69] He

---

58 *Calderbank v Calderbank* [1976] Fam 93 [1975] 3 All ER 332.
59 Arbitration Act 1950, s 22.
60 RSC Ord 73, r 2(1)(a), (c).
61 Ibid, r 5(1).
62 *Re Montgomery, Jones & Co and Liebenthal & Co's Arbitration* (1898) 78 LT 406, 409. Arbitration Act 1979, s 1.
63 *Mutual Shipping Corporation of New York v Bayshore Shipping Co of Monrovia. The Montan* [1985] 1 All ER 520.
64 *Odlum v Vancouver City and Canadian Northern Pacific Rly Co* (1915) 85 LJPC 95.
65 *Ardahalian v Unifert International SA. The Elissar* [1984] 2 Lloyd's Rep 84.
66 *Aiden Shipping Ltd v Interbulk Ltd. The Vimeira (No 1)* [1985] 2 Lloyd's Rep 410n.
67 *Davies v Price* (1862) 6 LT 713.
68 *Bache v Billingham* [1894] 1 QB 107.
69 *Kaukomarkkinat O/Y v Elbe Transport – Union GmbH. The Kelo* [1985] 2 Lloyd's Rep 85.

can also apply for an injunction against the enforcement of the award pending a decision as to validity. If proceedings are brought to enforce an award, it is a defence that the award is void.[70]

12.5.11 Appeals

An appeal lies to the High Court on a question of law arising from the arbitrator's award. An appeal can be brought only where all the parties consent or with leave of the court.[71] The award must set out the reasons for the decision to enable the court to consider the question of law. The court, on determination of the appeal, may by order confirm, vary or set aside the award, or remit the award for the reconsideration of the arbitrator having answered the point of law. Although it is sometimes possible for the parties to exclude the right of an appeal, this is prevented by statute[72] where the arbitration is a statutory arbitration as under the Agricultural Tenancies Act 1995.

The court cannot grant leave to appeal unless having regard to all the circumstances the question of law could substantially affect the rights of one or both of the parties.[73] Where that requirement has been fulfilled, so that the court has jurisdiction, it still has to consider whether leave to appeal should be granted. If the leave is sought on a point of construction which is a non-standard contractual term or on the application of law to an unusual set of facts, leave will not normally be granted. The point of law must be of general importance unless it appears to the judge on reading the award that the reasons on which it was made were clearly wrong.[74]

12.5.12 Enforcement of the award

Where a party fails to comply with an award, the other party may bring court proceedings to enforce the award.[75] The claim can be for judgment for the amount of the award, a declaration that the award is binding, damages for failure to perform the award, or an injunction restraining the other party from acting contrary to the award.[76] Instead of being enforced by action the award may, by leave of the High Court, be enforced as a judgment.[77]

12.6 RESOLUTION BY THIRD PARTIES

Instead of an arbitrator, the parties can provide in their tenancy agreement that an independent third party can settle disputes. In order to be effective the third party, whether or not acting as arbitrator, must be empowered by the terms of the tenancy to give a decision which is binding in law on the landlord and tenant.[78] Moreover, the

---

[70] *Davies v Price, supra.*
[71] Arbitration Act 1979, s 1.
[72] Arbitration Act 1950, s 31(1). Arbitration Act 1979, s 3(5).
[73] Arbitration Act 1979, s 1(4).
[74] *Pioneer Shipping Ltd v BTP Tioxide Ltd. The Nema* [1982] AC 724.
[75] *King v Bowen* (1841) 8 M&W 625.
[76] *Birtley District Co-operative Society Ltd v Windy Nook and District Industrial Co-operative Society Ltd (No 2)* [1960] 2 QB 1.
[77] Arbitration Act 1950, s 26(i).
[78] Agricultural Tenancies Act 1995, s 29.

tenancy agreement must not provide for the third party to be appointed without the consent or concurrence of both the landlord and tenant. When a dispute has arisen there must be a joint reference to the third party or, where one party makes the reference, notice must be served on the other informing him in writing that such a reference has been made. The person on whom the notice is served can, within four weeks from the notice, evoke the arbitration provisions of s 28 of the Agricultural Tenancies Act 1995. Under the provisions of that section, he must serve a notice in writing on the other party (ie in this situation the person who has given him the notice of reference made to the third party) specifying the dispute and stating that unless an arbitrator is appointed by agreement before the end of two months he intends to apply to the President of the Royal Institution of Chartered Surveyors for the appointment of an arbitrator. If he fails to do so then the independent third party named in the contract will have jurisdiction to settle the dispute.

12.7 RESOLUTION BY THE COURTS

The jurisdiction of the courts is preserved except for the cases already discussed where arbitration is mandatory (see para 12.2). The landlord or the tenant may decide to institute court proceedings. The other party then has the option of applying to the court for a stay of proceedings which, if granted, will mean that the dispute will have to be resolved by arbitration.[79]

The applicant must have taken no steps in the proceedings other than the acknowledgment of service. He must satisfy the court that he is, and was at the commencement of the proceedings, ready and willing to do everything necessary for the proper conduct of the case.[80]

The court has a discretion whether or not to grant a stay. Where there is a statutory provision for arbitration the presumption will be that a stay should be granted. The court may take into account the ability of the arbitrator to conduct the arbitration in a proper and impartial manner.[81] If there are points of law involved which are more suitable for determination by the court, a stay may be refused.[82] It may also be refused where the applicant has delayed in his application or where the matter is urgent.[83]

The court has a discretion as to the terms on which a stay will be granted. For instance, it might order a new arbitrator to be appointed who has a legal qualification.[84] Or it might grant a stay for part of the action only, so that some matters are decided by the court and others by arbitration.[85] Certain actions will have to be brought in the courts because the powers of the arbitrator are not wide enough to give the remedies sought. These include possession proceedings and relief in such proceedings and orders for

---

[79] Ibid, s 28(4).
[80] Arbitration Act 1950, s 4.
[81] *Bremer Handelsgesellschaft mbH v Ets Soules et Cie and Scott* [1984] 1 Lloyd's Rep 160.
[82] *Halifax Overseas Freighters v Rasno Export* [1958] 2 Lloyd's Rep 146.
[83] *Gilbert Ash (Northern) Ltd v Modern Engineering (Bristol) Ltd* [1974] AC 689 at 726.
[84] *John Mowlem & Co v Carlton Gate Development Co Ltd* (1990) 6 Const LJ 298 at 303.
[85] *Bristol Corporation v John Aird & Co* [1913] AC 241 at 261.

specific performance of a contract for the lease. Arbitration will not be available if the dispute concerns whether or not there is a contract at all.[86]

12.8 ALTERNATIVE DISPUTE RESOLUTION

The parties may decide to include a clause in their tenancy agreement providing for disputes to be resolved by mediation. Such a clause might be:

> 'Any dispute or difference between the parties arising out of or in connection with this tenancy agreement shall first be referred to mediation in accordance with the mediation procedures of . . .
>
> The mediator shall be agreed upon by the parties and failing such agreement within 15 days of one party requesting the appointment of a mediator and providing their suggestion therefor the mediator shall be appointed by the then President of the Law Society. Unless agreed otherwise the parties shall share equally the costs of mediation. The use of mediation will not be construed under the doctrines of laches, waiver or estoppel to affect adversely the rights of either party.'

Even without such a clause, if a dispute arises the parties may agree at that stage to try to resolve the matter by mediation.

The essence of mediation is that the parties themselves resolve their disputes with the aid of a mediator. Either party would be free to break off negotiations and apply for the appointment of an arbitrator or go to the courts in accordance with s 28 of the Agricultural Tenancies Act 1995.

Mediation takes place in private. The mediator is an independent third party who has been specially trained. His role is to help the parties negotiate with each other. He will help with problems of communication so that the landlord understands the concerns of the tenant and the tenant understands the concerns of the landlord. The mediator will ensure that any proposals for settlement are realistic and acceptable.

The procedure is informal. The parties are likely to contact an organisation which provides mediation services.[87] The mediator will require details of the case and will explain to the parties what is involved in mediation. He will want to see the tenancy agreement and any other relevant documents.

The mediator will then have a joint session with the parties at which they will present their case. After that, the mediator may meet the landlord and tenant separately to explore what are the real concerns of the parties and may suggest constructive solutions to the problems. When the parties are near to settling the dispute the mediator will bring them together to draw up and sign an agreement. This document is a contract containing the terms of the settlement.

Where mediation achieves a settlement, it will be quicker and cheaper than litigation or arbitration. It is especially appropriate where parties are in a continuing contractual

---

[86] *Heyman v Darwins Ltd* [1942] AC 356.
[87] Eg Centre for Dispute Resolution (CEDR), ADR Net Ltd, The Law Society.

relationship such as landlord and tenant. A constructive approach to problem solving is better than the acrimony which is caused by litigation. Even where the alternative dispute resolution procedure does not achieve a settlement, it is likely to clarify the issues to the benefit of any subsequent litigation or arbitration.

12.9 THE AGRICULTURAL HOLDINGS ACT 1986

Under the Agricultural Holdings Act 1986, most disputes are assigned to the Agricultural Land Tribunal or arbitration under the special rules laid down in Sch 11 to the Act. However, except where the Act specifically provides to the contrary, any right of action in the courts is preserved.

12.9.1 The courts

The main areas where the landlord or tenant will bring an action in the courts are as follows:

(i) actions for forfeiture where there is a forfeiture clause in the lease;

(ii) questions on the security protection in s 2 (lettings of land for less than from year to year) and s 3 (lettings of more than two years continue after the term dated as a letting from year to year);

(iii) actions for damages for breach of covenant brought during the continuation of the tenancy;

(iv) disputes on the construction of a tenancy or a notice to quit.

12.9.2 The Agricultural Land Tribunal

The Agricultural Land Tribunal is given jurisdiction in specific matters. The parties themselves cannot confer jurisdiction on the Tribunal. Therefore, the Agricultural Land Tribunal cannot deal with any matters arising under farm business tenancies.

A large part of the work of the Agricultural Land Tribunal concerns security of tenure. Applications for consent to the operation of a notice to quit[88] and applications for succession tenancies[89] have to be made to the Agricultural Land Tribunal for the area in which the holding is situated. There are no similar provisions in the Agricultural Tenancies Act 1995. If properly drafted and served, a notice to quit given to terminate a yearly tenancy or a fixed term of more than two years will operate to bring the tenancy to an end without the consent of the Tribunal. Moreover, there are no provisions in the 1995 Act for succession tenancies.

Another area of the Tribunal's work concerns applications by tenants for the provision of fixed equipment[90] and consent to the carrying out of long-term improvements.[91]

---

88 Agricultural Holdings Act 1986, s 27(2).
89 Ibid, Pt IV, ss 34–59.
90 Ibid, s 11.
91 Ibid, s 67(3).

There are no statutory provisions in the Agricultural Tenancies Act 1995 imposing an obligation on the landlord to supply fixed equipment. Where the landlord does not consent to an improvement, the tenant can demand that the question be referred to an arbitrator. The arbitrator's powers are governed by the Agricultural Tenancies Act 1995 and the Arbitration Acts 1950–1979.

12.10 NOTICES UNDER THE AGRICULTURAL TENANCIES ACT 1995

There are many sections in the Agricultural Tenancies Act 1995 which provide for the service of written notices before specified action can be taken. It is essential therefore that there should be clear rules setting out what amounts to service. The rules apply to both written and unwritten tenancies.

12.10.1 Method of service

A notice or other document is duly given if it is delivered to the person or left at his proper address.[92] The proper address is his last known address. Where the service is on a company the proper address is the registered or principal office of the company.[93]

Service may be effective by other means where there has been a prior written agreement between the person giving the notice and the recipient of the notice authorising service in that way.[94] This might, for instance, include the giving of notice by facsimile or other electronic means. Unless there is such written agreement, notice transmitted by these means is not duly given.[95]

A written agreement could provide for service by document exchange. Even if there were no such agreement, this method of service would be effective if it could be proved that the document was delivered to a person or left at his proper address.

12.10.2 Service on agents and companies

A notice or other document is duly given to a landlord of a farm business tenancy if it is given to an agent or servant of his who is responsible for the control and management of the holding. Likewise, a notice or document is duly given to a tenant if it is given to his agent or servant responsible for the carrying on of a business on the holding.[96] Service on an employee, of either the landlord or tenant, who does not have these responsibilities is not sufficient. Where a notice or document is given to a company, it must be served on the Secretary or Clerk of the company.[97]

12.10.3 Change of landlord

The tenant must be informed of any change of landlord. Unless he has received notice that the former landlord has ceased to be entitled to receive the rents and profits and

---

[92] Agricultural Tenancies Act 1995, s 36(2).
[93] Ibid, s 36(6).
[94] Ibid, s 36(2)(c).
[95] Ibid, s 36(3).
[96] Ibid, s 36(5).
[97] Ibid, s 36(4).

has been given the name and address of the new landlord, any notice or document given to the old landlord will be deemed to have been properly served.[98]

12.11 NOTICE UNDER LANDLORD AND TENANT ACT 1987

Under s 48 of the Landlord and Tenant Act 1987, a landlord must:

> 'by notice furnish the tenant with an address in England and Wales at which notices (including notices in proceedings) may be served on him by the tenant.'

Failure to do so will mean that any rent or service charge due from the tenant to the landlord will not be due until such notice is served.[99] These provisions apply to farm business tenancies.

---

[98] Ibid, s 36(7).
[99] For a liberal interpretation of this section, see *Rogan v Woodfield Buildings* [1995] 20 EG 132. Identity and address of landlord in tenancy agreement sufficient.

Appendix I

STATUTE AND ANNOTATIONS

Agricultural Tenancies Act 1995

(1995 c 8)

ARRANGEMENT OF SECTIONS

PART I

GENERAL PROVISIONS

PART II

RENT REVIEW UNDER FARM BUSINESS TENANCY

PART III

COMPENSATION ON TERMINATION OF FARM BUSINESS TENANCY

PART IV

MISCELLANEOUS AND SUPPLEMENTAL

Resolution of disputes

SCHEDULE

An Act to make further provision with respect to tenancies which include agricultural land.

[9th May 1995]

Part I

General Provisions

Farm business tenancies

1 Meaning of 'farm business tenancy'

(1) A tenancy is a 'farm business tenancy' for the purposes of this Act if—

- (a) it meets the business conditions together with either the agriculture condition or the notice conditions, and
- (b) it is not a tenancy which, by virtue of section 2 of this Act, cannot be a farm business tenancy.

(2) The business conditions are—

- (a) that all or part of the land comprised in the tenancy is farmed for the purposes of a trade or business, and
- (b) that, since the beginning of the tenancy, all or part of the land so comprised has been so farmed.

(3) The agriculture condition is that, having regard to—

- (a) the terms of the tenancy,
- (b) the use of the land comprised in the tenancy,
- (c) the nature of any commercial activities carried on on that land, and
- (d) any other relevant circumstances,

the character of the tenancy is primarily or wholly agriculture.

(4) The notice conditions are—

- (a) that, on or before the relevant day, the landlord and the tenant each gave the other a written notice—
    - (i) identifying (by name or otherwise) the land to be comprised in the tenancy or proposed tenancy, and
    - (ii) containing a statement to the effect that the person giving the notice intends that the tenancy or proposed tenancy is to be, and remain, a farm business tenancy, and
- (b) that, at the beginning of the tenancy, having regard to the terms of the tenancy and any other relevant circumstances, the character of the tenancy was primarily or wholly agricultural.

(5) In subsection (4) above 'the relevant day' means whichever is the earlier of the following—

- (a) the day on which the parties enter into any instrument creating the tenancy, other than an agreement to enter into a tenancy on a future date, or

(b) the beginning of the tenancy.

(6) The written notice referred to in subsection (4) above must not be included in any instrument creating the tenancy.

(7) If in any proceedings—

(a) any question arises as to whether a tenancy was a farm business tenancy at any time, and

(b) it is proved that all or part of the land comprised in the tenancy was farmed for the purposes of a trade or business at that time,

it shall be presumed, unless the contrary is proved, that all or part of the land so comprised has been so farmed since the beginning of the tenancy.

(8) Any use of land in breach of the terms of the tenancy, any commercial activities carried on in breach of those terms, and any cessation of such activities in breach of those terms, shall be disregarded in determining whether at any time the tenancy meets the business conditions or the agriculture condition, unless the landlord or his predecessor in title has consented to the breach or the landlord has acquiesced in the breach.

Explanatory text—see para **3.2**.

Subsection (1)(a)—Failure to comply with the business and agricultural or notice conditions will usually result in the tenancy being a business tenancy within the Landlord and Tenant Act 1954, Pt II.

Subsection (1)(b)—Tenancies beginning (for definition of 'beginning' see s 38(4)) before 1 September 1995 are excluded as are tenancies granted pursuant to a written contract before that date which indicates that the Agricultural Holdings Act 1986 shall apply, succession tenancies, implied surrenders and regrants, and tenancies granted under the Evesham custom. See notes to s 4.

Subsection (2)—Farming is defined by s 38(2) to 'include references to the carrying on in relation to land of any agricultural activity'. 'Agriculture' is defined in s 38(1) in similar terms to the Agricultural Holdings Act 1986, s 96(1).

Subsection (3)—No special weight is given to any of these activities.

Subsection (4)—There is no prescribed form for this notice. It must be given in accordance with the rules set out in s 36. The notice must be given before the date of the tenancy document or the beginning of the tenancy, whichever is earlier. It cannot be given in the tenancy agreement itself.

Subsection (7)—This creates a presumption that the business condition has been fulfilled.

Subsection (8)—Breaches of covenant which are not waived by the landlord are ignored when determining whether the business and agricultural conditions have been fulfilled. For waiver see *Central Estates (Belgravia) Ltd v Woolgar (No 2)* [1972] 1 WLR 1048; *Segal Securities Ltd v Thoseby* [1963] 1 QB 887.

---

2 Tenancies which cannot be farm business tenancies

(1) A tenancy cannot be a farm business tenancy for the purposes of this Act if—

(a) the tenancy begins before 1st September 1995, or

(b) it is a tenancy of an agricultural holding beginning on or after that date with respect to which, by virtue of section 4 of this Act, the Agricultural Holdings Act 1986 applies.

(2) In this section 'agricultural holding' has the same meaning as in the Agricultural Holdings Act 1986.

Explanatory text—see para **3.3**.

Subsection (1)—See note to subs (1)(b) above.

Subsection (2)—Agricultural Holdings Act 1986, s 1. 'In this Act "agricultural holdings" means the aggregate of the land (whether agricultural land or not) comprised in a contract of tenancy which is a contract for an agricultural tenancy, not being a contract under which the land is let to the tenant during his continuance in any office, appointment or employment under the landlord'.

3   Compliance with notice conditions in cases of surrender and regrant

(1) This section applies where—

   (a)   a tenancy ('the new tenancy') is granted to a person who, immediately before the grant, was the tenant under a farm business tenancy ('the old tenancy') which met the notice conditions specified in section 1(4) of this Act,

   (b)   the condition in subsection (2) below or the condition in subsection (3) below is met, and

   (c)   except as respects the matters mentioned in subsections (2) and (3) below and matters consequential on them, the terms of the new tenancy are substantially the same as the terms of the old tenancy.

(2) The first condition referred to in subsection (1)(b) above is that the land comprised in the new tenancy is the same as the land comprised in the old tenancy, apart from any changes in area which are small in relation to the size of the holding and do not affect the character of the holding.

(3) The second condition referred to in subsection (1)(b) above is that the old tenancy and the new tenancy are both fixed term tenancies, but the term date under the new tenancy is earlier than the term date under the old tenancy.

(4) Where this section applies, the new tenancy shall be taken for the purposes of this Act to meet the notice conditions specified in section 1(4) of this Act.

(5) In subsection (3) above, 'the term date', in relation to a fixed term tenancy, means the date fixed for the expiry of the term.

Explanatory text—see para **3.2.3**.

Further notices—There is no need for further notices to be exchanged where there is a new tenancy following an express or implied surrender and regrant if the conditions set out in the section are fulfilled. These are:

(i)   the notice condition must have been complied with for the original farm tenancy;

(ii)   the new tenancy must be to the same tenant;

(iii)   on substantially the same terms as the old tenancy; and

(iv)   either the tenancy is of the same land apart from small changes in area which do not affect the character of the holding or both the old and new tenancies were for a fixed term and the new tenancy expires earlier than the old tenancy.

A series of fixed-term tenancies which expire by effluxion of time would need new notices.

Exclusion of Agricultural Holdings Act 1986

4   Agricultural Holdings Act 1986 not to apply in relation to new tenancies except in special cases

(1) The Agricultural Holdings Act 1986 (in this section referred to as 'the 1986 Act') shall not apply in relation to any tenancy beginning on or after 1st September 1995

(including any agreement to which section 2 of that Act would otherwise apply beginning on or after that date), except any tenancy of an agricultural holding which—

(a) is granted by a written contract of tenancy entered into before 1st September 1995 and indicating (in whatever terms) that the 1986 Act is to apply in relation to the tenancy,

(b) is obtained by virtue of a direction of an Agricultural Land Tribunal under section 39 or 53 of the 1986 Act,

(c) is granted (following a direction under section 39 of that Act) in circumstances falling within section 45(6) of that Act,

(d) is granted on an agreed succession by a written contract of tenancy indicating (in whatever terms) that Part IV of the 1986 Act is to apply in relation to the tenancy,

(e) is created by the acceptance of a tenant, in accordance with the provisions as to compensation known as the 'Evesham custom' and set out in subsections (3) to (5) of section 80 of the 1986 Act, on the terms and conditions of the previous tenancy, or

(f) is granted to a person who, immediately before the grant of the tenancy, was the tenant of the holding, or of any agricultural holding which comprised the whole or a substantial part of the land comprised in the holding, under a tenancy in relation to which the 1986 Act applied ('the previous tenancy') and is so granted merely because a purported variation of the previous tenancy (not being an agreement expressed to take effect as a new tenancy between the parties) has effect as an implied surrender followed by the grant of the tenancy.

(2) For the purposes of subsection (1)(d) above, a tenancy ('the current tenancy') is granted on an agreed succession if, and only if—

(a) the previous tenancy of the holding or a related holding was a tenancy in relation to which Part IV of the 1986 Act applied, and

(b) the current tenancy is granted otherwise than as mentioned in paragraph (b) or (c) of subsection (1) above but in such circumstances that if—

(i)   Part IV of the 1986 Act applied in relation to the current tenancy, and

(ii) a sole (or sole surviving) tenant under the current tenancy were to die and be survived by a close relative of his,

the occasion on which the current tenancy is granted would for the purposes of subsection (1) of section 37 of the 1986 Act be taken to be an occasion falling within paragraph (a) or (b) of that subsection.

(3) In this section—

(a) 'agricultural holding' and 'contract of tenancy' have the same meaning as in the 1986 Act, and

(b) 'close relative' and 'related holding' have the meaning given by section 35(2) of that Act.

Explanatory text—see para **3.3**.

Basic rule—The basic rule is that tenancies beginning before 1 September 1995 are governed by the Agricultural Holdings Act 1986; those beginning on or after that date by the Agricultural Tenancies Act 1995. The exceptions are to protect parties' legitimate expectations where they are in contractual relationships which predate the introduction of the Act.

Subsection 8(1)—Section 38(3) provides that a tenancy granted pursuant to a contract shall be taken to have been granted when the contract was entered into. However, the term used in ss 2 and 4 is the beginning of the tenancy. See s 38(4). Tenancy begins when tenant is entitled to possession.

Subsection (1)(a)—A tenancy granted by a written contract of tenancy before that date which indicates that the Agricultural Holdings Act 1986 is to apply will be governed by that Act and will not be a farm business tenancy.

Subsection (1)(b)—This provision is derived from the Agricultural Holdings Act 1986, s 34 (1)(b)(i). Where an original tenancy was granted before 12 July 1984 then the rights of succession conferred by the Agriculture (Miscellaneous Provisions) Act 1976 were preserved. These rights continue to be preserved under the new Act. An eligible person can apply to the Agricultural Land Tribunal for a direction entitling him to a tenancy of the holding provided he applies within three months of the date of death, Agricultural Holdings Act 1986, s 39. The Agricultural Holdings Act 1984 introduced provisions for succession on a tenant's retirement at 65 or over. By the Agricultural Holdings Act 1986, s 53 the Tribunal has power to give a direction entitling the nominated successor to a tenancy of the holding. This right is also preserved by the new Act.

Subsection (1)(c)—This section is derived from the Agricultural Holdings Act 1986, s 34(1)(b)(ii). Sometimes, after a direction has been made but before a new tenancy has been vested in the tenant by deemed grant under the Agricultural Holdings Act 1986, s 45(1), the landlord and tenant will have negotiated terms and the landlord will have made a direct grant to the tenant. Where this happens the direction ceases to apply and there can be no arbitration under the Agricultural Holdings Act 1986, s 48.

Subsections (1)(d), (2) and (3)—This is derived from the Agricultural Holdings Act 1986, s 34(1)(b)(iii). It applies where a succession tenancy is granted to a close relative (wife, husband, brother, sister, child, 'treated' child of the deceased tenant) Agricultural Holdings Act 1986, s 35(2), by agreement which indicates that the succession and retirement provisions of Pt IV of the 1986 Act are to apply, even though the original tenancy was concluded after 12 July 1984. The original tenancy must have been entered into before the coming into force of the Agricultural Tenancies Act 1995 and have indicated that Pt IV of the Agricultural Holdings Act 1986 was to apply. Where the succession provisions are 'contracted into' in this way, there is a limitation of two succession tenancies, Agricultural Holdings Act 1986, s 37(1).

Agricultural holding—see note to s 2(2) above.

Contract of tenancy—'. . . a contract of tenancy relating to land is a contract for an agricultural tenancy if having regard to—
(a) the terms of the tenancy
(b) the actual or contemplated use of the land at the time of the conclusion of the contract and subsequently, and
(c) any other relevant circumstances, the whole of the land comprised in the contract, subject to such exceptions only as do not substantially affect the character of the tenancy, is let for use as agricultural land' Agricultural Holdings Act 1986, s 1(2).

Subsection (1)(e)—Where a tenancy of a market garden is terminated by a notice to quit given by the tenant, or by reason of the tenant becoming insolvent, a landlord will not be liable to pay compensation for tenant's improvements unless he refuses to accept a new tenant, being a substantial and otherwise suitable tenant, procured by the outgoing tenant. Incoming tenants have been paying not only the compensation to the outgoing tenant but a premium for obtaining a tenancy with lifetime security. This practice will continue by virtue of the sub-section. Existing tenants are therefore not prejudiced as they will be able to recoup the premium they paid when they acquired their tenancies by obtaining a similar premium from an incoming tenant. Were those new tenants not protected under the Agricultural Holdings Act 1986, they would not be prepared to pay the premium.

It is estimated that there are about 600 tenancies which are subject to the Evesham custom.

Subsection (1)(f)—This subsection applies to *implied* surrenders and regrants only where there is a purported variation of the previous tenancy. Where there is an express surrender and regrant the Agricultural Tenancies Act 1995 will apply. On what amounts to a surrender and regrant, see *Saunders Trustees v Ralph* [1993] 28 EG 127, *Fredco Estates Ltd v Bryant* [1961] 1 All ER 34, *Jenkin R Lewis & Son v Kerman* [1971] Ch 477 at 487.

Termination of the tenancy

5 Tenancies for more than two years to continue from year to year unless terminated by notice

(1) A farm business tenancy for a term of more than two years shall, instead of terminating on the term date, continue (as from that date) as a tenancy from year to year, but otherwise on the terms of the original tenancy so far as applicable, unless at least twelve months but less than twenty-four months before the term date a written notice has been given by either party to the other of his intention to terminate the tenancy.

(2) In subsection (1) above 'the term date', in relation to a fixed term tenancy, means the date fixed for the expiry of the term.

(3) For the purposes of section 140 of the Law of Property Act 1925 (apportionment of conditions on severance of reversion), a notice under subsection (1) above shall be taken to be a notice to quit.

(4) This section has effect notwithstanding any agreement to the contrary.

Explanatory text—see para **11.1.1**.

Subsections (1) and (4)—For the service of notices see s 36. At least 12 but not less than 24 months' notice must be served before expiry date of fixed-term tenancy of over two years. Otherwise, tenancy will continue as yearly tenancy. It is not possible to contract out of this section. Tenancies for fixed terms of two years or less will expire automatically on the term date.

Subsection (3)—Where there is a right to serve a notice to quit and the reversion is severed, any landlord of the severed part can serve a notice to quit of that part, even though the tenancy remains a single tenancy, *Jelly v Buckman* [1974] QB 488.

6 Length of notice to quit

(1) Where a farm business tenancy is a tenancy from year to year, a notice to quit the holding or part of the holding shall (notwithstanding any provision to the contrary in the tenancy) be invalid unless—

(a) it is in writing,
(b) it is to take effect at the end of a year of the tenancy, and
(c) it is given at least twelve months but less than twenty-four months before the date on which it is to take effect.

(2) Where, by virtue of section 5(1) of this Act, a farm business tenancy for a term of more than two years is to continue (as from the term date) as a tenancy from year to year, a notice to quit which complies with subsection (1) above and which is to take effect on the first anniversary of the term date shall not be invalid merely because it is given before the term date; and in this subsection 'the term date' has the meaning given by section 5(2) of this Act.

(3) Subsection (1) above does not apply in relation to a counter-notice given by the tenant by virtue of subsection (2) of section 140 of the Law of Property Act 1925 (apportionment of conditions on severance of reversion).

Explanatory text—see para **11.1.2**.

Subsection (1)—This is a similar provision to the Agricultural Holdings Act 1986, s 25

Subsection (2)—The notice can be served during the last year of the fixed term to terminate the yearly tenancy which arises on the expiry of the fixed term.

Subsection (3)—If a landlord of a severed reversion has served a notice to quit of part of the holding the tenant can elect to quit the whole holding by serving a counter-notice on the other reversioners. The counter-notice has to be served within one month of the notice to expire at the same time as the original notice. It does not have to comply with the rules set out in s 6(1).

7   Notice required for exercise of option to terminate tenancy or resume possession of part

(1) Where a farm business tenancy is a tenancy for a term of more than two years, any notice to quit the holding or part of the holding given in pursuance of any provision of the tenancy shall (notwithstanding any provision to the contrary in the tenancy) be invalid unless it is in writing and is given at least twelve months but less than twenty-four months before the date on which it is to take effect.

(2) Subsection (1) above does not apply in relation to a counter-notice given by the tenant by virtue of subsection (2) of section 140 of the Law of Property Act 1925 (apportionment of conditions on severance of reversion).

(3) Subsection (1) above does not apply to a tenancy which, by virtue of subsection (6) of section 149 of the Law of Property Act 1925 (lease for life or lives or for a term determinable with life or lives or on the marriage of the lessee), takes effect as such a term of years as is mentioned in that subsection.

Explanatory text—see paras **11.1.6** and **11.1.7**.

Subsection (1)—Break clauses in tenancies of more than two years must be operated by a notice of at least 12 but less than 24 months.

Subsection (2)—Where a break clause is operated by a landlord of the severed reversion, in relation to his part the tenant can serve a counter-notice on the other landlords if he wants to determine the lease in respect of the rest of the land. The counter-notice has to be served within one month to expire at the same time as the original notice but does not have to comply with the rules in s 7(1).

Subsection (3)—The Law of Property Act 1925, s 149(6) converts a lease at a rent or a fine for life or lives or for a term determinable with a life or lives or on the marriage of the lessee into a term of 90 years. The lease continues after the death or marriage but can be determined by either party giving one month's notice expiring on one of the quarter days applicable to the tenancy or, if there are none, on one of the usual quarter days.

Tenant's right to remove fixtures and buildings

8   Tenant's right to remove fixtures and buildings

(1) Subject to the provisions of this section—

(a)   any fixture (of whatever description) affixed, whether for the purposes of agriculture or not, to the holding by the tenant under a farm business tenancy, and

(b) any building erected by him on the holding,

may be removed by the tenant at any time during the continuance of the tenancy or at any time after the termination of the tenancy when he remains in possession as tenant (whether or not under a new tenancy), and shall remain his property so long as he may remove it by virtue of this subsection.

(2) Subsection (1) above shall not apply—

(a) to a fixture affixed or a building erected in pursuance of some obligation,

(b) to a fixture affixed or a building erected instead of some fixture or building belonging to the landlord,

(c) to a fixture or building in respect of which the tenant has obtained compensation under section 16 of this Act or otherwise, or

(d) to a fixture or building in respect of which the landlord has given his consent under section 17 of this Act on condition that the tenant agrees not to remove it and which the tenant has agreed not to remove.

(3) In the removal of a fixture or building by virtue of subsection (1) above, the tenant shall not do any avoidable damage to the holding.

(4) Immediately, after removing a fixture or building by virtue of subsection (1) above, the tenant shall make good all damage to the holding that is occasioned by the removal.

(5) This section applies to a fixture or building acquired by a tenant as it applies to a fixture or building affixed or erected by him.

(6) Except as provided by subsection (2)(d) above, this section has effect notwithstanding any agreement or custom to the contrary.

(7) No right to remove fixtures that subsists otherwise than by virtue of this section shall be exercisable by the tenant under a farm business tenancy.

Explanatory text—see para **8.2**.

General rule—The general rule is 'quicquid plantatur solo, solo cedit', whatever is attached to the soil becomes part of it. Whether or not a chattel has become a fixture depends on: (1) the degree of annexation; and (2) the purpose of annexation. If an article is not a fixture, but remains a chattel, then it can be removed by the person bringing it onto the land or his successor in title (subject to any contractual provisions to the contrary). Generally, fixtures belong to the fee simple owner and cannot be removed. Exceptions to this rule are trade and ornamental fixtures and agricultural fixtures under the Agricultural Holdings Act 1986.

Trade fixtures are those fixtures which a tenant attaches for the purpose of his trade or business. Although he is entitled to remove them during the continuance of the tenancy they are, until removed, the property of the landlord. At common law, agricultural fixtures were not regarded as trade fixtures. A statutory right was given to agricultural tenants to remove fixtures, see the Agricultural Holdings Act 1986, s 10. The Agricultural Tenancies Act 1995, s 8 is a combination of the common law rules and the statutory provisions.

Subsection (1)—Any fixture affixed by a tenancy and any building erected by him can be removed by a tenant during the continuance of the tenancy or when he continues in possession either as a tenant at will or under a new tenancy. See *New Zealand Government Property Corporation v HM&S Ltd* [1982] QB 1145 (tenant does not surrender his right of removal by surrendering his existing tenancy in return for the grant of a new tenancy). This provision differs in two important respects from the rules for trade fixtures. First, it extends to the removal of buildings (*cf Whitehead v Bennett* [1858] 27 LJ Ch 474) and, secondly, the fixture remains the property of the tenant. It also differs from the Agricultural Holdings Act 1986, s 10 in that there is not a two-month period after termination of the tenancy when the fixture can be removed, nor is there an option for the landlord to purchase the fixture.

Subsection (2)(a)—This is a similar provision to the Agricultural Holdings Act 1986, s 10(2)(a). Note: it is not limited to an obligation in the tenancy agreement. It would include a statutory obligation eg to comply with pollution regulations.

Subsection (2)(b)—This is a similar provision to the Agricultural Holdings Act 1986, s 10(2)(b).

Subsection (2)(c)—Section 16 confers the right to compensation on a tenant who fulfils the conditions in ss 17 and 18. Section 8(2)(c) of the Act provides that a tenant cannot remove a fixture or building 'in respect of which the tenant has obtained compensation'. This is different from the equivalent provision in s 10(2)(c) which refers 'to a building in respect of which the tenant is entitled to compensation'.

Subsection (2)(d)—Before a tenant is entitled to compensation under s 18 the landlord must have given his consent in writing to the making of the improvement. Such a consent may be subject to a specified variation in the terms of the tenancy. The consent might stipulate that any improvement, being a fixture or building, should not be removed by the tenant. This paragraph is an exception to s 8(6) which prevents contracting out.

Subsections (3) and (4)—These subsections reproduce the common law rules and are similar to the Agriculture Holdings Act 1986, s 10(5).

Subsection (5)—This subsection reproduces the Agricultural Holdings Act 1986, s 10(7).

Subsection (6)—It is not possible to contract out of s 8 except to the extent provided for in s 8(2)(d), ie where consent is given to an improvement on condition that it shall not be removed.

Subsection (7)—The Agricultural Holdings Act 1986, s 10(8) provides 'This section shall not be taken as prejudicing any right to remove a fixture that subsists otherwise than by virtue of this section'. The position is reversed under the Agricultural Tenancy Act 1995. For farm business tenancies the common law rules, so far as not reproduced in the section, are excluded as are the rules under the Agricultural Holdings Act 1986.

PART II

RENT REVIEW UNDER FARM BUSINESS TENANCY

9 Application of Part II

This Part of this Act applies in relation to a farm business tenancy (notwithstanding any agreement to the contrary) unless the tenancy is created by an instrument which—

(a) expressly states that the rent is not to be reviewed during the tenancy, or

(b) provides that the rent is to be varied, at a specified time or times during the tenancy—

  (i) by or to a specified amount, or

  (ii) in accordance with a specified formula which does not preclude a reduction and which does not require or permit the exercise by any person of any judgment or discretion in relation to the determination of the rent of the holding,

but otherwise is to remain fixed.

Explanatory text—see paras **6.3, 6.4** and **6.5.**

Subsection (a)—It is not enough merely to have no review clause. The tenancy agreement must expressly state that there shall not be one. This reverses the normal position that there will be no review unless there is a contractual provision so providing.

Subsection (b)—The tenancy agreement can provide for phased rents or adjustments of rent up and down by reference to objective criteria.

---

10   Notice requiring statutory rent review

(1) The landlord or tenant under a farm business tenancy in relation to which this Part of this Act applies may by notice in writing given to the other (in this Part of this Act referred to as a 'statutory review notice') require that the rent to be payable in respect of the holding as from the review date shall be referred to arbitration in accordance with this Act.

(2) In this Part of this Act 'the review date', in relation to a statutory review notice, means a date which—

    (a)   is specified in the notice, and
    (b)   complies with subsections (3) to (6) below.

(3) The review date must be at least twelve months but less than twenty-four months after the day on which the statutory review notice is given.

(4) If the parties have agreed in writing that the rent is to be, or may be, varied as from a specified date or dates, or at specified intervals, the review date must be a date as from which the rent could be varied under the agreement.

(5) If the parties have agreed in writing that the review date for the purposes of this Part of this Act is to be a specified date or dates, the review date must be that date or one of those dates.

(6) If the parties have not agreed as mentioned in subsection (4) or (5) above, the review date—

    (a)   must be an anniversary of the beginning of the tenancy or, where the landlord and the tenant have agreed in writing that the review date for the purposes of this Act is to be some other day of the year, that day of the year, and
    (b)   must not fall before the end of the period of three years beginning with the latest of any of the following dates—

        (i)   the beginning of the tenancy,
        (ii)   any date as from which there took effect a previous direction of an arbitrator as to the amount of the rent,
        (iii)   any date as from which there took effect a previous determination as to the amount of the rent made, otherwise than as arbitrator, by a person appointed under an agreement between the landlord and the tenant, and
        (iv)   any date as from which there took effect a previous agreement in writing between the landlord and the tenant, entered into since the grant of the tenancy, as to the amount of the rent.

Explanatory text—see paras **6.7** and **6.8**.

Subsection (1)—For service of notices see s 36. The relevant date for determining the rent is the review date, cf Agricultural Holdings Act 1986, s 12(2) when the rent is determined at the date of reference.

Subsection (2)—The review date must:
(i) be specified in the notice;
(ii) be at least 12 but less than 24 months after the notice is given;
(iii) comply with any written agreement between the parties as to date or dates or intervals when the rent can be varied;
(iv) be the review date agreed by the parties in writing or, in default, the anniversary of the beginning of the tenancy. For the definition of beginning of the tenancy see s 38(4).

Subsection (6)(b)—Where the parties have not agreed on the intervals for a rent review then there is a fall-back provision. Either party can demand a rent review at not less than three-yearly intervals.
(iii) If the parties agree in writing as to the amount of the rent, the three years runs from that date, ie the parties could agree to increase or reduce the rent or that it should remain the same, cf Agricultural Holdings Act 1986, s 12, Sch 2, para 4(1)(b) 'the date as from which there took effect a previous increase of reduction of rent'. Therefore, under the 1986 Act an agreement by the parties for the rent to remain the same does not affect the three-year cycle.
NB There are no statutory provisions excluding from the three-year rule, alterations in rent where:
(i) there is a resumption of part;
(ii) adjustments in the boundaries are made; or
(iii) the landlord makes improvements. The parties can agree for rent reviews on these occasions either in the original tenancy agreement or in writing subsequently. A notice of at least 12 but less than 24 months would still have to be given in accordance with s 10(1), (2) and (3) above.

11 Review date where new tenancy of severed part of reversion

(1) This section applies in any case where a farm business tenancy ('the new tenancy') arises between—

(a) a person who immediately before the date of the beginning of the tenancy was entitled to a severed part of the reversionary estate in the land comprised in a farm business tenancy ('the original tenancy') in which the land to which the new tenancy relates was then comprised, and

(b) the person who immediately before that date was the tenant under the original tenancy,

and the rent payable under the new tenancy as its beginning represents merely the appropriate portion of the rent payable under the original tenancy immediately before the beginning of the new tenancy.

(2) In any case where this section applies—

(a) references to the beginning of the tenancy in subsection (6) of section 10 of this Act shall be taken to be references to the beginning of the original tenancy, and

(b) references to rent in that subsection shall be taken to be references to the rent payable under the original tenancy,

until the first occasion following the beginning of the new tenancy on which any such direction, determination or agreement with respect to the rent of the new holding as is mentioned in that subsection takes effect.

Explanatory text—see para **6.9**.

Subsection (1)—A severance of the reversion does not affect the tenancy which remains a single tenancy,

Jelly v Buckman [1974] QB 488, [1973] 3 All ER 853, [1973] 3 WLR 585. However, the landlords of the severed reversions could decide to enter into separate tenancies with the tenant. If the rent under the new tenancy is merely an apportioned amount of the rent under the original tenancy then it is the beginning of the original tenancy which is taken into account in ascertaining the three-year rent review period. After the first post-severance rent review the severed portion of the land will have its own separate rent review cycle.

12 Appointment of arbitrator

Where a statutory review notice has been given in relation to a farm business tenancy, but—

(a) no arbitrator has been appointed under an agreement made since the notice was given, and

(b) no person has been appointed under such an agreement to determine the question of the rent (otherwise than as arbitrator) on a basis agreed by the parties,

either party may, at any time during the period of six months ending with the review date, apply to the President of the Royal Institution of Chartered Surveyors (in this Act referred to as 'the RICS') for the appointment of an arbitrator by him.

Explanatory text—see para **6.12.2**.

Statutory review notice—To preclude application to the Royal Institution of Chartered Surveyors the agreement as to the appointment of an arbitrator or third party must be made after the statutory review notice has been given. For the service of notices, see s 36. The arbitrator has to determine the rent on an open market basis. The third party, however, can determine the rent 'on a basis agreed by the parties'. This could be more or less than the open market.

13 Amount of rent

(1) On any reference made in pursuance of a statutory review notice, the arbitrator shall determine the rent properly payable in respect of the holding at the review date and accordingly shall, with effect from that date, increase or reduce the rent previously payable or direct that it shall continue unchanged.

(2) For the purposes of subsection (1) above, the rent properly payable in respect of a holding is the rent at which the holding might reasonably be expected to be let on the open market by a willing landlord to a willing tenant, taking into account (subject to subsections (3) and (4) below) all relevant factors, including (in every case) the terms of the tenancy (including those which are relevant for the purposes of section 10(4) to (6) of this Act, but not those relating to the criteria by reference to which any new rent is to be determined).

(3) The arbitrator shall disregard any increase in the rental value of the holding which is due to tenant's improvements other than—

(a) any tenant's improvement provided under an obligation which was imposed on the tenant by the terms of his tenancy or any previous tenancy and which arose on or before the beginning of the tenancy in question,

(b) any tenant's improvement to the extent that any allowance or benefit has been made or given by the landlord in consideration of its provision, and

(c) any tenant's improvement to the extent that the tenant has received any compensation from the landlord in respect of it.

(4) The arbitrator—

(a) shall disregard any effect on the rent of the fact that the tenant who is a party to the arbitration is in occupation of the holding, and

(b) shall not fix the rent at a lower amount by reason of any dilapidation or deterioration of, or damage to, buildings or land caused or permitted by the tenant.

(5) In this section 'tenant's improvement', and references to the provision of such an improvement, have the meaning given by section 15 of this Act.

Explanatory text—see para **6.10**.

Subsection (1)—The powers of the arbitrators are similar to those in the Agricultural Holdings Act 1986, s 2(2), although the relevant date for determining the rent under the 1995 Act is the review date, not the date of reference.

Subsection (2)—The landlord and tenant have to be willing, see *FR Evans (Leeds) Ltd v English Electric Co Ltd* [1978] 36 P&CR 185 (hypothetical lessor and lessee). The arbitrator has to take into account, inter alia, any contractual terms as to the timing and frequency of rent reviews but not any terms as to the method of ascertaining the amount of rent.

Subsection (3)(a)—This is derived from the Agricultural Holdings Act 1986, s 12, Sch 2, para 2(1)(a).

Subsection (3)(b) and (c)—This prevents any double counting.

---

14 Interpretation of Part II

In this Part of this Act, unless the context otherwise requires—

'the review date', in relation to a statutory review notice, has the meaning given by section 10(2) of this Act;

'statutory review notice' has the meaning given by section 10(1) of this Act.

PART III

COMPENSATION ON TERMINATION OF FARM BUSINESS TENANCY

Tenant's entitlement to compensation

15 Meaning of 'tenant's improvement'

For the purposes of this Part of this Act a 'tenant's improvement', in relation to any farm business tenancy, means—

(a) any physical improvement which is made on the holding by the tenant by his own effort or wholly or partly at his own expense, or

(b) any intangible advantage which—

(i) is obtained for the holding by the tenant by his own effort or wholly or partly at his own expense, and

(ii) becomes attached to the holding,

and references to the provision of a tenant's improvement are references to the making by the tenant of any physical improvement falling within paragraph (a) above or the obtaining by the tenant of any intangible advantage falling within paragraph (b) above.

Explanatory text—see para **8.3.2**.

Tenant's improvements—This section defines tenant's improvements. The section is wider than physical improvements specified in the Agricultural Holdings Act 1986. There are no Schedules of improvements and the term includes intangible improvements as well as physical improvements, for example quotas which are attached to land, water abstraction licences, goodwill, provided these benefits remain with the holding.

---

16 Tenant's right to compensation for tenant's improvement

(1) The tenant under a farm business tenancy shall, subject to the provisions of this Part of this Act, be entitled on the termination of the tenancy, on quitting the holding, to obtain from his landlord compensation in respect of any tenant's improvement.

(2) A tenant shall not be entitled to compensation under this section in respect of—

    (a)   any physical improvement which is removed from the holding, or

    (b)   any intangible advantage which does not remain attached to the holding.

(3) Section 13 of, and Schedule 1 to, the Agriculture Act 1986 (compensation to outgoing tenants for milk quota) shall not apply in relation to a farm business tenancy.

Explanatory text—see para **8.3.4**.

Compensation—This section gives the tenant a right to compensation provided that the improvement remains with the holding. Where a tenant removes buildings or fixtures under s 8, he will not be entitled to compensation. Any compensation for milk quota attached to land on the termination of a farm business tenancy will be payable under this section and not under the Agriculture Act 1986.

Contracting out—See s 26.

Successive tenancies—For successive tenancies see s 23.

Conditions of eligibility

17 Consent of landlord as condition of compensation for tenant's improvement

(1) A tenant shall not be entitled to compensation under section 16 of this Act in respect of any tenant's improvement unless the landlord has given his consent in writing to the provision of the tenant's improvement.

(2) Any such consent may be given in the instrument creating the tenancy or elsewhere.

(3) Any such consent may be given either unconditionally or on condition that the tenant agrees to a specified variation in the terms of the tenancy.

(4) The variation referred to in subsection (3) above must be related to the tenant's improvement in question.

(5) This section does not apply in any case where the tenant's improvement consists of planning permission.

Explanatory text—see para **8.3.5**.

Compensation—This section applies to improvements other than planning permission. In order for the tenant to be entitled to compensation he must have obtained the landlord's consent to the making of the improvement. The consent must be in writing but does not have to be in the tenancy agreement. It can be given before or after the making of the improvement. The consent can be conditional or unconditional. Where conditional, the conditions must relate to the improvement and not the amount of compensation, cf Agricultural Holdings Act 1986, s 67(2). The consent can be specific or general (eg permission to plant standing crops which will not be harvested before termination). Where the landlord refuses or fails to give consent or gives it subject to conditions unacceptable to the tenant, the tenant has the right under s 19 to go to arbitration. For definition of planning permission, see the Town and Country Planning Act 1990, s 336(1).

---

18 Conditions in relation to compensation for planning permission

(1) A tenant shall not be entitled to compensation under section 16 of this Act in respect of a tenant's improvement which consists of planning permission unless—

(a) the landlord has given his consent in writing to the making of the application for planning permission,

(b) that consent is expressed to be given for the purpose—

(i) of enabling a specified physical improvement falling within paragraph (a) of section 15 of this Act lawfully to be provided by the tenant, or

(ii) of enabling the tenant lawfully to effect a specified change of use, and

(c) on the termination of the tenancy, the specified physical improvement has not been completed or the specified change of use has not been effected.

(2) Any such consent may be given either unconditionally or on condition that the tenant agrees to a specified variation in the terms of the tenancy.

(3) The variation referred to in subsection (2) above must be related to the physical improvement or change of use in question.

Explanatory text—see para **8.3.5**.

Compensation—This section imposes special conditions where the consent relates to an application for planning permission which has not been implemented by the time the tenancy is terminated. For implemented planning permission, see s 20(4). The landlord must have given written consent for an application for planning permission for a specified physical improvement or a specified change of use. This is to give effect to the Joint Industry Statement (see Appendix III) that compensation should only be payable in respect of planning permission gained by a tenant which is related to activities on a holding permitted by the terms of the tenancy agreement. No compensation is payable insofar as the planning permission enables development other than for the specified purpose for which the landlord gave consent.

There are no special provisions under the Landlord and Tenant Act 1927 (compensation for improvements for business tenancies) relating to planning permission. In the private residential section, there are no statutory compensation provisions for improvements of any kind. For definition of planning permission, see the Town and Country Planning Act 1990, s 336(1).

---

19   Reference to arbitration of refusal or failure to give consent or of condition attached to consent

(1) Where, in relation to any tenant's improvement, the tenant under a farm business tenancy is aggrieved by—

   (a)   the refusal of his landlord to give his consent under section 17(1) of this Act,
   (b)   the failure of his landlord to give such consent within two months of a written request by the tenant for such consent, or
   (c)   any variation in the terms of the tenancy required by the landlord as a condition of giving such consent,

the tenant may by notice in writing given to the landlord demand that the question shall be referred to arbitration under this section; but this subsection has effect subject to subsections (2) and (3) below.

(2) No notice under subsection (1) above may be given in relation to any tenant's improvement which the tenant has already provided or begun to provide, unless that improvement is a routine improvement.

(3) No notice under subsection (1) above may be given—

   (a)   in a case falling within paragraph (a) or (c) of that subsection, after the end of the period of two months beginning with the day on which notice of the refusal or variation referred to in that paragraph was given to the tenant, or
   (b)   in a case falling within paragraph (b) of that subsection, after the end of the period of four months beginning with the day on which the written request referred to in that paragraph was given to the landlord.

(4) Where the tenant has given notice under subsection (1) above but no arbitrator has been appointed under an agreement made since the notice was given, the tenant or the landlord may apply to the President of the RICS, subject to subsection (9) below, for the appointment of an arbitrator by him.

(5) The arbitrator shall consider whether, having regard to the terms of the tenancy and any other relevant circumstances (including the circumstances of the tenant and the landlord), it is reasonable for the tenant to provide the tenant's improvement.

(6) Subject to subsection (9) below, the arbitrator may unconditionally approve the provision of the tenant's improvement or may withhold his approval, but may not give his approval subject to any condition or vary any condition required by the landlord under section 17(3) of this Act.

(7) If the arbitrator gives his approval, that approval shall have effect for the purposes of this Part of this Act and for the purposes of the terms of the farm business tenancy as if it were the consent of the landlord.

(8) In a case falling within subsection (1)(c) above, the withholding by the arbitrator of his approval shall not affect the validity of the landlord's consent or of the condition subject to which it was given.

(9) Where, at any time after giving a notice under subsection (1) above in relation to any tenant's improvement which is not a routine improvement, the tenant begins to provide the improvement—

(a) no application may be made under subsection (4) above after that time,

(b) where such an application has been made but no arbitrator has been appointed before that time, the application shall be ineffective, and

(c) no award may be made by virtue of subsection (6) above after that time except as to the costs of the reference and award in a case where the arbitrator was appointed before that time.

(10) For the purposes of this section—

'fixed equipment' includes any building or structure affixed to land and any works constructed on, in, over or under land, and also includes anything grown on land for a purpose other than use after severance from the land, consumption of the thing grown or its produce, or amenity;

'routine improvement', in relation to a farm business tenancy, means any tenant's improvement which—

(a) is a physical improvement made in the normal course of farming the holding or any part of the holding, and

(b) does not consist of fixed equipment or an improvement to fixed equipment,

but does not include any improvement whose provision is prohibited by the terms of the tenancy.

Explanatory text—see para **8.3.7**.

Subsection (1)—This subsection is based on the Agricultural Holdings Act 1986, s 67, Sch, Pt II. It enables an aggrieved tenant to refer to an arbitrator the refusal or failure of the landlord to give consent or the landlord's imposition of unsatisfactory conditions. The section does not apply to the landlord's refusal to consent for an application for planning permission. There is no appeal to an arbitrator if the landlord refuses his consent to the tenant making an application for planning permission. The section will not apply if the tenant has begun to provide the improvement, ie the notice to the landlord must be served before the improvement is begun, unless it is a routine improvement cf s 17(1) improvement may be made before landlord's consent. For service of notice see s 36.

Subsection (2)—These time-limits are strict and must be complied with.

Subsection (4)—Any user clauses in the tenancy agreement will be relevant as will the length of the term. The circumstances of the tenant and landlord must also be taken into account.

Subsections (5) and (7)—The effect is that where a landlord imposes conditions, the arbitrator can give unconditional approval so that the tenant has consent free of the landlord's conditions. However, if he refuses consent then the landlord's consent and conditions will stand. The arbitrator cannot impose his own conditions or vary the landlord's conditions, cf Agricultural Holdings Act 1986, s 67(4).

Subsections (9) and (10)—These subsections were introduced at Report Stage in the House of Commons to deal with the problem of tenant-right. It was argued that many tenants would not realise the need for consent to routine acts of husbandry such as planting crops. If these crops were not harvested when the tenancy was terminated then, because the consent of the landlord had not been obtained, the tenant could not obtain compensation. If the landlord refused consent, it would be too late to apply for the consent of the arbitrator as the improvement would have already been begun. The effect of the subsections is that an application can be made for the arbitrator's consent to routine improvements even after the improvement has been made. The definition of fixed equipment is derived from the Agricultural Holdings Act 1986, s 96 and would include hedges, fences and walls, etc.

Amount of compensation

20 Amount of compensation for tenant's improvement not consisting of planning permission

(1) The amount of compensation payable to the tenant under section 16 of this Act in respect of any tenant's improvement shall be an amount equal to the increase attributable to the improvement in the value of the holding at the termination of the tenancy as land comprised in a tenancy.

(2) Where the landlord and the tenant have entered into an agreement in writing whereby any benefit is given or allowed to the tenant in consideration of the provision of a tenant's improvement, the amount of compensation otherwise payable in respect of that improvement shall be reduced by the proportion which the value of the benefit bears to the amount of the total cost of providing the improvement.

(3) Where a grant has been or will be made to the tenant out of public money in respect of a tenant's improvement, the amount of compensation otherwise payable in respect of that improvement shall be reduced by the proportion which the amount of the grant bears to the amount of the total cost of providing the improvement.

(4) Where a physical improvement which has been completed or a change of use which has been effected is authorised by any planning permission granted on an application made by the tenant, section 18 of this Act does not prevent any value attributable to the fact that the physical improvement or change of use is so authorised from being taken into account under this section in determining the amount of compensation payable in respect of the physical improvement or in respect of any intangible advantage obtained as a result of the change of use.

(5) This section does not apply where the tenant's improvement consists of planning permission.

Explanatory text—see para **8.3.10**.

Compensation—This section sets out the amount of compensation.

Subsection (1)—Land comprised in a tenancy means the tenanted value. It is not limited to the tenanted value of an agricultural holding.

Subsection (2)—This provision is based on the Agricultural Holdings Act 1986, s 66(3) but is much wider in application. Section 66(3) applies only to the improvements set out in Pt I of Sch 8 to the Agricultural Holdings Act 1986 (improvements for which the consent of the landlord is not necessary).

Subsection (3)—The money can come from any public source including the European Union, cf Agricultural Holdings Act 1986, s 66(5) which applies only in respect of money provided by Parliament or local government, and requires such grants to be taken into account.

Subsection (4)—If a planning permission is not implemented by the time the tenancy is terminated, compensation may be payable under s 16 provided the conditions in that section have been complied with. Section 20(4) enables the obtaining of planning permission to be taken into account as an element of compensation when the planning permission has been implemented.

---

21 Amount of compensation for planning permission

(1) The amount of compensation payable to the tenant under section 16 of this Act in respect of a tenant's improvement which consists of planning permission shall be an

amount equal to the increase attributable to the fact that the relevant development is authorised by the planning permission in the value of the holding at the termination of the tenancy as land comprised in a tenancy.

(2) In subsection (1) above, 'the relevant development' means the physical improvement or change of use specified in the landlord's consent under section 18 of this Act in accordance with subsection (1)(b) of that section.

(3) Where the landlord and the tenant have entered into an agreement in writing whereby any benefit is given or allowed to the tenant in consideration of the obtaining of planning permission by the tenant, the amount of compensation otherwise payable in respect of that permission shall be reduced by the proportion which the value of the benefit bears to the amount of the total cost of obtaining the permission.

Explanatory text—see para **8.3.11**.

Compensation—This section deals with compensation for planning permission.

Subsection (2)—The conditions in s 16 have to be met if compensation is to be made.

Subsection (3)—Benefits given or allowed to the tenant have to be deducted from the compensation. This is a similar provision to s 20(3) (see note above) and the Agricultural Holdings Act 1986, s 66(5). For definition of planning permission see the Town and Country Planning Act, s 336(1).

---

22   Settlement of claims for compensation

(1) Any claim by the tenant under a farm business tenancy for compensation under section 16 of this Act shall, subject to the provisions of this section, be determined by arbitration under this section.

(2) No such claim for compensation shall be enforceable unless before the end of the period of two months beginning with the date of the termination of the tenancy the tenant has given notice in writing to his landlord of his intention to make the claim and of the nature of the claim.

(3) Where—

    (a) the landlord and the tenant have not settled the claim by agreement in writing, and

    (b) no arbitrator has been appointed under an agreement made since the notice under subsection (2) above was given,

either party may, after the end of the period of four months beginning with the date of the termination of the tenancy, apply to the President of the RICS for the appointment of an arbitrator by him.

(4) Where—

    (a) an application under subsection (3) above relates wholly or partly to compensation in respect of a routine improvement (within the meaning of section 19 of this Act) which the tenant has provided or has begun to provide, and

    (b) that application is made at the same time as an application under section 19(4) of this Act relating to the provision of that improvement, the President of the RICS shall appoint the same arbitrator on both applications and, if both applications are made by the same person, only one fee shall be payable by virtue of section 30(2) of this Act in respect of them.

(5) Where a tenant lawfully remains in occupation of part of the holding after the termination of a farm business tenancy, references in subsections (2) and (3) above to the termination of the tenancy shall, in the case of a claim relating to that part of the holding, be construed as references to the termination of the occupation.

Explanatory text—see para **8.3.12**.

Settlement of claims for compensation—This section provides for settlement by arbitration. The jurisdiction of the courts is excluded.

Subsection (2)—The two-month time-limit must be complied with. Presumably, a notice served before the termination of the tenancy would be good, as it would be given 'before the end of the period of two months beginning with the date of termination of the tenancy'. There is a similar provision in the Agricultural Holdings Act 1986, s 83(2). For service of notice, see s 36.

Subsection (3)—Four months is a shorter time-limit than is provided under the equivalent provision in the Agricultural Holdings Act 1986. Section 83(4) provides for a period of eight months to elapse before an arbitrator can be appointed.

Supplementary provisions with respect to compensation

23 Successive tenancies

(1) Where the tenant under a farm business tenancy has remained in the holding during two or more such tenancies, he shall not be deprived of his right to compensation under section 16 of this Act by reason only that any tenant's improvement was provided during a tenancy other than the one at the termination of which he quits the holding.

(2) The landlord and tenant under a farm business tenancy may agree that the tenant is to be entitled to compensation under section 16 of this Act on the termination of the tenancy even though at that termination the tenant remains in the holding under a new tenancy.

(3) Where the landlord and the tenant have agreed as mentioned in subsection (2) above in relation to any tenancy ('the earlier tenancy'), the tenant shall not be entitled to compensation at the end of any subsequent tenancy in respect of any tenant's improvement provided during the earlier tenancy in relation to the land comprised in the earlier tenancy.

Explanatory text—see para **8.3.13**.

Compensation for successive tenancies—This section preserves the right of compensation where a tenant is granted further tenancies on the same holding albeit on different terms. It is similar to the Agricultural Holdings Act 1986, s 69(1).

Subsection (2)—This enables the parties to settle compensation on the old tenancy even where a new one is granted.

Subsection (2)—This ensures that the tenant is not compensated twice.

---

24   Resumption of possession of part of holding

(1) Where—

(a) the landlord under a farm business tenancy resumes possession of part of the holding in pursuance of any provision of the tenancy, or

(b) a person entitled to a severed part of the reversionary estate in a holding held under a farm business tenancy resumes possession of part of the holding by virtue of a notice to quit that part given to the tenant by virtue of section 140 of the Law of Property Act 1925,

the provisions of this Part of this Act shall, subject to subsections (2) and (3) below, apply to that part of the holding (in this section referred to as 'the relevant part') as if it were a separate holding which the tenant had quitted in consequence of a notice to quit and, in a case falling within paragraph (b) above, as if the person resuming possession were the landlord of that separate holding.

(2) The amount of compensation payable to the tenant under section 16 of this Act in respect of any tenant's improvement provided for the relevant part by the tenant and not consisting of planning permission shall, subject to section 20(2) to (4) of this Act, be an amount equal to the increase attributable to the tenant's improvement in the value of the original holding on the termination date as land comprised in a tenancy.

(3) The amount of compensation payable to the tenant under section 16 of this Act in respect of any tenant's improvement which consists of planning permission relating to the relevant part shall, subject to section 21(3) of this Act, be an amount equal to the increase attributable to the fact that the relevant development is authorised by the planning permission in the value of the original holding on the termination date as land comprised in a tenancy.

(4) In a case falling within paragraph (a) or (b) of subsection (1) above, sections 20 and 21 of this Act shall apply on the termination of the tenancy, in relation to the land then comprised in the tenancy, as if the reference in subsection (1) of each of those sections to the holding were a reference to the original holding.

(5) In subsections (2) to (4) above—

'the original holding' means the land comprised in the farm business tenancy—

(a) on the date when the landlord gave his consent under section 17 or 18 of this Act in relation to the tenant's improvement, or

(b) where approval in relation to the tenant's improvement was given by an arbitrator, on the date on which that approval was given,

'the relevant development', in relation to any tenant's improvement which consists of planning permission, has the meaning given by section 21(2) of this Act, and 'the termination date' means the date on which possession of the relevant part was resumed.

Explanatory text—see para **8.3.14**.

Compensation—This section deals with compensation where possession of part of the holding is regained. It is modelled on the Agricultural Holdings Act 1986, ss 74(2), (3) and 75. However, compensation is not apportioned on the basis of the amount of land repossessed. It is payable on the value of the improvement on the land taken or land retained to the entire original holding.

Subsection (1)(b)—The Law of Property Act 1925, s 140 does not give a right to serve a notice to quit but where one exists, it enables the owner of the severed reversion to serve a notice relating to his interest. It is therefore a statutory exception to the common law rule that there cannot be a notice to quit of part of a holding in the absence of a contractual provision.

Subsections (2) and (3)—Refer to compensation for improvements on the land repossessed. Deductions from compensation are made for benefits or allowances given by the landlord to the tenant for the improvements or grants received or to be received by the tenant from public funds. Should the tenant fail to apply for such grants then no deduction can be made.

Subsection (4)—This refers to land which remains within the tenancy, after resumption of possession of part of the holding, at the termination of the tenancy. The tenant is entitled to compensation based on the increased letting value of the original holding as defined in subs (5). The landlord at the time of resumption of part under s 24(1)(a) or (b) needs to be aware of this contingent liability.

25 Compensation where reversionary estate in holding is severed

(1) Where the reversionary estate in the holding comprised in a farm business tenancy is for the time being vested in more than one person in several parts, the tenant shall be entitled, on quitting the entire holding, to require that any compensation payable to him under section 16 of this Act shall be determined as if the reversionary estate were not so severed.

(2) Where subsection (1) applies, the arbitrator shall, where necessary, apportion the amount awarded between the persons who for the purposes of this Part of this Act together constitute the landlord of the holding, and any additional costs of the award caused by the apportionment shall be directed by the arbitrator to be paid by those persons in such proportions as he shall determine.

Explanatory text—see para **8.3.15**.

Compensation—This section entitles the tenant to require that compensation be paid in relation to the whole holding where the reversionary estate has been severed. It is based on the Agricultural Holdings Act 1986, s 75(1) but applies only to compensation payable under the Agricultural Tenancies Act 1995, s 16. It does not cover any additional contractual compensation which may have been agreed by the parties.

26 Extent to which compensation recoverable under agreements

(1) In any case for which apart from this section the provisions of this Part of this Act provide for compensation, a tenant shall be entitled to compensation in accordance with those provisions and not otherwise, and shall be so entitled notwithstanding any agreement to the contrary.

(2) Nothing in the provisions of this Part of this Act, apart from this section, shall be construed as disentitling a tenant to compensation in any case for which those provisions do not provide for compensation.

Explanatory text—see **8.3.16**.

Subsection (1)—No contracting out of the Act is permitted.

Subsection (2)—Additional compensation may be agreed by the parties for matters not covered by the Act, for example game damage, or where a break clause is operated.

27 Interpretation of Part III

In this Part of this Act, unless the context otherwise requires—

'planning permission' has the meaning given by section 336(1) of the Town and Country Planning Act 1990;

'tenant's improvement', and references to the provision of such an improvement, have the meaning given by section 15 of this Act.

PART IV

MISCELLANEOUS AND SUPPLEMENTAL

Resolution of disputes

28 Resolution of disputes

(1) Subject to subsections (4) and (5) below and to section 29 of this Act, any dispute between the landlord and the tenant under a farm business tenancy, being a dispute concerning their rights and obligations under this Act, under the terms of the tenancy or under any custom, shall be determined by arbitration.

(2) Where such a dispute has arisen, the landlord or the tenant may give notice in writing to the other specifying the dispute and stating that, unless before the end of the period of two months beginning with the day on which the notice is given the parties have appointed an arbitrator by agreement, he proposes to apply to the President of the RICS for the appointment of an arbitrator by him.

(3) Where a notice has been given under subsection (2) above, but no arbitrator has been appointed by agreement, either party may, after the end of the period of two months referred to in that subsection, apply to the President of the RICS for the appointment of an arbitrator by him.

(4) Subsection (1) above does not affect the jurisdiction of the courts, except to the extent provided by section 4(1) of the Arbitration Act 1950 (staying of court proceedings where there is submission to arbitration), as applied to statutory arbitrations by section 31 of that Act.

(5) Subsections (1) to (3) above do not apply in relation to—

(a) the determination of rent in pursuance of a statutory review notice (as defined in section 10(1) of this Act),
(b) any case falling within section 19(1) of this Act, or
(c) any claim for compensation under Part III of this Act.

Explanatory text—see paras **12.2.1**, **12.2.2** and **12.2.3**.

Subsection (1)—Arbitration is under the Arbitration Acts 1950–1979. The special arbitration procedures under the Agricultural Holdings Act 1986 will not apply. An arbitrator has no jurisdiction to decide whether there is a binding tenancy between the parties. *Heyman v Darwins Ltd* [1942] AC 356.

Custom—The Agricultural Holdings Act 1986 abolished customary rights to compensation but did not abolish custom relating to other matters. Custom can be excluded by the tenancy agreement. If not excluded, it must be proved by the party who wants to rely on it and must be reasonable. See Muir Watt *Agricultural Holdings* 13th edn (Sweet & Maxwell, 1987) pp 255–260.

Subsection (4)—Jurisdiction of the courts is concurrent except for matters specified in subs (5).

29   Cases where right to refer claim to arbitration under section 28 does not apply

(1) Section 28 of this Act does not apply in relation to any dispute if—

(a)   the tenancy is created by an instrument which includes provision for disputes to be resolved by any person other than—

    (i)   the landlord or the tenant, or

    (ii)   a third party appointed by either of them without the consent or concurrence of the other, and

(b)   either of the following has occurred—

    (i)   the landlord and the tenant have jointly referred the dispute to the third party under the provision, or

    (ii)   the landlord or the tenant has referred the dispute to the third party under the provision and notified the other in writing of the making of the reference, the period of four weeks beginning with the date on which the other was so notified has expired and the other has not given a notice under section 28(2) of this Act in relation to the dispute before the end of that period.

(2)   For the purposes of subsection (1) above, a term of the tenancy does not provide for disputes to be 'resolved' by any person unless that person (whether or not acting as arbitrator) is enabled under the terms of the tenancy to give a decision which is binding in law on both parties.

Explanatory text—see para **12.6**.

Disputes resolution—The aim of the legislation is to allow the parties to specify their own disputes resolution procedure. Even if there is a term in the tenancy agreement allowing for a third party to resolve disputes unless both parties refer the dispute to that third party, there is still the option to evoke the arbitration provisions of s 28.

Subsection (2)—The third party under the terms of the tenancy agreement must be able to make a binding decision. It used to be considered that the jurisdiction of the courts could not be ousted in this way. However, recent cases have established that an independent third party can make binding decisions which cannot be challenged in the courts except on a point of law. *Campbell v Edwards* [1976] CLY 1533; *Baber v Kenwood Manufacturing Co* [1978] CLY 325; *Jones v Sherwood Computer Service* [1992] 1 WLR 277 CA (independent accountant acting as expert); *Pontsam Investments v Kansallis – Osake – Pankki* [1992] 22 EG 103 (expert surveyor had addressed himself to the correct question, whether or not his answer was wrong, and so his decision was final and binding).

Immunity from actions—Although arbitrators enjoy immunity from actions for negligence in the performance of their duties, experts do not. *Aarensen v Casson Beckman Rutley & Co* [1977] AC 405.

30 General provisions applying to arbitrations under Act

(1) Any matter which is required to be determined by arbitration under this Act shall be determined by the arbitration of a sole arbitrator.

(2) Any application under this Act to the President of the RICS for the appointment of an arbitrator by him must be made in writing and must be accompanied by such reasonable fee as the President may determine in respect of the costs of making the appointment.

(3) Where an arbitrator appointed for the purposes of this Act dies or is incapable of acting and no new arbitrator has been appointed by agreement, either party may apply to the President of the RICS for the appointment of a new arbitrator by him.

Miscellaneous

31 Mortgages of agricultural land

(1) Section 99 of the Law of Property Act 1925 (leasing powers of mortgagor and mortgagee in possession) shall be amended in accordance with subsections (2) and (3) below.

(2) At the beginning of subsection (13), there shall be inserted 'Subject to subsection (13A) below,'.

(3) After that subsection, there shall be inserted—

'(13A) Subsection (13) of this section—

  (a) shall not enable the application of any provision of this section to be excluded or restricted in relation to any mortgage of agricultural land made after 1st March 1948 but before 1st September 1995, and
  (b) shall not enable the power to grant a lease of an agricultural holding to which, by virtue of section 4 of the Agricultural Tenancies Act 1995, the Agricultural Holdings Act 1986 will apply, to be excluded or restricted in relation to any mortgage of agricultural land made on or after 1st September 1995.

(13B) In subsection (13A) of this section—

  'agricultural holding' has the same meaning as in the Agricultural Holdings Act 1986; and
  'agricultural land' has the same meaning as in the Agriculture Act 1947.'

(4) Paragraph 12 of Schedule 14 to the Agricultural Holdings Act 1986 (which excludes the application of subsection (13) of section 99 of the Law of Property Act 1925 in relation to a mortgage of agricultural land and is superseded by the amendments made by subsections (1) to (3) above) shall cease to have effect.

Explanatory text—see para **9.7**.
  Since 1948, agricultural holdings legislation has prevented mortgagees from restricting the letting of agricultural land. This has led to some cases of land being let to avoid possession being obtained by the

mortgagee on default of the borrower. See *Agricultural Mortgage Corporation v Woodward* [1994] EGCS 98. The section enables lenders to place restrictions on letting agricultural land where mortgages are created on or after 1 September 1995 provided the tenancies will not be agricultural holdings governed by the Agricultural Holdings Act 1986 by virtue of s 4 of the 1995 Act.

32 Power of limited owners to give consents etc.

The landlord under a farm business tenancy, whatever his estate or interest in the holding, may, for the purposes of this Act, give any consent, make any agreement or do or have done to him any other act which he might give, make, do or have done to him if he were owner in fee simple or, if his interest is an interest in a leasehold, were absolutely entitled to that leasehold.

Explanatory text—see para **9.2**.

Derivation—This is derived from the Agricultural Holdings Act 1986, s 88.

33 Power to apply and raise capital money

(1) The purposes authorised by section 73 of the Settled Land Act 1925 (either as originally enacted or as applied in relation to trusts for sale by section 28 of the Law of Property Act 1925) or section 26 of the Universities and College Estates Act 1925 for the application of capital money shall include—

(a) the payment of expenses incurred by a landlord under a farm business tenancy in, or in connection with, the making of any physical improvement on the holding,

(b) the payment of compensation under section 16 of this Act, and

(c) the payment of the costs, charges and expenses incurred by him on a reference to arbitration under section 19 or 22 of this Act.

(2) The purposes authorised by section 71 of the Settled Land Act 1925 (either as originally enacted or as applied in relation to trusts for sale by section 28 of the Law of Property Act 1925) as purposes for which money may be raised by mortgage shall include the payment of compensation under section 16 of this Act.

(3) Where the landlord under a farm business tenancy—

(a) is a tenant for life or in a fiduciary position, and

(b) is liable to pay compensation under section 16 of this Act,

he may require the sum payable as compensation and any costs, charges and expenses incurred by him in connection with the tenant's claim under that section to be paid out of any capital money held on the same trusts as the settled land.

(4) In subsection (3) above—

'capital money' includes any personal estate held on the same trusts as the land; and 'settled land' includes land held on trust for sale or vested in a personal representative.

Explanatory text—see para **9.3**.

Subsection (1)—The Settled Land Act 1925, s 73 sets out the investment powers of the Trustees under a strict settlement. These powers are given to trustees of a trust for sale by the Law of Property Act 1925, s 28. The Universities and Colleges Estates Act 1925 applies to the universities of Oxford (including Christchurch), Cambridge and Durham and their colleges and the schools of Winchester and Eton. Section 26 sets out the modes of investment and application of capital money. The Agricultural Tenancies Act 1995, s 33 provides that capital money may be applied under those Acts for improvements executed by the landlord or compensation paid to the tenant for approved improvements made by the tenant. Capital money may also be spent on costs, charges and expenses where a tenant goes to arbitration on the refusal, failure or imposition of unacceptable conditions, for consent to an improvement, or where there is a reference to arbitration for the settlement of a compensation claim.

These provisions reverse the position under the Agricultural Holdings Act 1986, s 88. Statutory interpretation of that section (and its predecessors) prevented capital money from being paid for compensation to a tenant for improvements but enabled capital money to be paid for repairs. See *Re Duke of Wellington's Estate* [1971] 2 All ER 1140, *Re Duke of Northumberland* [1950] 2 All ER 1181, *Re Lord Brougham and Vaux's Settled Estates* [1953] 2 All ER 1039, Harman J in *Re Sutherland Settlement Trusts* [1953] 2 All ER 27 declined to follow *Re Duke of Northumberland* where expenditure on repairs had been incurred on repairs before the coming into force of the Agricultural Holdings Act 1948. In *Re Winn* [1955] 2 All ER 865, Harman J refused to extend the principle of *Re Duke of Northumberland* to a life tenant under a trust for sale. In *Re Boston's Wills Trust*, Vaisey J the judge in *Re Duke of Northumberland* and *Re Lord Brougham and Vaux's Settled Estates* showed some unease about his earlier decisions.

The Agricultural Tenancy Act 1995, s 32 is in accord with the general principles of accounting between the life tenant and remaindermen under a trust and also with the Landlord and Tenant Act 1927, s 13.

Subsection (2)—The Settled Land 1925, s 71 enables a tenant for life to raise money by legal mortgage for specified purposes. These purposes are extended by s 33(2) to include payment of compensation to a tenant for improvements.

Subsection (3)—This gives the tenant for life power to demand that compensation under s 16 and any costs, charges or expenses in connection with the claim should be paid out of capital money.

---

34   Estimation of best rent for purposes of Acts and other instruments

(1) In estimating the best rent or reservation in the nature of rent of land comprised in a farm business tenancy for the purposes of a relevant instrument, it shall not be necessary to take into account against the tenant any increase in the value of that land arising from any tenant's improvements.

(2) In subsection (1) above—

'a relevant instrument' means any Act of Parliament, deed or other instrument which authorises a lease to be made on the condition that the best rent or reservation in the nature of rent is reserved;

'tenant's improvement' has the meaning given by section 15 of this Act.

Explanatory text—see para **9.5**

Derivation—This is derived from the Agricultural Holdings Act 1986, s 90.

Best rent—The Settled Land Act 1925, s 41 gives the tenant for life power to grant leases provided the conditions in s 42 are fulfilled. One of these conditions is that the best rent must be obtained. The Law of Property Act 1925, s 99 gives the mortgagor and mortgagee in possession power to grant leases provided the best rent is reserved. The Law of Property Act 1925, s 54(2) provides that leases taking effect in possession for a term not exceeding three years at the best rent which can reasonably be obtained without taking a fine can be made orally or in writing. The disregards reflect the disregards on a rent review; see s 13.

---

35   Preparation of documents etc. by valuers and surveyors

(1) Section 22 of the Solicitors Act 1974 (unqualified person not to prepare certain instruments) shall be amended as follows.

(2) In subsection (2), after paragraph (ab) there shall be inserted—

'(ac) any accredited person drawing or preparing any instrument—

   (i)   which creates, or which he believes on reasonable grounds will create, a farm business tenancy (within the meaning of the Agricultural Tenancies Act 1995), or

   (ii)   which relates to an existing tenancy which is, or which he believes on reasonable grounds to be, such a tenancy;'.

(3) In subsection (3A), immediately before the definition of 'registered trade mark agent' there shall be inserted—

'"accredited person" means any person who is—

(a)   a Full Member of the Central Association of Agricultural Valuers,

(b)   an Associate or Fellow of the Incorporated Society of Valuers and Auctioneers, or

(c)   an Associate or Fellow of the Royal Institution of Chartered Surveyors;'.

Explanatory text—see para **4.6**.

Preparing the farm business tenancy—Under the Solicitors Act 1974, s 22 it is an offence for an unqualified person (someone who is not a solicitor, barrister, licensed conveyancer, a notary public, an authorised practitioner and some public officers) to draw up for fee or reward a lease or a contract for a lease exceeding three years. This enables surveyors and others belonging to authorised bodies to draw up farm business tenancies even where they exceed three years.

Supplemental

36   Service of notices

(1) This section applies to any notice or other document required or authorised to be given under this Act.

(2) A notice or other document to which this section applies is duly given to a person if—

(a)   it is delivered to him,

(b)   it is left at his proper address, or

(c)   it is given to him in a manner authorised by a written agreement made, at any time before the giving of the notice, between him and the person giving the notice.

(3) A notice or other document to which this section applies is not duly given to a person if its text is transmitted to him by facsimile or other electronic means otherwise than by virtue of subsection (2)(c) above.

(4) Where a notice or other document to which this section applies is to be given to a body corporate, the notice or document is duly given if it is given to the secretary or clerk of that body.

(5) Where—

   (a) a notice or other document to which this section applies is to be given to a landlord under a farm business tenancy and an agent or servant of his is responsible for the control of the management of the holding, or

   (b) such a document is to be given to a tenant under a farm business tenancy and an agent or servant of his is responsible for the carrying on of a business on the holding,

the notice or document is duly given if it is given to that agent or servant.

(6) For the purposes of this section, the proper address of any person to whom a notice or other document to which this section applies is to be given is—

   (a) in the case of the secretary or clerk of a body corporate, the registered or principal office of that body, and

   (b) in any other case, the last known address of the person in question.

(7) Unless or until the tenant under a farm business tenancy has received—

   (a) notice that the person who before that time was entitled to receive the rents and profits of the holding ('the original landlord') has ceased to be so entitled, and

   (b) notice of the name and address of the person who has become entitled to receive the rents and profits,

any notice or other document given to the original landlord by the tenant shall be deemed for the purposes of this Act to have been given to the landlord under the tenancy.

Explanatory text—see para **12.10**.

Methods of service—Many provisions of the Act rely on the prior service of notices. It is therefore important that there are clear rules as to what amounts to service. Although it seems that service by facsimile is effective service (see *The Pendrecht* [1980] 2LL R 56, at p 65, service by telex valid service of notice for the purpose of arbitration), for the purposes of the Agricultural Tenancies Act 1995, it will be effective only if it has been authorised in a written agreement between the parties. The parties could specify other methods of service including Document Exchange. If there were no agreement then it would be a question of proving that a notice has been delivered to a person or left at his proper address.

Subsection (2)—The tenant should be informed of a change of landlord otherwise notice served on a former landlord by a tenant will be deemed to have been duly served. The Landlord and Tenant Act 1987, s 48 applies to farm business tenancies. See *Dallhold Estates (UK) Pty Ltd v Lindsey Trading Properties Inc* [1994] 17 EG 148; *Rogan v Woodfield Buildings* [1995] 20 EG 132.

---

37 Crown land

(1) This Act shall apply in relation to land in which there subsists, or has at any material time subsisted, a Crown interest as it applies in relation to land in which no such interest subsists or has ever subsisted.

(2) For the purposes of this Act—

   (a) where an interest belongs to Her Majesty in right of the Crown and forms part of the Crown Estate, the Crown Estate Commissioners shall be treated as the owner of the interest,

(b) where an interest belongs to Her Majesty in right of the Crown and does not form part of the Crown Estate, the government department having the management of the land or, if there is no such department, such person as Her Majesty may appoint in writing under the Royal Sign Manual shall be treated as the owner of the interest,

(c) where an interest belongs to Her Majesty in right of the Duchy of Lancaster, the Chancellor of the Duchy shall be treated as the owner of the interest,

(d) where an interest belongs to a government department or is held in trust for Her Majesty for the purposes of a government department, that department shall be treated as the owner of the interest, and

(e) where an interest belongs to the Duchy of Cornwall, such person as the Duke of Cornwall or the possessor for the time being of the Duchy of Cornwall appoints shall be treated as the owner of the interest and, in the case where the interest is that of landlord, may do any act or thing which a landlord is authorised or required to do under this Act.

(3) If any question arises as to who is to be treated as the owner of a Crown interest, that question shall be referred to the Treasury, whose decision shall be final.

(4) In subsections (1) and (3) above 'Crown interest' means an interest which belongs to Her Majesty in right of the Crown or of the Duchy of Lancaster or to the Duchy of Cornwall, or to a government department, or which is held in trust for Her Majesty for the purposes of a government department.

(5) Any compensation payable under section 16 of this Act by the Chancellor of the Duchy of Lancaster may be raised and paid under section 25 of the Duchy of Lancaster Act 1817 (application of monies) as an expense incurred in improvement of land belonging to Her Majesty in right of the Duchy.

(6) In the case of land belonging to the Duchy of Cornwall, the purposes authorised by section 8 of the Duchy of Cornwall Management Act 1863 (application of monies) for the advancement of parts of such gross sums as are there mentioned shall include the payment of compensation under section 16 of this Act.

(7) Nothing in subsection (6) above shall be taken as prejudicing the operation of the Duchy of Cornwall Management Act 1982.

Explanatory text—see para **9.6**.

---

38 Interpretation

(1) In this Act, unless the context otherwise requires—

'agriculture' includes horticulture, fruit growing, seed growing, dairy farming and livestock breeding and keeping, the use of land as grazing land, meadow land, osier land, market gardens and nursery grounds, and the use of land for woodlands where that use is ancillary to the farming of land for other agricultural purposes, and 'agricultural' shall be construed accordingly;

'building' includes any part of a building;

'fixed term tenancy' means any tenancy other than a periodic tenancy;

'holding', in relation to a farm business tenancy, means the aggregate of the land comprised in the tenancy;

'landlord' includes any person from time to time deriving title from the original landlord;

'livestock' includes any creature kept for the production of food, wool, skins or fur or for the purpose of its use in the farming of land;

'the RICS' means the Royal Institution of Chartered Surveyors;

'tenancy' means any tenancy other than a tenancy at will, and includes a sub-tenancy and an agreement for a tenancy or sub-tenancy;

'tenant' includes a sub-tenant and any person deriving title from the original tenant or sub-tenant;

'termination', in relation to a tenancy, means the cesser of the tenancy by reason of effluxion of time or from any other cause.

(2) References in this Act to the farming of land include references to the carrying on in relation to land of any agricultural activity.

(3) A tenancy granted pursuant to a contract shall be taken for the purposes of this Act to have been granted when the contract was entered into.

(4) For the purposes of this Act a tenancy begins on the day on which, under the terms of the tenancy, the tenant is entitled to possession under that tenancy; and references in this Act to the beginning of the tenancy are references to that day.

(5) The designations of landlord and tenant shall continue to apply until the conclusions of any proceedings taken under this Act in respect of compensation.

Subsection (1)—Agriculture is defined in the same terms as under the Agricultural Holdings Act 1986, s 96. Cases on the Agricultural Holdings Act 1986 may be relevant. The difference is that where notices have been served before the beginning of a farm business tenancy the tenancy may shift from being primarily or wholly agricultural at the start to being minimally agricultural.

Amendments to extend the meaning of agriculture and livestock were defeated in both the House of Lords and Commons. The list of agricultural activities is not exhaustive and so there was considered to be no need for a modern definition. The main argument against a change in definition was that the Agricultural Tenancies Act 1995 definition should be in accord with the definition of agriculture in other statutes.

Subsections (3) and (4)—There is a distinction between the grant of a tenancy and the beginning of a tenancy.

---

39   Index of defined expressions
In this Act the expressions listed below are defined by or otherwise fall to be construed in accordance with the provisions indicated—

agriculture, agricultural	section 38(1)
begins, beginning (in relation to a tenancy)	section 38(4)
building	section 38(1)
farm business tenancy	section 1
farming (of land)	section 38(2)
fixed term tenancy	section 38(1)

grant (of a tenancy)	section 38(3)
holding (in relation to a farm business tenancy)	section 38(1)
landlord	section 38(1) and (5)
livestock	section 38(1)
planning permission (in Part III)	section 27
provision (of a tenant's improvement) (in Part III)	section 15
the review date (in Part II)	section 10(2)
the RICS	section 38(1)
statutory review notice (in Part II)	section 10(1)
tenancy	section 38(1)
tenant	section 38(1) and (5)
tenant's improvement (in Part III)	section 15
termination (of a tenancy)	section 38(1).

Definitions—It is unusual, but useful, to have an index of definitions.

40   Consequential amendments

The Schedule to this Act (which contains consequential amendments) shall have effect.

41   Short title, commencement and extent

(1) This Act may be cited as the Agricultural Tenancies Act 1995.

(2) This Act shall come into force on 1st September 1995.

(3) Subject to subsection (4) below, this Act extends to England and Wales only.

(4) The amendment by a provision of the Schedule to this Act of an enactment which extends to Scotland or Northern Ireland also extends there, except that paragraph 9 of the Schedule does not extend to Northern Ireland.

Commencement—The Act was given a definite starting date, rather than a specified period after Royal Assent, for greater clarity. It enabled parties to plan ahead especially for new lettings beginning at Michaelmas 1995.

SECTION 40

SCHEDULE

CONSEQUENTIAL AMENDMENTS

The Small Holdings and Allotments Act 1908 (c 36)

1 (1) Section 47 of the Small Holdings and Allotments Act 1908 (compensation for improvements) shall be amended as follows.

(2) In subsection (1), after 'to any tenant' there shall be inserted 'otherwise than under a farm business tenancy'.

(3) In subsection (2), after 'small holdings or allotments' there shall be inserted 'otherwise than under a farm business tenancy'.

(4) In subsection (3), after 'if' there shall be inserted 'he is not a tenant under a farm business tenancy and'.

(5) In subsection (4), after 'allotment' there shall be inserted 'who is not a tenant under a farm business tenancy'.

(6) After that subsection, there shall be inserted—

'(5) In this section, 'farm business tenancy' has the same meaning as in the Agricultural Tenancies Act 1995.'

The Law of Distress Amendment Act 1908 (c 53)

2 In section 4(1) of the Law of Distress Amendment Act 1908 (exclusion of certain goods), for 'to which that section applies' there shall be substituted 'on land comprised in a tenancy to which that Act applies'.

The Allotments Act 1922 (c 51)

3 In section 3(7) of the Allotments Act 1922 (provision as to cottage holdings and certain allotments), after 'landlord' there shall be inserted 'otherwise than under a farm business tenancy (within the meaning of the Agricultural Tenancies Act 1995)'.

4 In section 6(1) of that Act (assessment and recovery of compensation), after 'contract of tenancy' there shall be inserted '(not being a farm business tenancy within the meaning of the Agricultural Tenancies Act 1995)'.

The Landlord and Tenant Act 1927 (c 36)

5 In section 17(1) of the Landlord and Tenant Act 1927 (holdings to which Part I applies), for the words from 'not being' to the end there is substituted 'not being—

(a) agricultural holdings within the meaning of the Agricultural Holdings Act 1986 held under leases in relation to which that Act applies, or
(b) holdings held under farm business tenancies within the meaning of the Agricultural Tenancies Act 1995.'

6 In section 19(4) of that Act (provisions as to covenants not to assign etc. without licence or consent), after 'the Agricultural Holdings Act 1986' there shall be inserted 'which are leases in relation to which that Act applies, or to farm business tenancies within the meaning of the Agricultural Tenancies Act 1995'.

The Agricultural Credits Act 1928 (c 43)

7 In section 5(7) of the Agricultural Credits Act 1928 (agricultural charges on farming stock and assets) in the definition of 'other agricultural assets', after 'otherwise' there shall be inserted 'a tenant's right to compensation under section 16 of the Agricultural Tenancies Act 1995,'.

The Leasehold Property (Repairs) Act 1938 (c 34)

8 In section 7(1) of the Leasehold Property (Repairs) Act 1938 (interpretation), at the end there shall be added 'which is a lease in relation to which that Act applies and not being a farm business tenancy within the meaning of the Agricultural Tenancies Act 1995'.

The Reserve and Auxiliary Forces (Protection of Civil Interests) Act 1951 (c 65)

9 (1) Section 27 of the Reserve and Auxiliary Forces (Protection of Civil Interests) Act 1951 (renewal of tenancy expiring during period of service or within two months thereafter) shall be amended as follows.

(2) In subsection (1), for the words from 'are an agricultural holding' onwards there shall be substituted—

'(a) are an agricultural holding (within the meaning of the Agricultural Holdings Act 1986) held under a tenancy in relation to which that Act applies,
(b) are a holding (other than a holding excepted from this provision) held under a farm business tenancy, or
(c) consist of or comprise premises (other than premises excepted from this provision) licensed for the sale of intoxicating liquor for consumption on the premises.'

(3) In subsection (5), after paragraph (b) there shall be inserted—

'(bb) the expressions 'farm business tenancy' and 'holding', in relation to such a tenancy, have the same meaning as in the Agricultural Tenancies Act 1995;'.

(4) After that subsection, there shall be inserted—

'(5A) In paragraph (b) of the proviso to subsection (1) of this section the reference to a holding excepted from the provision is a reference to a holding held under a farm business tenancy in which there is comprised a dwelling-house occupied by the person responsible for the control (whether as tenant or servant or agent of the tenant) of the management of the holding.'

(5) In subsection (6), for the words from the beginning to 'liquor' there shall be substituted 'In paragraph (c) of the proviso to subsection (1) of this section, the reference to premises excepted from the provision'.

The Landlord and Tenant Act 1954 (c 56)

10   In section 43(1) of the Landlord and Tenant Act 1954 (tenancies excluded from Part II)—

(a)   in paragraph (a), for the words from 'or a tenancy' to '1986' there shall be substituted 'which is a tenancy in relation to which the Agricultural Holdings Act 1986 applies or a tenancy which would be a tenancy of an agricultural holding in relation to which that Act applied if subsection (3) of section 2 of that Act', and

(b)   after that paragraph there shall be inserted—

'(aa)   to a farm business tenancy;'.

11   In section 51(1) of that Act (extension of Leasehold Property (Repairs) Act 1938), for paragraph (c) there shall be substituted—

'(c)   that the tenancy is neither a tenancy of an agricultural holding in relation to which the Agricultural Holdings Act 1986 applies nor a farm business tenancy'.

12   In section 69(1) of that Act (interpretation), after the definition of 'development corporation' there shall be inserted—

'farm business tenancy' has the same meaning as in the Agricultural Tenancies Act 1995;'.

The Opencast Coal Act 1958 (c 69)

13   (1) Section 14 of the Opencast Coal Act 1958 (provisions as to agricultural tenancies in England and Wales) shall be amended as follows.

(2) In subsection (1)(b), for 'or part of an agricultural holding' there shall be substituted 'held under a tenancy in relation to which the Agricultural Holdings Act 1986 (in this Act referred to as 'the Act of 1986') applies or part of such an agricultural holding'.

(3) In subsection (2), for the words from 'Agricultural' to 'of 1986')' there shall be substituted 'Act of 1986'.

14   After section 14A of that Act, there shall be inserted—

'14B   Provisions as to farm business tenancies
(1) Without prejudice to the provisions of Part III of this Act as to matters arising between landlords and tenants in consequence of compulsory rights orders, the provisions of this section shall have effect where—

(a)   opencast planning permission has been granted subject to a restoration condition, and

(b)   immediately before that permission is granted, any of the land comprised therein consists of the holding or part of the holding held under a farm business tenancy,

whether any of that land is comprised in a compulsory rights order or not.

(2) For the purposes of section 1 of the Agricultural Tenancies Act 1995 (in this Act referred to as 'the Act of 1995'), the land shall be taken, while it is occupied or used for the permitted activities, to be used for the purposes for which it was used immediately before it was occupied or used for the permitted activities.

(3) For the purposes of the Act of 1995, nothing done or omitted by the tenant or by the landlord under the tenancy by way of permitting any of the land in respect of which opencast planning permission has been granted to be occupied for the purpose of carrying on any of the permitted activities, or by way of facilitating the use of any of that land for that purpose, shall be taken to be a breach of any term or condition of the tenancy, either on the part of the tenant or on the part of the landlord.

(4) In determining under subsections (1) and (2) of section 13 of the Act of 1995 the rent which should be properly payable for the holding, in respect of any period for which the person with the benefit of the opencast planning permission is in occupation of the holding, or of any part thereof, for the purpose of carrying on any of the permitted activities, the arbitrator shall disregard any increase or diminution in the rental value of the holding in so far as that increase or diminution is attributable to the occupation of the holding, or of that part of the holding, by that person for the purpose of carrying on any of the permitted activities.

(5) In this section 'holding', in relation to a farm business tenancy, has the same meaning as in the Act of 1995.

(6) This section does not extend to Scotland.'

15 (1) Section 24 of that Act (tenant's right to compensation for improvements and other matters) shall be amended as follows.

(2) In subsection (1)(a), after 'holding' there shall be inserted 'held under a tenancy in relation to which the Act of 1986 applies'.

(3) In subsection (10), after 'Scotland' there shall be inserted 'the words "held under a tenancy in relation to which the Act of 1986 applies" in subsection (1)(a) of this section shall be omitted and'.

16 After section 25 of that Act, there shall be inserted—

'25A Tenant's right to compensation for improvements etc.: farm business tenancies

(1) The provisions of this section shall have effect where—

    (a) any part of the land comprised in a compulsory rights order is held, immediately before the date of entry, under a farm business tenancy;

    (b) there have been provided in relation to the land which is both so comprised and so held ('the tenant's land') tenant's improvements in respect of which, immediately before that date, the tenant had a prospective right to compensation under section 16 of the Act of 1995 on quitting the holding on the termination of the tenancy;

(c) at the end of the period of occupation, the tenant's land has lost the benefit of any such improvement; and

(d) immediately after the end of that period, the tenant's land is comprised in the same tenancy as immediately before the date of entry, or is comprised in a subsequent farm business tenancy at the end of which the tenant is not deprived, by virtue of section 23(3) of that Act, of his right to compensation under section 16 of that Act in respect of any tenant's improvement provided during the earlier tenancy in relation to the tenant's land.

(2) For the purposes of subsection (1) of this section, subsection (2) of section 22 of the Act of 1995 (which requires notice to be given of the intention to make a claim) shall be disregarded.

(3) Subject to subsection (4) of this section, Part III of the Act of 1995 shall apply as if—

(a) the tenant's land were in the state in which it was immediately before the date of entry, and

(b) the tenancy under which that land is held at the end of the period of occupation had terminated immediately after the end of that period and the tenant had then quitted the holding.

(4) Where the tenant's land has lost the benefit of some tenant's improvements but has not lost the benefit of all of them, Part III of the Act of 1995 shall apply as mentioned in subsection (3) above, but as if the improvements of which the tenant's land has not lost the benefit had not been tenant's improvements.

(5) For the purposes of subsections (1) and (4) of this section, the tenant's land shall be taken to have lost the benefit of a tenant's improvement if the benefit of that improvement has been lost (wholly or in part) without being replaced by another improvement of comparable benefit to the land.

(6) In this section 'holding', in relation to a farm business tenancy, 'tenant's improvement', 'termination', in relation to a tenancy, and references to the provision of a tenant's improvement have the same meaning as in the Act of 1995.

(7) This section does not extend to Scotland.'

17 (1) Section 26 of that Act (compensation for short-term improvements and related matters) shall be amended as follows.

(2) In subsection (1), after 'agricultural land' there shall be inserted 'and was not comprised in a farm business tenancy'.

(3) In subsection (6), after 'Scotland' there shall be inserted—

'(za) in subsection (1) of this section, the words 'and was not comprised in a farm business tenancy' shall be omitted;'.

18 (1) Section 28 of that Act (special provision as to market gardens) shall be amended as follows.

(2) In subsection (1), after 'market garden' there shall be inserted 'and was not comprised in a farm business tenancy.'

(3) In subsection (6), after 'Scotland' there shall be inserted 'in subsection (1) of this section, the words 'and was not comprised in a farm business tenancy' shall be omitted; and'.

19 In section 51 of that Act (interpretation) in subsection (1)—

(a) after the definition of 'the Act of 1986' there shall be inserted—

'"the Act of 1995" means the Agricultural Tenancies Act 1995;' and

(b) after the definition of 'emergency powers' there shall be inserted—

'"farm business tenancy" has the same meaning as in the Act of 1995;'.

20 (1) Schedule 7 to that Act (adjustments between landlords and tenants and in respect of mortgages and mining leases and orders) shall be amended as follows.

(2) After paragraph 1, there shall be inserted—

'1A (1) The provisions of this paragraph shall have effect where—

(a) paragraphs (a) and (b) of subsection (1) of section 25A of this Act apply, and
(b) the farm business tenancy at the end of which the tenant could have claimed compensation for tenant's improvements terminates on or after the date of entry, but before the end of the period of occupation, without being succeeded by another such subsequent tenancy.

(2) In the circumstances specified in sub-paragraph (1) of this paragraph, the provisions of Part III of the Act of 1995—

(a) shall apply, in relation to the tenancy mentioned in that sub-paragraph, as if, at the termination of that tenancy, the land in question were in the state in which it was immediately before the date of entry, and
(b) if the tenant under that tenancy quitted the holding before the termination of his tenancy, shall so apply as if he had quitted the holding on the termination of his tenancy.

(3) In sub-paragraph (2) of this paragraph, 'holding', in relation to a farm business tenancy, and 'termination', in relation to a tenancy, have the same meaning as in the Act of 1995.'

(3) In paragraph 2, in sub-paragraph (1), after 'agricultural holding' there shall be inserted 'held under a tenancy in relation to which the Act of 1986 applies'.

(4) After that paragraph there shall be inserted—

'2A (1) The provisions of this paragraph shall have effect where land comprised in a farm business tenancy is comprised in a compulsory rights order (whether any other land is comprised in the holding, or comprised in the order, or not), and—

(a) before the date of entry there had been provided in relation to the land in question tenant's improvements (in this paragraph referred to as 'the former tenant's improvements') in respect of which, immediately before that date, the tenant had a prospective right to compensation under section 16 of the Act of 1995 on quitting the holding on the termination of the tenancy, and

(b) at the end of the period of occupation the circumstances are such that Part III of that Act would have applied as mentioned in subsections (3) and (4) of section 25A of this Act, but for the fact that the benefit of the former tenant's improvements has been replaced, on the restoration of the land, by other improvements (in this paragraph referred to as 'the new improvements') of comparable benefit to the land.

(2) In the circumstances specified in sub-paragraph (1) of this paragraph, Part III of the Act of 1995 shall have effect in relation to the new improvements as if those improvements were tenant's improvements.

(3) Subsections (2) and (6) of section 25A of this Act shall apply for the purposes of this paragraph as they apply for the purposes of that section.'

(5) After paragraph 3 there shall be inserted—

'**3A** Where by virtue of section 25A of this Act a tenant is entitled to compensation for tenant's improvements as mentioned in that section and—

(a) after the end of the period of occupation expenses are incurred in replacing the benefit of the tenant's improvements by other improvements of comparable benefit to the land, and

(b) the person incurring those expenses (whether he is the landlord or not) is entitled to compensation in respect of those expenses under section 22 of this Act,

section 13 of the Act shall apply as if the works in respect of which those expenses are incurred were not tenant's improvements, if apart from this paragraph they would constitute such improvements.'

(6) At the end of paragraph 4, there shall be added—

'(7) In this paragraph "agricultural holding" does not include an agricultural holding held under a farm business tenancy.'

(7) After that paragraph there shall be inserted—

'**4A** (1) The provisions of this paragraph shall apply where—

(a) immediately before the operative date of a compulsory rights order, any of the land comprised in the order is subject to a farm business tenancy, and

(b) that tenancy continues until after the end of the period of occupation.

(2) The landlord or tenant under the tenancy may, by notice in writing served on his tenant or landlord, demand a reference to arbitration of the question whether any of the terms and conditions of the tenancy (including any term or condition relating to rent) should be varied in consequence of any change in the state of the land resulting from the occupation or use of the land in the exercise of rights conferred by the order; and subsection (3) of section 28 of the Act of 1995 shall apply in relation to a notice under this sub-paragraph as it applies in relation to a notice under subsection (2) of that section.

(3) On a reference by virtue of this paragraph, the arbitrator shall determine what variations (if any) should be made in the terms and conditions of the tenancy, and the date (not being earlier than the end of the period of occupation) from which any such variations are to take effect or to be treated as having taken effect; and as from that date the tenancy shall have effect, or, as the case may be, shall be treated as having had effect, subject to any variations determined by the arbitrator under this paragraph.

(4) The provisions of this paragraph shall not affect any right of the landlord or the tenant, or the jurisdiction of the arbitrator, under Part II of the Act of 1995; but where—

    (a)   there is a reference by virtue of this paragraph and a reference under Part II of that Act in respect of the same tenancy, and

    (b)   it appears to the arbitrator that the reference under Part II of that Act relates wholly or mainly to the consequences of the occupation or use of the land in the exercise of rights conferred by the order,

he may direct that proceedings on the two references shall be taken concurrently.'

(8) In paragraph 5(1), after 'agricultural holding' there shall be inserted 'held under a tenancy in relation to which the Act of 1986 applies'.

(9) In paragraph 6—

    (a)   in sub-paragraph (1), for 'an agricultural holding' there shall be substituted '—

        (a)   an agricultural holding held under a tenancy in relation to which the Act of 1986 applies, or

        (b)   a holding under a farm business tenancy,'; and

    (b)   after sub-paragraph (2) there shall be added—

'(2A) In sub-paragraph (1) of this paragraph, 'holding', in relation to a farm business tenancy, has the same meaning as in the Act of 1995.'

(10) In paragraph 7—

    (a)   after 'The provisions of' there shall be inserted 'sub-paragraphs (1) to (6) of';
    (b)   for 'that paragraph' there shall be substituted 'those sub-paragraphs'; and
    (c)   after 'subject to a mortgage' there shall be inserted 'but not comprised in a farm business tenancy'.

(11) After that paragraph there shall be inserted—

'**7A** The provisions of paragraph 4A of this Schedule shall apply in relation to mortgages of land comprised in farm business tenancies as they apply in relation to such tenancies, as if any reference in that paragraph to such a tenancy were a reference to such a mortgage, and any reference to a landlord or to a tenant were a reference to a mortgagee or to a mortgagor, as the case may be.'

(12) In paragraph 12(1)(a), for the words from 'did' to 'holding' there shall be substituted 'was not comprised in a tenancy in relation to which the Act of 1986 applies or in a farm business tenancy'.

(13) In paragraph 13, after 'or to a tenancy' there shall be inserted '(other than a reference to a tenancy in relation to which the Act of 1986 applies or a farm business tenancy)'.

(14) In paragraph 25—

   (a) in sub-paragraph (a), at the beginning there shall be inserted 'subject to sub-paragraphs (ba), (bc), (bd)(i) and (be) of this paragraph,';
   (b) after sub-paragraph (b), there shall be inserted—

   '(ba) in sub-paragraph (1) of paragraph 2, the words 'held under a tenancy in relation to which the Act of 1986 applies' shall be omitted;
   (bb) sub-paragraph (7) of paragraph 4 shall be omitted;
   (bc) in sub-paragraph (1) of paragraph 5, the words 'held under a tenancy in relation to which the Act of 1986 applies' shall be omitted;
   (bd) in paragraph (6)—

      (i) for paragraphs (a) and (b) of sub-paragraph (1) there shall be substituted the words 'an agricultural holding'; and
      (ii) sub-paragraph (2A) shall be omitted;

   (be) in sub-paragraph (1)(a) of paragraph 12, for the words 'was not comprised in a tenancy in relation to which the Act of 1986 applies or in a farm business tenancy' there shall be substituted the words 'did not constitute or form part of an agricultural holding';' and

   (c) in sub-paragraph (c), for '7' there shall be substituted '1A, 2A, 3A, 4A, 7, 7A'.

The Agriculture (Miscellaneous Provisions) Act 1963 (c 11)

21 (1) Section 22 of the Agriculture (Miscellaneous Provisions) Act 1963 (allowances to persons displaced from agricultural land) shall be amended as follows.

(2) In subsection (1), for paragraph (a) there shall be substituted—

'(a) the land—

   (i) is used for the purposes of agriculture (within the meaning of the Agricultural Tenancies Act 1995) and is so used by way of a trade or business, or
   (ii) is not so used but is comprised in a farm business tenancy (within the meaning of the Agricultural Tenancies Act 1995) and used for the purposes of a trade or business,'.

(3) In subsection (6)(c), for 'the Agricultural Holdings Act 1986' there shall be substituted ', the Agricultural Tenancies Act 1995'.

The Leasehold Reform Act 1967 (c 88)

22 In section 1(3) of the Leasehold Reform Act 1967 (tenants entitled to enfranchisement or extension), for paragraph (b) there shall be substituted—

'(b) it is comprised in—

   (i) an agricultural holding within the meaning of the Agricultural Holdings Act 1986 held under a tenancy in relation to which that Act applies, or

(ii)   the holding held under a farm business tenancy within the meaning of the
        Agricultural Tenancies Act 1995.'

The Agriculture (Miscellaneous Provisions) Act 1968 (c 34)

23   In section 12 of the Agriculture (Miscellaneous Provisions) Act 1968 (additional
payments in consequence of compulsory acquisition etc of agricultural holdings), after
subsection (1) there shall be inserted—

'(1A) No sum shall be payable by virtue of subsection (1) of this section in respect of
any land comprised in a farm business tenancy within the meaning of the Agricultural Tenancies Act 1995.'

The Land Compensation Act 1973 (c 26)

24   In section 48 of the Land Compensation Act 1973 (compensation in respect of
agricultural holdings) at the beginning of subsection (1) there shall be inserted 'Subject
to subsection (1A) below' and after subsection (1) there shall be inserted—

'(1A) This section does not have effect where the tenancy of the agricultural
holding is a tenancy to which, by virtue of section 4 of the Agricultural Tenancies
Act 1995, the Agricultural Holdings Act 1986 does not apply.'

The Rent (Agriculture) Act 1976 (c 80)

25   (1) Section 9 of the Rent (Agriculture) Act 1976 (effect of determination of
superior tenancy, etc) shall be amended as follows.

(2) In subsection (3), after 'the Agricultural Holdings Act 1986' there shall be inserted
'held under a tenancy in relation to which that Act applies and land comprised in a
farm business tenancy within the meaning of the Agricultural Tenancies Act 1995.'

(3) In subsection (4), for the words from 'or' at the end of paragraph (b) onwards there
shall be substituted—

'(c)   a tenancy of an agricultural holding within the meaning of the Agricultural
        Holdings Act 1986 which is a tenancy in relation to which that Act applies; or
(d)   a farm business tenancy within the meaning of the Agricultural Tenancies Act
        1995.'

26   In Schedule 2 to that Act (meaning of 'relevant licence' and 'relevant tenancy'), in
paragraph 2 for the words from 'and a tenancy' to the end there shall be substituted ', a
tenancy of an agricultural holding within the meaning of the Agricultural Holdings
Act 1986 which is a tenancy in relation to which that Act applies, and a farm business
tenancy within the meaning of the Agricultural Tenancies Act 1995.'

The Rent Act 1977 (c 42)

27   For section 10 of the Rent Act 1977 there shall be substituted—

'10 'Agricultural holdings etc

(1) A tenancy is not a protected tenancy if—

(a) the dwelling-house is comprised in an agricultural holding and is occupied by the person responsible for the control (whether as tenant or as servant or agent of the tenant) of the farming of the holding, or

(b) the dwelling-house is comprised in the holding held under a farm business tenancy and is occupied by the person responsible for the control (whether as tenant or as servant or agent of the tenant) of the management of the holding.

(2) In subsection (1) above—

'agricultural holding' means any agricultural holding within the meaning of the Agricultural Holdings Act 1986 held under a tenancy in relation to which that Act applies, and

'farm business tenancy', and 'holding' in relation to such a tenancy, have the same meaning as in the Agricultural Tenancies Act 1995.'

28 (1) Section 137 of that Act (effect on sub-tenancy of determination of superior tenancy) shall be amended as follows.

(2) In subsection (3), after 'the Agricultural Holdings Act 1986' there shall be inserted 'held under a tenancy to which that Act applies and land comprised in a farm business tenancy within the meaning of the Agricultural Tenancies Act 1995.'

(3) In subsection (4), in paragraph (c), for the words from 'applies' onwards there shall be substituted 'applies—

(i) a tenancy of an agricultural holding within the meaning of the Agricultural Holdings Act 1986 which is a tenancy in relation to which that Act applies, or

(ii) a farm business tenancy within the meaning of the Agricultural Tenancies Act 1995.'

The Protection from Eviction Act 1977 (c 43)

29 In section 8(1) of the Protection from Eviction Act 1977 (interpretation)—

(a) in paragraph (d), after 'Agricultural Holdings Act 1986' there shall be inserted 'which is a tenancy in relation to which that Act applies', and

(b) at the end there shall be added—

'(g) a farm business tenancy within the meaning of the Agricultural Tenancies Act 1995.'

The Housing Act 1985 (c 68)

30 In Schedule 1 to the Housing Act 1985 (tenancies which are not secure tenancies), for paragraph 8 there shall be substituted—

'Agricultural holdings etc.

8 (1) A tenancy is not a secure tenancy if—

(a) the dwelling-house is comprised in an agricultural holding and is occupied by the person responsible for the control (whether as tenant or as servant or agent of the tenant) of the farming of the holding, or

(b) the dwelling-house is comprised in the holding held under a farm business tenancy and is occupied by the person responsible for the control (whether as tenant or as servant or agent of the tenant) of the management of the holding.

(2) In sub-paragraph (1) above—

'agricultural holding' means any agricultural holding within the meaning of the Agricultural Holdings Act 1986 held under a tenancy in relation to which that Act applies, and

'farm business tenancy', and 'holding' in relation to such a tenancy, have the same meaning as in the Agricultural Tenancies Act 1995.'

The Landlord and Tenant Act 1985 (c 70)

31   In section 14(3) of the Landlord and Tenant Act 1985 (leases to which section 11 does not apply), at the end there shall be added 'and in relation to which that Act applies or to a farm business tenancy within the meaning of the Agricultural Tenancies Act 1995.'

The Agricultural Holdings Act 1986 (c 5)

32   In Schedule 6 to the Agricultural Holdings Act 1986 (eligibility to apply for a new tenancy under Part IV of that Act), in paragraph 6 (occupation to be disregarded for purposes of occupancy condition), in sub-paragraph (1) after paragraph (d) there shall be inserted—

'(dd) under a farm business tenancy, within the meaning of the Agricultural Tenancies Act 1995, for less than five years (including a farm business tenancy which is a periodic tenancy),'.

The Housing Act 1988 (c 50)

33   In section 101(2) of the Housing Act 1988 (which relates to tenancies and licences affecting property proposed to be acquired under Part IV of that Act), after 'smallholdings)' there shall be inserted 'nor the Agricultural Tenancies Act 1995 (farm business tenancies)'.

34   In Schedule 1 to that Act (tenancies which cannot be assured tenancies), for paragraph 7 there shall be substituted—

'Tenancies of agricultural holdings etc

7 (1) A tenancy under which the dwelling-house—

(a) is comprised in an agricultural holding, and

(b) is occupied by the person responsible for the control (whether as tenant or as servant or agent of the tenant) of the farming of the holding.

(2) A tenancy under which the dwelling-house—

(a) is comprised in the holding held under a farm business tenancy, and

(b)   is occupied by the person responsible for the control (whether as tenant or as servant or agent of the tenant) of the management of the holding.

(3) In this paragraph—

'agricultural holding' means any agricultural holding within the meaning of the Agricultural Holdings Act 1986 held under a tenancy in relation to which that Act applies, and
'farm business tenancy' and 'holding', in relation to such a tenancy, have the same meaning as in the Agricultural Tenancies Act 1995.'

The Town and Country Planning Act 1990 (c 8)

35 (1) Section 65 of the Town and Country Planning Act 1990 (notice etc. of applications for planning permissions) shall be amended as follows.

(2) In subsection (2), for 'a tenant of any agricultural holding any part of which is comprised in that land' there shall be substituted 'an agricultural tenant of that land'.

(3) In subsection (8), for the definition of 'agricultural holding' there shall be substituted—

'"agricultural tenant", in relation to any land, means any person who—

(a)   is the tenant, under a tenancy in relation to which the Agricultural Holdings Act 1986 applies, of an agricultural holding within the meaning of that Act any part of which is comprised in that land; or
(b)   is the tenant, under a farm business tenancy (within the meaning of the Agricultural Tenancies Act 1995), of land any part of which is comprised in that land;'.

The Coal Mining Subsidence Act 1991 (c 45)

36 In section 21 of the Coal Mining Subsidence Act 1991 (property belonging to protected tenants) in subsection (3), after paragraph (a) there shall be inserted—

'(aa) a tenant under a farm business tenancy within the meaning of the Agricultural Tenancies Act 1995;'.

37 In Schedule 3 to that Act (property belonging to protected tenants) in paragraph 1(2), after paragraph (b) there shall be inserted—

'(bb) section 20 of the Agricultural Tenancies Act 1995;'.

Appendix II
NOTICES UNDER THE AGRICULTURAL TENANCIES ACT 1995

The Agricultural Tenancies Act 1995 does not prescribe the form of any notice served under it. The precedents set out below are guidelines only. The essential requirement is that the notices comply with the relevant section of the Act and that they are served in accordance with section 36.

1. LANDLORD'S NOTICE OF INTENTION AS TO THE TENANCY UNDER SECTION 1(4)

AGRICULTURAL TENANCIES ACT 1995

Section 1(1)(a), (4)

THE HOLDING
[name and identification of holding, by address, Ordnance Survey number or plan].

TO TENANT

[Name and Address]

I   of
[name and address of Landlord] give you notice that I intend the proposed tenancy of the above Holding to be and remain a farm business tenancy and that at its beginning the character of the tenancy will be primarily or wholly agricultural.

Signed:

Dated:

Explanation: These notices must be exchanged before the beginning of the tenancy (ie when the tenant is entitled to possession under the tenancy) or the signing of the tenancy agreement, whichever is earlier. The notice cannot be contained in the agreement itself.

2. TENANT'S NOTICE OF INTENTION AS TO THE TENANCY UNDER SECTION 1(4)

AGRICULTURAL TENANCIES ACT 1995

Section 1(1)(a), (4)

THE HOLDING
[name and identification of holding, by address, Ordnance
Survey number or plan].

TO LANDLORD

[Name and Address]

I   of
[name and address of Tenant] give you notice that I intend the proposed
tenancy of the above Holding to be and remain a farm business tenancy and
that at its beginning the character of the tenancy will be primarily or wholly
agricultural.

Signed:

Dated:

Explanation: These notices must be exchanged before the beginning of the
tenancy (ie when the tenant is entitled to possession under the
tenancy) or the signing of the tenancy agreement, whichever is
earlier. The notice cannot be contained in the agreement itself.

3. LANDLORD'S NOTICE TO TERMINATE FIXED TERM TENANCY OF OVER 2 YEARS

AGRICULTURAL TENANCIES ACT 1995

Section 5

THE HOLDING
[name and identification of holding, by address, Ordnance
Survey number or plan].

TO TENANT

[Name and Address]

I   of
[name and address of Landlord] give you notice that I intend to terminate
the tenancy of the above Holding dated   and made between
[original Landlord] (1) and [original Tenant] (2), on   being the
date fixed by the lease for the expiry of the term granted by the lease.

Signed:

Dated:

Explanation: Notice has to be served of at least twelve but less than twenty-four
months to expire on the contractual term date. Failure to serve the
notice correctly will mean that the tenancy will continue as a yearly
tenancy. For terminating a yearly tenancy, use Form 5.

Fixed term tenancies of two years and under expire automatically on
the term date without the service of any notice.

4. TENANT'S NOTICE TO TERMINATE FIXED TERM TENANCY OF OVER 2 YEARS

AGRICULTURAL TENANCIES ACT 1995

Section 5

THE HOLDING
[name and identification of holding, by address, Ordnance
Survey number or plan].

TO LANDLORD

[Name and Address]

    I   of
[name and address of Tenant] give you notice that I intend to terminate the
tenancy of the above Holding dated   and made between
[original Landlord] (1) and [original Tenant] (2), on   being the
date fixed by the lease for the expiry of the term granted by the lease.

Signed:

Dated:

Explanation: Notice has to be served of at least twelve but less than twenty-four
months to expire on the contractual term date. Failure to serve the
notice correctly will mean that the tenancy will continue as a yearly
tenancy. For terminating a yearly tenancy, use Form 6.

Fixed term tenancies of two years and under expire automatically on
the term date without the service of any notice.

5. LANDLORD'S NOTICE TO TERMINATE TENANCY FROM YEAR TO YEAR

AGRICULTURAL TENANCIES ACT 1995

Section 6

THE HOLDING
[name and identification of holding, by address, Ordnance
Survey number or plan].

TO TENANT

[Name and Address]

I   of
[name and address of Landlord] give you notice to quit the above Holding of
which you are tenant on   or at the expiration of the year of
your tenancy which shall expire next after the end of twelve months from the
service of this notice.

Signed:

Dated:

Explanation: Notice must be served of at least twelve but less than twenty-four
months expiring at the completed year of the tenancy, or where it is
a yearly tenancy which arises automatically on the expiration of the
fixed term, between twelve and twenty-four months expiring on the
anniversary of the fixed term.

6. TENANT'S NOTICE TO TERMINATE TENANCY FROM YEAR TO YEAR

AGRICULTURAL TENANCIES ACT 1995

Section 6

THE HOLDING
[name and identification of holding, by address, Ordnance
Survey number or plan].

TO LANDLORD

[Name and Address]

> I   of
> [name and address of Tenant] give you notice of my intention to quit and
> deliver up possession of the above Holding which I hold as tenant from you
> on   or at the expiration of the year of the tenancy which shall
> expire after the end of twelve months from the date of service of this notice.

Signed:

Dated:

Explanation: Notice must be served of at least twelve but less than twenty-four
months expiring at the completed year of the tenancy, or where it is
a yearly tenancy which arises automatically on the expiration of the
fixed term, between twelve and twenty-four months expiring on the
anniversary of the fixed term.

7. LANDLORD'S NOTICE TO EXERCISE OPTION TO TERMINATE TENANCY OF WHOLE OR PART

AGRICULTURAL TENANCIES ACT 1995

Section 7

THE HOLDING
[name and identification of holding, by address, Ordnance
Survey number or plan].

TO TENANT

[Name and Address]

I   of
[name and address of Landlord] in accordance with Clause   of the
Tenancy Agreement of the above Holding dated   and made
between [original Landlord] (1) and [original Tenant] (2) hereby exercise the
option to terminate the tenancy of the Holding [part of the Holding as
described in the Schedule] on

Signed:

Dated:

The Schedule
[identification of part of Holding, to which the notice relates,
by Ordnance Survey number with area and plan]

Explanation: Whether or not a landlord can exercise a break clause in relation to
the whole or part of the holding depends on the tenancy agreement.
The date to be inserted in the notice must accord with the
contractual provisions and must be given at least twelve but less than
twenty-four months before it is to take effect.

8. TENANT'S NOTICE TO EXERCISE OPTION TO TERMINATE TENANCY OF WHOLE OR PART

AGRICULTURAL TENANCIES ACT 1995

Section 7

THE HOLDING
[name and identification of holding, by address, Ordnance
Survey number or plan].

TO LANDLORD

[Name and Address]

I   of
[name and address of Tenant] in accordance with Clause   of the
Tenancy Agreement of the above Holding dated   and made
between [original Landlord] (1) and [original Tenant] (2) hereby exercise the
option to terminate the tenancy of the Holding [part of the Holding as
described in the Schedule] on

Signed:

Dated:

The Schedule
[identification of part of Holding, to which the notice relates,
by Ordnance Survey number with area and plan]

Explanation: Whether or not a tenant can exercise a break clause in relation to the
whole or part of the holding depends on the tenancy agreement. The
date to be inserted in the notice must accord with the contractual
provisions and must be given at least twelve but less than twenty-four
months before it is to take effect.

9. LANDLORD'S NOTICE DEMANDING STATUTORY REVIEW OF RENT

AGRICULTURAL TENANCIES ACT 1995

Section 10

THE HOLDING
[name and identification of holding, by address, Ordnance Survey number or plan].

TO TENANT

[Name and Address]

I   of
[name and address of Landlord] demand that the question of rent to be paid in respect of the above Holding as from   shall be referred to arbitration in accordance with Section 10 of the Agricultural Tenancies Act 1995.

Signed:

Dated:

Explanation: The date must be at least twelve but less than twenty-four months after the service of the notice and accord with any contractual review dates and specified intervals. If there are non-such then the review date must be the anniversary of the beginning of the tenancy. In the absence of any contractual provision the rent cannot be reviewed at less than three yearly intervals.

10. TENANT'S NOTICE DEMANDING STATUTORY REVIEW OF RENT

AGRICULTURAL TENANCIES ACT 1995

Section 10

THE HOLDING
[name and identification of holding, by address, Ordnance
Survey number or plan].

TO LANDLORD

[Name and Address]

I   of
[name and address of Tenant] demand that the question of rent to be paid in
respect of the above Holding as from   shall be referred to
arbitration in accordance with Section 10 of the Agricultural Tenancies Act
1995.

Signed:

Dated:

Explanation: The date must be at least twelve but less than twenty-four months
after the service of the notice and accord with any contractual review
dates and specified intervals. If there are non-such then the review
date must be the anniversary of the beginning of the tenancy. In the
absence of any contractual provision the rent cannot be reviewed at
less than three yearly intervals.

11. TENANT'S NOTICE DEMANDING ARBITRATION ON CONSENT TO IMPROVEMENTS

AGRICULTURAL TENANCIES ACT 1995

Section 19

THE HOLDING
[name and identification of holding, by address, Ordnance
Survey number or plan].

TO LANDLORD

[Name and Address]

I   of
[name and address of Tenant] demand that [your refusal to give consent to
the improvement specified below] [your failure to give consent within two
months of my written request for the improvement specified below] [your
variation in the terms of the tenancy specified below as a condition of giving
consent to the improvement specified below] be referred to arbitration in
accordance with Section 19 of the Agricultural Tenancies Act 1995.

[insert details of improvement and any variations in terms of the tenancy]

Signed:

Dated:

Explanation: The tenant can make an application to an arbitrator only where he
has not begun to provide the improvement unless it is a routine
improvement. An application or refusal or variation must be made
within two months beginning with the day on which the refusal or
variation was given to the tenant. An application on failure to give
consent must be made within four months beginning with the day on
which the written request was given to the landlord.

12. TENANT'S NOTICE OF INTENTION TO MAKE A CLAIM FOR COMPENSATION

AGRICULTURAL TENANCIES ACT 1995

Section 22

THE HOLDING
[name and identification of holding, by address, Ordnance
Survey number or plan].

TO LANDLORD

[Name and Address]

I   of
[name and address of Tenant] intend to make a claim for compensation for the
improvements specified below in accordance with Section 22 of the Agricultural
Tenancies Act 1995. Consent for the improvement was given by you in writing on
            [approval was given by the (name of Arbitrator) acting as
Arbitrator on   ].

Signed:

Dated:

Explanation: In order to obtain compensation the tenant must before the end of
            the period of two months beginning with the date of the termination
            of the tenancy give notice in writing to his landlord of his intention to
            make the claim and the nature of the claim.

13. LANDLORD'S NOTICE OF PROPOSAL TO APPLY FOR THE APPOINTMENT OF AN ARBITRATOR

AGRICULTURAL TENANCIES ACT 1995

Section 22

THE HOLDING
[name and identification of holding, by address, Ordnance Survey number or plan].

TO TENANT

[Name and Address]

     I   of
[name and address of Landlord] propose to apply to the President of the Royal Institution of Chartered Surveyors for the appointment of an arbitrator by him to settle the dispute specified below unless within two months from the service of this notice you and I have appointed an arbitrator by agreement.

[Nature of Dispute]

Signed:

Dated:

Explanation: This notice should not be used where the dispute relates to determination of rent (a statutory review notice must be served – see notice 9). If no arbitrator is appointed by agreement within two months of the service of notice either party can apply to the President of the Royal Institution of Chartered Surveyors for an appointment of an arbitrator by him.

14. TENANT'S NOTICE OF PROPOSAL TO APPLY FOR THE APPOINTMENT OF AN ARBITRATOR

AGRICULTURAL TENANCIES ACT 1995

Section 28

THE HOLDING
[name and identification of holding, by address, Ordnance
Survey number or plan].

TO LANDLORD

[Name and Address]

I   of
[name and address of Tenant] propose to apply to the President of the Royal
Institution of Chartered Surveyors for the appointment of an arbitrator by
him to settle the dispute specified below unless within two months from the
service of this notice you and I have appointed an arbitrator by agreement.

[Nature of Dispute]

Signed:

Dated:

Explanation: This notice should not be used where the dispute relates to
determination of rent (a statutory review notice must be served – see
notice 10) or to consent for improvements (use notice 11) or
compensation claims (use notice 12). If no arbitrator is appointed by
agreement within two months of the service of notice either party
can apply to the President of the Royal Institution of Chartered
Surveyors for an appointment of an arbitrator by him.

15. LANDLORD'S NOTICE OF REFERENCE OF DISPUTE TO THIRD PARTY

AGRICULTURAL TENANCIES ACT 1995

Section 29

THE HOLDING
[name and identification of holding, by address, Ordnance
Survey number or plan].

TO TENANT

[Name and Address]

I   of
[name and address of Landlord] in accordance with Clause   of the
Tenancy Agreement dated   made between [original
Landlord] (1) and [original Tenant] (2) have made reference to
[specify third party named in tenancy agreement] to settle the
dispute specified below.

[Nature of Dispute]

Signed:

Dated:

Explanation: If the tenancy agreement makes provision for the appointment of an
independent third party to settle disputes and a joint reference by the
landlord and tenant is made to that person after the dispute has
arisen the arbitration provisions will not apply. However where one
party only makes the application he must serve a notice on the other
informing him that an application has been made. The recipient of
the notice has four weeks in which to serve a notice under Section
28(2) instigating the arbitration procedure (see notice 14). If he fails
to do this then the dispute will be resolved by the third party in
accordance with the tenancy agreement.

16. TENANT'S NOTICE OF REFERENCE OF DISPUTE TO THIRD PARTY

AGRICULTURAL TENANCIES ACT 1995

Section 29

THE HOLDING
[name and identification of holding, by address, Ordnance
Survey number or plan].

TO LANDLORD

[Name and Address]

I   of
[name and address of Tenant] in accordance with Clause   of the
Tenancy Agreement dated   made between [original
Landlord] (1) and [original Tenant] (2) have made reference to
[specify third party named in tenancy agreement] to settle the
dispute specified below.

[Nature of Dispute]

Signed:

Dated:

Explanation: If the tenancy agreement makes provision for the appointment of an
independent third party to settle disputes and a joint reference by the
landlord and tenant is made to that person after the dispute has
arisen the arbitration provisions will not apply. However where one
party only makes the application he must serve a notice on the other
informing him that an application has been made. The recipient of
the notice has four weeks in which to serve a notice under Section
28(2) instigating the arbitration procedure (see notice 13). If he fails
to do this then the dispute will be resolved by the third party in
accordance with the tenancy agreement.

Appendix III

JOINT INDUSTRY STATEMENT

AGRICULTURAL TENANCY REFORM

Introduction

1. The CLA, NFU, TFA and NFYFC have agreed to submit the following proposals for the reform of agricultural tenancy law to Ministers.

Definition

2. The farm business tenancy legislation will apply to the letting of any property provided its use is primarily agricultural and will then cover all other uses. A written agreement by the parties that the letting is a farm business tenancy will protect that character throughout that letting.

Term

3. There will be no provision for a minimum term.

Compensation

4. (a) There will be mandatory compensation at the end of the tenancy for any improvements made with the landlord's consent on the basis of the value they add to the holding. It will not be possible to contract out of this rule nor substitute an alternative basis for compensation.

   (b) Where a landlord refuses consent or there is a dispute regarding the terms of the consent, the tenant will be entitled to apply to an independent arbitrator under the Arbitration Acts 1950–1979 who will consider whether it is reasonable for consent to be granted.

   (c) Independent arbitration at the instigation of either party under the same Acts will be available to settle disputes over compensation on the termination of the tenancy.

   (d) Consideration will be given by the parties to imposing time-limits to prevent delays in gaining consent and settling compensation.

5. Improvements will include all physical additions to the property and, in some cases, intangible improvements such as planning permissions which attach to the premises. The tenant may be entitled to claim compensation for a planning permission he has gained where it is related to the tenant's activities on the holding and is permitted by the lease, but not otherwise. It is not intended that the tenant should obtain a share of the development potential by being compensated for planning permission on a development unrelated to his use of the holding.

6. Tenant's fixtures (including agricultural buildings erected without consent) will be handled under the rules for trade fixtures, so that tenants may remove them.

Notices to quit

7. For a fixed-term tenancy of more than two years, a full year's notice expiring on the termination date would be necessary to bring the tenancy to a conclusion. Failing this, the tenancy will then run from year to year. A full year's notice will be required to end the tenancy under any break clause in the tenancy agreement. Yearly tenancies would also require a full year's notice terminating on the anniversary of the tenancy.

Rent review

8. (a) The parties shall be free to decide whether the tenancy agreement will provide for rent reviews or not. The frequency of the rent review could be specified by the parties. In default of a contactual provision as to the frequency, it would be not less than three years from the grant of the tenancy or three years from the last rent review date.

(b) For adjusting the rent on a pre-determined basis the parties may agree other clear procedures which do not involve a review and so are not covered by the following paragraphs (c) and (d). This means that rent may be adjusted at stated intervals with reference to some objective criterion.

(c) Either party may refer any dispute over the rent to be set at a review to an independent arbitrator operating under the Arbitration Acts 1950–1979.

(d) The arbitrator must assess the rent on the basis of the open market value which would be agreed between willing parties taking into account the terms of the tenancy (including any premium or equivalent) and the uses, facilities and equipment available on the holding at the time of the review but disregarding the fact of the tenant's possession and tenant's improvements.

Disputes resolution

9. Where the tenancy agreement does not make provision for a procedure for disputes to be resolved by an independent third party, either party may refer a dispute arising under the tenancy to arbitration under the Arbitration Acts 1950–1979. If the independence of the third party is challenged by either party the dispute can be referred to arbitration.

10. The organisations subscribing to this paper will work together to identify and promote appropriate methods of alternative disputes resolution so that litigation may be a last resort only.

Repairing clauses

11. Since there will be no fall-back clauses on repairs, the organisations subscribing to this paper, representing both landlords and tenants, will work with the RICS and CAAV to agree clauses on the repair and maintenance of fixed equipment adapted to the special needs of the farm business tenancy which the organisations will recommend to their members for use on a voluntary basis.

Conclusion

12. With this agreement, the four organisations seek a commitment from Government to the earliest possible introduction of legislation on the above basis.

Appendix IV

DATES AND HANSARD REFERENCES

PARLIAMENTARY STAGES OF THE AGRICULTURAL TENANCIES BILL

Lords	Date	Column	Volume
1st Reading	17.11.94	25	559 no 2
2nd Reading	28.11.94	485–532	559 no 6
Committee	12.12.94	1098–98: 1112–1154	559 no 14
	13.12.94	1205–1264	559 no 15
Report	24.1.95	862–869: 884–925	560 no 27
3rd Reading	30.1.95	1258–1273: 1279–1290	560 no 27
Commons Amendments	2.5.95	1348–1359	563 no 80
Royal Assent	9.5.95	4	564 no 84

Commons	Date	Column	Volume
1st Reading	30.1.95	Not printed	
2nd Reading	6.2.95	23–114	254 no 45
Committee (SCA)	21.2.95	Standing Committee Hansard	
	23.2.95	Standard Committee Hansard	
	28.2.95	Standing Committee Hansard	
Report and Third Reading	19.4.95	230–272	258 no 88

INDEX